HAVE A NICE DOOMSDAY

Have a Nice
DOOMSDAY

Why Millions of Americans Are Looking
Forward to the End of the World

NICHOLAS GUYATT

HARPER PERENNIAL

NEW YORK • LONDON • TORONTO • SYDNEY

HARPER ● PERENNIAL

P.S.™ is a trademark of HarperCollins Publishers.

HarperCollins books may be purchased for educational, business, or
sales promotional use. For information please write: Special Markets
Department, HarperCollins Publishers, 10 East 53rd Street, New
York, NY 10022.

FIRST EDITION

Designed by Jamie Kerner-Scott

Library of Congress Cataloging-in-Publication Data is available upon
request.

ISBN: 978-0-06-115224-5
ISBN-10: 0-06-115224-2

07 08 09 10 11 ID/RRD 10 9 8 7 6 5 4 3 2 1

For Tess

For in such an hour as ye think not,
the Son of man cometh.

—Jesus Christ, Matthew 24:44

Contents

PROLOGUE: The Beginning of the End   1

1   Jews and a Furious Christ   9

2   In Search of a Perfect Red Heifer   39

3   Of Horns, Little Horns, and Antichrists   61

4   Riding the White Elephant   83

5   American Apocalypse   111

6   The Dirty Old Fishpond   137

7   Nuking the Hill   161

8   Tom Clancy with Prayer   189

9   Armageddon Comes Later   215

EPILOGUE: An Intercept from God   245

Further Reading   271

Acknowledgments   275

Prologue

The Beginning of the End

I t's June 6, 2006—6/6/06—and I'm standing in Mardel's, a Christian superstore in Littleton, Colorado, waiting for the arrival of Tim LaHaye and Jerry Jenkins. LaHaye and Jenkins are the biggest stars in the Christian publishing industry, the authors of blockbuster books about the end of the world—the *Left Behind* series—which have sold more than 60 million copies since 1995. Today, they've come to this suburb on the southwestern side of Denver to plug their new book, *The Rapture*. Littleton is a place you already know about—three miles down the road is Columbine High School, where twelve students and one teacher lost their lives in 1999 during America's most notorious school massacre. But there's no trace of that tragedy in the gathering crowd at Mardel's, which snakes around the bookstacks in a long and cheerful line that ends at the empty signing table. The authors are due to arrive in ten minutes, and a couple of hundred fans are already here to greet them.

Over the past ten years, the fifteen novels in the *Left Behind* series have assured Americans that they're on the verge of the End Times, the last moments before the apocalyptic prophecies of the Bible are fulfilled. Tim LaHaye, like most Bible prophecy enthusiasts in the United States, believes that our current world system—governments, economies, religions, cultures—is about to collapse. The warning signs are already there for the faithful to observe; in fact, God will rescue true Christians before things get really bad in a massive spiritual airlift known as the Rapture. This is where the *Left Behind* series begins, with the baffling, instantaneous disappearance of all true believers.

The hero of the books isn't one of these lucky few who are snatched away by God. He's a 747 pilot named Rayford Steele who misses out on the Rapture because he doesn't share his wife's faith in Christ. In the dramatic first scene of the original *Left Behind* novel, Rayford is hitting on one of his flight attendants at precisely the moment when dozens of Christian passengers vanish into thin air. Seven years (and twelve books) later, the series ends with the Second Coming, and Rayford gets to meet Jesus Christ himself.

It's hard to think of a more blockbuster ending to a fictional saga—the final book is called *The Glorious Appearing*—but along the way things get very nasty for Christians. The Antichrist, a loyal servant of Satan called Nicolae Carpathia, becomes the leader of the world. Christians are persecuted for their faith and ordered to worship Nicolae. A giant earthquake kills more than a billion people. Worst of all, the United States falls by the wayside. America, for once, does not ride in to save the world from the bad guy. Satan manages to install Nicolae as secretary-general of the United Nations, and repeatedly bests the White House. (By the third book in the series, a UN army has bombed Chicago and other American cities.) The Antichrist sets up his world headquarters in the rebuilt Iraqi city of Babylon, and America fades from view. This period is known as the Tribulation, and it's going to be as bad as that sounds.

All of this may seem implausible, but the point of these books is to jar us from our everyday reality and remind us that God is in charge of our future. In the real world, Bill Clinton managed to remove the troublesome UN secretary-general, Boutros Boutros-Ghali back in 1996, and George W. Bush invaded Iraq in 2003 against the wishes of the Security Council. In the *Left Behind* universe, it's the Antichrist who bosses the UN and seizes Iraq, and only Jesus Christ can sort out the ensuing mess.

Littleton is as patriotic as any other American suburb. By the entrance to Mardel's, there's a prayer tree inviting shoppers to write the names of loved ones or friends serving in the military on blue leaves, so that other customers can pray for them. The tree is crammed with leaves, filled out with tiny handwriting. Many of them say "President Bush" as well as the names of soldiers and units. But the *Left Behind* books suggest that the current world order is on the verge of collapse, and that the "war on terror" is about to be overshadowed by a much grander conflict in which America plays no role. The Antichrist may already be among us, suggest Tim LaHaye and Jerry Jenkins, and when he comes to power there'll be nothing that the United States can do about it.

WHEN TIM AND JERRY finally arrive, the crowd bursts into applause and the signing begins. LaHaye turned eighty in April, and he looks at least ten years younger. He has a full head of red hair and a bright smile as he meets his readers, but there is something a little too healthy about his appearance: he's sprightly in a rather artificial way, like a bagged salad. Jerry Jenkins is much younger, tall with a smartly trimmed gray goatee.

As they sit at the table, Tim LaHaye's wife, Beverly, joins him and helps with the signing. Beverly is also a conservative celebrity. Back in 1978, she was so appalled by the liberal agenda of feminists that she founded Concerned Women for America, a pressure group dedicated to fighting the Equal Rights Amendment (which was intended to make sex discrimination unconstitutional) and the "spiritual forces of darkness" more generally. Nearly thirty years later, Beverly's organization has successfully kept that amendment at bay through fund-raising and Washington lobbying, and CWA has branched out. These days, it runs campaigns against gay rights, abortion, sexually active teens, and even popular music. Sometimes these issues overlap in exciting ways: "iPods Keep Teens from Saying No!" declares a recent news story on the CWA Web site.

Tim's hand is giving him trouble, so the publicity people have preprinted his signature on a book plate and only Jerry is signing the books. Beverly is busy sticking plates into the new copies of *The Rapture*. The authors seem genuinely happy to chat with the customers, and there's a cheery air. The posters for the event had darkly trailed the release date—"6/6/6—Will You Be Ready?"—but Mardel's seems unruffled by the arrival of the Antichrist's special day.

"We picked this date a long time ago, but then they scheduled *The Omen* for a Tuesday release." I've found my way to LaHaye's publicist, a smart and wary woman who's also called Beverly. She put together the *Rapture* signing tour and has arranged for me to chat with Tim when the event is over. "Movies come out on Fridays, not Tuesdays—books come out on Tuesdays, but they've taken our slot." Beverly has been handling interviews with LaHaye and Jenkins all day, and she's been too busy to read the short piece in the *New York Times* that mentions the book in passing. (The *Times* article also reports that 216 people have bet an average of $2 each that the world will end today, at odds of 100,000 to 1. It's not clear how they intend to collect.) In addition to the many suitors from the local media, Fox News sent someone to the afternoon press junket to do a piece on LaHaye and Jenkins and the 6/6/6 tie-in, but Beverly has just found out that it's been bumped from the evening broadcast: "They found an exorcist instead," she says with a familiar resignation.

The crowd continues to move toward the signing table. There are quite a few younger people in the line, as well as some children who seem to have been dragged along by their parents. (The kids perk up when they're handed an empty box by the Mardel's staff: "LEFT BEHIND: ETERNAL FORCES—THE VIDEOGAME. Preorder your copy today!") Many of the readers have stories to tell about how the *Left Behind* books have helped them in their own spiritual lives. Tim LaHaye isn't standoffish, but Jerry Jenkins, who lives just down the road in Colorado Springs, directs the banter. Jenkins actually writes the books; LaHaye helps with the plotting, and ensures that the spiritual message is clear and biblically consistent.

These responsibilities seem to inform the public reception of the authors: LaHaye is the revered elder; Jenkins is the stand-to guy who brings LaHaye's world to life. A man in his forties approaches the table, wearing what looks like a Nike cap. When he comes closer, I notice that the red swoosh is actually followed by "ESUS" in black italics. (On even closer inspection, there's a bar at the top of the J—it's a crucifix swoosh.) The man is telling LaHaye and Jenkins how he met his wife protesting outside an abortion clinic. Tim and Jerry tell him to keep up the good work, and he collects his signed copy. Another happy reader moves down the line, and dozens more wait for their moment.

I FIRST HEARD about Tim LaHaye nearly ten years ago. I grew up in Britain, but in 1997 I moved to Princeton to do a Ph.D. in American history. Back then, Tim was already a legend in evangelical circles, but he wasn't well known more generally in America. Soon after arriving in New Jersey, I read a review of *Left Behind* in a magazine and I was intrigued. I'd come to America to study "manifest destiny," the idea that God had a special plan for the United States. The Americans that I was writing about described their nation with a mixture of pride and spiritual confidence. John Winthrop, who led the Puritan migration to Massachusetts in 1630, thought that New England could be a "city on a hill," a community set up by God for the rest of the world to admire. Abraham Lincoln filled his Civil War speeches with religious rhetoric about America's "vast future." Woodrow Wilson told cheering crowds that God had given the United States a special responsibility to spread democracy throughout the world. In the 1980s, Ronald Reagan liked to talk about his "eternal optimism" for America, and his belief that God had planted the nation as an outpost of freedom. Tim LaHaye, on the other hand, believed that America's days were numbered. This seemed like a very un-American idea, and yet *Left Behind* was at the top of the bestseller lists. As I worked on my thesis about the United States as a chosen nation, I kept wondering about the Christians in contemporary America who were abandoning their faith in the nation's redemptive potential.

Then, around 2000, Tim LaHaye suddenly crossed over and became a household name. *Left Behind* and its sequels had now sold tens of millions of copies. A New York publisher offered Tim a $40 million advance for a new series of apocalyptic novels. The original *Left Behind* books were made into movies. Tim was the subject of a cover story in *Time* magazine. The market for religious books and films had taken off, fueled by the upsurge of interest in the apocalypse. Tim was at the center of this, but an entire industry was growing up around him.

This apocalyptic mood was fired by two events that changed America. In December 2000, the bitter presidential election was finally decided in favor of George W. Bush, a born-again Christian who spoke on the campaign trail about how Jesus had "changed my heart." Evangelical voters—precisely the people who were buying *Left Behind* and other apocalyptic books—had been instrumental in swinging the narrow election toward Bush. The following September, the 9/11 attacks seemed to confirm for many Christians that the nation was on the verge of the End Times predicted by prophecy. As thousands died in New York and Washington, D.C., and the United States was besieged by a terrorism of apocalyptic proportions, many evangelicals could see the events of *Left Behind* leap onto the front pages of their newspapers.

By 2002, according to a poll commissioned by *Time* and CNN, nearly 60 percent of Americans had come to believe that the Bible's scariest prophecies—in the Book of Revelation—would literally come true. Nearly 20 percent—more than 50 million Americans—believed that the apocalypse would take place in their own lifetime. While I was writing a thesis about the enormous confidence and optimism of American Christians in the past, evangelicals in twenty-first-century America seemed to be adopting a much bleaker view. God hadn't created America to save the world, because the world wasn't going to be saved. It was going to be destroyed by Satan and the Antichrist, and the end was nigh.

I SPENT SEVEN YEARS in the United States, from the beginning of Bill Clinton's second term until the end of George W. Bush's first term. During that period, I lived in New Jersey, New York, and California. I never met an apocalyptic Christian, and none of my friends or acquaintances had any contact with the 50 million people who had apparently embraced the apocalypse. But by 2004, many of my secular friends—and large sections of the liberal media—had become skittish about the influence of evangelical Christians on American politics. Books and articles had started to appear about the rise of the Religious Right and its ominous agenda for remaking America and the world at large.

Even moderate Republicans were worried. In 2006, the veteran conservative commentator Kevin Phillips published a book called *American Theocracy*, which argued that the American government had been taken over by evangelical zealots with apocalyptic beliefs. At a press conference in Cleveland, President Bush was asked directly whether the war in Iraq and the attacks of 9/11 were "signs of the apocalypse," and he gave a typically nervous answer:

> The answer is—I haven't really thought of it that way. Here's how I think of it. The first I've heard of that, by the way. I guess I'm more of a practical fellow.

Phillips wasn't happy with the president's response. In a follow-up interview he declared that the president saw himself as an instrument of God's will; and, worse, that many Republicans had come to view Bush as a kind of prophet, a man with a hotline to God himself who had been placed in the White House by Divine Providence at a crucial moment in American history.

As a lapsed Catholic, I was drawn to those liberal warnings of evangelicals run amok. But I couldn't figure out one thing: Why would apocalyptic Christians, who believe that the world is about to be ruined by the Antichrist, want to get involved in politics? Historically, prophecy enthusiasts have tended to withdraw from the political scene and to wait for Christ to return, or for the world to end. If God is in charge, what's the point of electing a Republican Congress or an evangelical president?

Even after reading countless liberal assaults on *Left Behind* and the Religious Right, I didn't know what prophecy enthusiasts actually believed. Are their lives totally overshadowed by the End Times? What do they think about America? If any of them have made it to Washington, what are they trying to do there? So I decided to take a trip through the world of apocalyptic Christianity. I read books on prophecy, watched apocalyptic movies, and even played the *Left Behind* video game. I interviewed some of the most influential apocalyptic Christians, traveling through the Bible Belt and exploring their world from the inside. In my reading and on my travels, I was guided by two questions in particular: Why do so many Americans believe that the world is about to end? And should the rest of us be worried that they do?

1

Jews and a Furious Christ

t's a little after eight on a muggy Sunday morning and I'm standing outside Cornerstone Church in San Antonio, Texas. The parking lot is vast, filling up with minivans, pickups, and SUVs nearly half an hour before the service begins. The church itself, set back from the road, looks like a resort hotel: there's one of those semicircular drives just in front of the main doors, and I'm half expecting to see valet parking. Cornerstone is the headquarters of John Hagee, one of the most influential Christian leaders in America. Pastor Hagee, like tens of millions of evangelicals, believes that the apocalypse is imminent.

A few months earlier, in a secondhand bookstore in New York, I'd stumbled upon *Jerusalem Countdown*, Hagee's "warning to the world" about the looming nuclear confrontation between Iran and the United States. The first paragraph got my attention.

Jerusalem Countdown is a page-turning heart-stopper! Using my confidential sources in Israel, information from military experts around the world, and electrifying revelations from Bible prophecy, I will expose this reality: unless the entire world—including America, Israel, and the Middle East—reaches soon a diplomatic and peaceful solution to Iran's nuclear threat, Israel and America will be on a nuclear collision course with Iran!

The book was brand new, and I guessed that some jaded New York reviewer had discarded it. I bought a copy but I didn't think that anyone else would.

When I arrive in Texas in May 2006, *Jerusalem Countdown* has sold more than six hundred thousand copies and reached number 14 on the *USA Today* bestseller list. Since Hagee completed the draft of the book the previous autumn, President Mahmoud Ahmadinejad has steered Iran toward a diplomatic showdown with the United States. Right on the Hagee schedule, Ahmadinejad has just announced to the world that Iran has succeeded in producing weapons-grade uranium. Even though the war in Iraq is going badly for America, some pundits are predicting that the Bush administration will go to war with Iran. Does John Hagee know something that the rest of us don't? "We are standing on the brink of a nuclear Armageddon," Hagee warns in the first part of the book. "The coming showdown with Iran is a certainty!"

Cornerstone is just off a major freeway, and as you drive into the parking lot you pass beneath an enormous sign that flashes the times of church services, the names of upcoming church speakers and events, and a billowing Stars and Stripes. The sign is also a billboard for the latest products from the Hagee commercial empire. Today, it's plugging *Jerusalem Countdown*, but Pastor Hagee isn't just a minister and author. He's the president of John Hagee Ministries, a sprawling enterprise that sells sermons, videos, Israel tours, and even high-speed Internet access that filters out unsavory Web sites. ("John Hagee Online can protect you and your children from the dangers of the Internet!") He appears regularly on Trinity Broadcasting Network, the nation's leading Christian TV station, and he has his own "television ministry"—Global Evangelism Television—to broadcast Cornerstone services and events to subscribers and across the Internet.

According to the local newspaper, Hagee made $1.25 million in 2001, more than three times as much as other nonprofit directors and executives in this part of Texas. He lives in an exclusive gated community, the Dominion, near the stars of the San Antonio Spurs. When he was challenged by a journalist to justify his income, he pointed out that he worked an eighty-hour week and was entitled to a decent living: "I deserve every dime I'm getting."

Jerusalem Countdown has been keeping Hagee busy. Since it was published in January 2006, the pastor has been touting his "confidential sources" and styling himself as an Iran expert. Some journalists have taken him at his word. Earlier in the year, I saw him interviewed on Fox News, probed by the anchor for some indication of Ahmadinejad's next move. "Make no mistake," Pastor Hagee assured viewers. "Iran will use nuclear weapons against Israel and use nuclear weapons against the United States of America." Hagee has made a number of appearances on Fox, though curiously he isn't introduced as an apocalyptic preacher.

When evangelicals cross over to a mainstream audience, things don't always turn out well. On September 13, 2001, the veteran televangelist Pat Robertson interviewed his old friend Jerry Falwell. The pair of them agreed that the 9/11 attacks were God's revenge on an America that tolerated pagans, gays, feminists, and the American Civil Liberties Union. Although Falwell apologized the following day, both men remained in the headlines for their extreme views about the war on terror. In 2002, Falwell told *60 Minutes* that "Muhammad was a terrorist." (Another apology was issued.) In 2005, Pat Robertson suggested on his TV show that President Bush should assassinate the troublesome Venezuelan leader Hugo Chavez.

Evangelicals like Falwell (who died in May 2007) and Robertson have made an impact on mainstream culture since 9/11, but I don't think they've found a lot of new converts this way. I remember being on the immigration line at Newark Airport in January 2006 watching a CNN report on Pat Robertson's latest assertion. Ariel Sharon, the Israeli prime minister, had just been felled by a stroke after removing Israeli settlers from the Gaza Strip. Robertson saw this as a simple case of divine vengeance. (The CNN headline: "Robertson suggests God smote Sharon.") As the story played out on the video screen at Newark, I watched Americans and visitors in the arrivals hall react to the story with a mixture of amusement and disgust.

John Hagee's relationship with the media seems very different. CNN has invited him to chat about the end of the world as if he were discussing the congressional elections. Fox News treats him like an expert from the Council on Foreign Relations. In spite of his open embrace of doomsday in *Jerusalem Countdown*, John Hagee has become an authority on the Middle East even while the region has been gripped by unprecedented instability and violence. He isn't just offering a bleak commentary on this debate: he's helping to shape it.

There's another thing I can't work out about John Hagee, and I see some evidence of it even as I'm walking through the Cornerstone parking lot toward the church building. To the left of the main entrance is a honey-colored stone wall about six feet high. Most of the churchgoers head straight for the entrance, but a group of them linger in front of this wall and seem lost in the moment. There's an inscription running across the top, taken from one of Pastor Hagee's favorite psalms: "Pray for the Peace of Jerusalem. They shall prosper that love thee." The message here is a little misleading. While it sounds as if the pastor is a strong advocate of the Middle East peace process, he's actually a staunch and unrelenting supporter of Israel. Right now, he's organizing a new evangelical lobbying group called Christians United for Israel, which will put pressure on the White House and Congress to adopt a biblical foreign policy in the Middle East: God gave the land to Israel, and the President of the United States doesn't have the authority to give any of it to the Palestinians. In an even-handed touch, Hagee insists that the Israelis can't give any away either.

The wall outside Cornerstone Church is more than just a political statement. John Hagee claims not only to support Israel but to *love* it, and his San Antonio "prayer wall" is a homage to the Holy Land. It's a scale model of the Western Wall in the Old City of Jerusalem, which Israel captured in the Six-Day War of 1967. The Western Wall is the last remaining part of the Jewish Temple that was destroyed by the Romans after the siege of Jerusalem in AD 70, and it's revered as the holiest place for religious Jews. People flock from around the world to pray at the wall, and for centuries pilgrims have written their divine requests on scraps of paper that they've jammed into cracks between the ancient stones.

These days, you can send your prayer via the Internet and—if you have the money to spare—an Israeli firm will print your message and squeeze it into the Western Wall within thirty minutes. ("This is express service," says their cheerful Web site, "and it costs $120.00.") Or you can visit Cornerstone Church and deposit your prayer in the Texas substitute. John Hagee asked his builders to leave gaps between the stones for the same reason. He's asking the people of San Antonio—and pilgrims from farther afield—to exit the freeway, dodge the strip malls, and push their problems and desires into his miniature Jerusalem.

I've come to Texas to find out why John Hagee thinks the world is going to end, and how he's persuaded people to accept him as a commentator on the increasingly unstable Middle East. But the wall reminds me of another thing about Hagee that takes some explaining. How does a Christian fundamentalist come to love Israel and the Jews? And how do Jews feel about their apocalyptic cheerleader?

———

"I LOVE HIM, I respect him, I admire him, I pray for his wel-fare." This glowing testimony to Pastor Hagee came from Aryeh Scheinberg, a conservative rabbi who's lived in San Antonio for nearly forty years. I heard that Rabbi Scheinberg was a regular at Cornerstone, and a guide on Hagee's tours of the Holy Land, so I went to see him a few days before my visit to the church. The rabbi had recently gotten into a spot of trouble. In an interview with the *Jerusalem Post* about Pastor Hagee, he apparently implied that his good friend believed Jews could be saved without believ-ing in Jesus. Worse, the rabbi suggested that Hagee had persuaded Jerry Falwell that this was true. Predictably, the *Post* splashed this "revelation" in its headline: "Falwell: Jews Can Get To Heaven."

A flurry of denials followed, including a particularly wither-ing one from Falwell, and I felt rather sorry for Scheinberg. He's a very friendly man, and completely sincere in his regard for Hagee. I found him in his office at the heart of the Congrega-tion Rodfei Shalom compound, which is a retirement community cum synagogue for Orthodox Jews. There are a lot of Jews in San Antonio, I discovered, though not all of them agree with Rabbi Scheinberg about John Hagee.

"That was based on an incorrect communication! A genuine mistake!" The rabbi lays out a complicated story involving an old interview that Hagee did with the *Houston Chronicle*, and a misstep by the reporter for the *Jerusalem Post*. Scheinberg is an animated man of sixty with a wispy white beard. He stumbled into this mess after agreeing to be the Jewish face of Christians United for Israel, the lobbying group that Hagee founded in February 2006. CUFI has already made national headlines, and Pastor Hagee is busy organizing a "Washington-Israel Summit" for early July. Rabbi Scheinberg and three thousand delegates from across the country will take Hagee's pro-Israel message directly to Congress.

You may think that Congress already does a pretty good job

of supporting Israel, or that there are active lobbying groups, including the formidable American-Israel Public Affairs Committee (AIPAC), which have this covered. But John Hagee wants something more reliable than AIPAC, and he sees CUFI as the best way to ensure that the United States government stays on Israel's side in its many disputes with its neighbors.

I ask Rabbi Scheinberg how he met John Hagee. "It was 1981, when Israel bombed the Osirak nuclear reactor in Iraq. So, of course, there was worldwide condemnation of Israel's action, including the United States, and that's when Pastor Hagee thought of having a Night to Honor Israel for what she did." Hagee, like most evangelical Christians, feels a special attachment to the land of Israel. His epiphany came in April 1979 when, on his first visit to the Holy Land, he was overwhelmed by "the courageous enthusiasm of these sons and daughters of Gideon." From this point onward, Hagee became a staunch supporter of Israel.

The Israeli bombing of the Osirak reactor in 1981 caused quite a stir at the time, not least since the Iraqis pointed out that Israel had introduced nuclear weapons to the region during the 1960s. Hagee saw this as a chance to formalize the revelation he'd had in Jerusalem two years earlier. "A Night to Honor Israel"—part fundraising event, part Judeo-Christian variety performance—has taken place in San Antonio every year since then, invariably with Rabbi Scheinberg representing the Jewish community. It has even spread to other cities. The week before my visit to Cornerstone Church, Hagee flew up to Canada to attend ANTHI in Toronto. $649,000 was raised for Israeli charities in a single evening, though the flagship event at Cornerstone doles out nearly ten times that sum.

According to Scheinberg, Hagee originally met with resistance from Jews in San Antonio when he suggested an event that would honor Israel. "Their first question was 'Well, what is the hidden agenda? What missionary activity lies behind all this?'" But the rabbi himself decided to see if John Hagee was for real. The relationship between the two men grew stronger over the years, and Scheinberg insists that Hagee has never tried to convert him or any other Jew. Meanwhile, "A Night to Honor Israel" became more and more successful, and with Scheinberg's blessing attracted prominent Israelis as well as American politicians. Recent speakers include Tom DeLay, the former leader of the House of Representatives; Gary Bauer, an adviser to Ronald Reagan who ran for the Republican presidential nomination in 2000; and even Ariel Sharon and Benjamin Netanyahu. South Texas seems like an unlikely destination for the movers and shakers of Israeli politics, but Hagee's quarter century of unstinting support for Israel has put San Antonio on the map.

What makes this procession of Israeli and American leaders more odd is the backdrop to Hagee's views about the Middle East. Like Tim LaHaye, John Hagee insists that the End Times are fast approaching. His support for Israel is grounded not only in the shared ancestry of Jews and Christians but in the belief that the apocalyptic events prophesied by the Bible will actually come to pass in the next few years. These events are focused on Israel, and on the fate of the Jews as well as Christians—so Hagee believes that Christians have a special responsibility to follow Middle East politics for signs that the end is nigh. For more than a decade, he's been delivering bestsellers that map current events onto the apocalyptic scheme. They appear to be growing in popularity.

PERHAPS THE EASIEST WAY to understand John Hagee's love for Israel is to look at his ideas about how, exactly, the end of the world is going to come about. Hagee, Tim LaHaye, and other doomsday preachers have a remarkably consistent view of how the Bible's prophetic promises will shape tomorrow's headlines. The Antichrist will take over the world; Christ will return in person to vanquish him; and Jesus will preside over a peaceful and harmonious world for a thousand years.

Apocalyptic Christians like Hagee and LaHaye have derived this scheme from a number of different parts of the Bible, but they stick to it with remarkable faithfulness. It's the plot that drives the *Left Behind* books, and the strategic scenario that informs John Hagee's views about Iran in *Jerusalem Countdown*. Israel has the starring role, from the first scene to the last.

1. Israel will be restored to the Middle East as a nation, after nearly two thousand years in which the Jews have been scattered throughout the world.

You can check this off: Israel won its independence in 1948, and this inspired the current wave of enthusiasm for Bible prophecy. In his books, Hagee often recalls listening to the radio with his father as an eight-year-old boy on the day that the United Nations recognized Israel. His dad—himself a prophecy enthusiast—apparently told him: "We have just heard the most important prophetic message that will ever be delivered until Jesus Christ returns to earth."

2. The world will gravitate toward a single government, a single economy, and a single religion.

This one-world system only becomes truly evil when the Antichrist rises up to become its leader, but Bible prophecy Christians view "globalization" as evidence that the satanic takeover of the world is already under way. Although most of the world recognizes that the United Nations is a toothless creature, and that America is the superpower, prophecy believers imagine that the UN could be the vehicle for the Antichrist's rise. (It's the route to power favored by Nicolae Carpathia in *Left Behind*.) The IMF and the World Bank also unnerve Bible prophecy Christians, and their fear of economic consolidation makes them wary of ATMs, credit cards, and even barcodes.

3. All true believers will be "Raptured" by God. Faithful Christians will instantly vanish from the earth, creating political and social chaos.

Although this is where things start to sound farfetched, the idea of a massive disappearance of true believers has some foundation in scripture: it's based on a verse in a letter from St. Paul to the Thessalonians. (You can hear Tim LaHaye reading the verse in question, and admire a Flash animation of the Rapture, at timlahaye.com.) The Rapture is absolutely central to the prophetic scheme of most apocalyptic Christians in America. In a Christian superstore like Mardel's in Littleton, you can buy bumper stickers that read:

IN CASE OF RAPTURE, THIS VEHICLE WILL BE UNMANNED

Prophecy believers use chat rooms to debate how they can reconcile public safety with the unknowable timing of the Rapture. Some have suggested that true believers should think twice before becoming surgeons or airline pilots, because they could easily endanger non-Christians by disappearing suddenly when God gathers up the faithful.

John Hagee sincerely believes that he will be Raptured. In fact, some of his books contain a rider in which he anticipates this scenario: "*For those who have missed the Rapture*: you may be confused and terrified by the momentous events you are experiencing. You may be in hiding. Take heed to this book, then lift up your heads—your redemption draws near."

From this point onward in the End Times scheme, you should keep in mind that the world will have to fare without the help of Bible prophecy teachers and true Christians like John Hagee and Tim LaHaye. The effort to resist Satan will be waged only by those "left behind."

4. Russia, in alliance with Arab and/or Islamic nations, will attack Israel. Israel will be miraculously spared destruction, and virtually all of the invading forces will be destroyed.

Pastor Hagee admits that he's not totally sure about the sequence here. It's possible that the Russian attack may come before the Rapture, as in the *Left Behind* books. But he doesn't doubt that a war involving Russia, Iran, and Israel will be a crucial part of the apocalyptic sequence. This assumption is based on a prophetic vision in the Book of Ezekiel, which describes an attack on Israel by a prince called Gog. Gog ruled over the kingdom of Magog which equates roughly to Turkey, Iran, and Central Asia. Or perhaps to Russia.

On the basis of this ancient and mysterious prediction, Hagee suggests that "it is reasonable to assume Russia will lead a massive Pan-Islamic military force to invade Jerusalem." The same passage in Ezekiel leads Hagee to believe that the invasion will be a complete failure. God will strike down the Russians and their Muslim allies with earthquakes and brimstone. Or perhaps these references are metaphorical. "The fire and brimstone might refer to Israel's release of nuclear weapons in a last-ditch attempt to prevent annihilation," Hagee helpfully suggests. "In either case, the results are equally catastrophic."

There's an unnerving aside in the Ezekiel passage that promises brimstone not only for the unfortunate aggressors of Magog but also for those who are "living in security in the coastlands." In *Jerusalem Countdown*, Hagee lingers on this clause: "Could it be that America, which refuses to defend Israel from the Russian invasion, will experience nuclear warfare on our east and west coasts?" He adds, rather disingenuously for a San Antonio resident, "That's exactly where most of us live today." When he thinks about the sins that could provoke such a calamitous judgment from God, Hagee returns to anti-

Semitism: "Right now in America's major universities, professors, many of whose positions are funded by Saudi Arabian oil money, blast Israel as the cancer on the soul of humanity." The liberal elite, and its anti-Israel rhetoric, might eventually draw down God's vengeance on the entire nation.

Hagee likes to tell a story about a trip he made to Berlin during the 1980s. He'd been invited to give a speech to American GIs, and he was taken around the western half of the city by a German guide. When they got to Checkpoint Charlie, and looked over at Soviet East Berlin, the guide asked Hagee sadly why God had "permitted the communists to build a wall around us." Hagee, who'd been to Dachau the day before, instantly replied: "Everything your parents did to the Jewish people, son, the communists are doing to you." This is a general rule, repeated in Hagee's books: "What a nation or an individual does to the nation of Israel is what God repays to them."

5. In the aftermath of this terrible war, the world will reach a peace agreement brokered by a charismatic leader, probably from Europe. This leader is the Antichrist, and the peace treaty marks the beginning of the "Tribulation," the seven-year period in which he takes over the planet. He will unify the world under a single government and will purge Christians and anyone opposed to his reign. With the aid of his sidekick, the "false prophet," the Antichrist persuades or compels everyone to worship him.

If you've accepted the logic of the story so far, perhaps this won't seem bizarre. The Antichrist is the embodiment of evil, a false version of Jesus who seems to solve the world's problems but actually serves Satan himself. He isn't the literal incarnation of Satan, but he's the instrument through which the devil will attempt to destroy the world.

Naturally, he's European. (There's a reason for this in the Book of Daniel, but it must be intuitive for many Bible prophecy enthusiasts.) He capitalizes on the chaos following the Russian war and the Rapture, and he manages to fool the world into accepting him as a peacemaker, a leader, and eventually as a god. By the time people realize what's happening, the Antichrist is already in charge.

Here's where the one-world government really takes off. The Antichrist places the "mark of the Beast" on everyone, and insists that this mark is used in every transaction. Perhaps the mark will appear on coins and banknotes. Or perhaps the Antichrist will abolish cash and insist on credit cards embossed with his insignia. Some prophecy enthusiasts have an eye on more elaborate technologies—RFID chips that could be implanted beneath the skin, for example—but everyone agrees that the Beast's stranglehold on economic activity will make it impossible to survive without accepting his mark. A growing number of people (Jews and recent converts to Christianity) will try to reject the Antichrist's rule, but he's brutal in suppressing their dissent.

6. *Things get very bleak indeed. The Antichrist is assassinated by two Jews who realize his true identity, but then he rises from the dead with Satan's help, a trick that only strengthens his control over the world. Everyone who refuses to worship him is killed.*

This is a good place to reflect on why it's better to become a Christian before the Rapture than afterward.

7. *The Antichrist is attacked by armies from Russia and China, but then somehow persuades the Russians and the Chinese to team up with him. This is just as well, since they are now facing the ultimate enemy: Jesus Christ himself comes down from heaven with an army of wrathful angels and fights the hostile armies on the plains of Armageddon.*

Seven years have passed since the peace treaty between Israel and its enemies, and the Antichrist has ravaged the world. Now Christ is back. So are all the believers who were Raptured by Christ at the start of the apocalyptic sequence. Hagee reminds us that Christ isn't the gentle hippie that he's sometimes portrayed as: "This is no weak-wristed, smiling Jesus come to pay the earth a condolence call. This is a furious Christ, ready to confront the gathered armies of the world."

It seems odd that the Russians and the Chinese, who originally set out to attack the Antichrist, would switch sides at precisely the moment that Christ crashes through the heavens with an invincible army of saints. But the misguided opponents of the Lord, led by the Antichrist himself, take up arms and are soundly defeated. Everyone who continues to reject Jesus is slaughtered by him (including any Jews who, like the Russians and the Chinese, defy the furious Christ).

Armageddon is a real place in northern Israel. This vast plain is one of the highlights of the Holy Land vacations organized by Hagee, Tim LaHaye, and other prophecy enthusiasts.

8. The Antichrist and the false prophet are chained to a lake of fire, condemned to perpetual torment. Christ establishes a new kingdom on earth, which will last for a thousand years. This period is the "millennium" that's promised in the Bible. Satan is locked away in hell throughout the millennium, and the Christians who were Raptured before the seven years of the Tribulation return to live on earth.

This is the earliest that any of us can expect to find true peace in the world. Christ himself will rule over the Christians that he Raptured, as well as anyone who came to Jesus during the Tribulation. (Like the heroes of the *Left Behind* books.) Pastor Hagee expects that he will return to earth with Christ and lead a normal life when the apocalyptic dust has settled. People will be born and will die during the millennium, though some evangelicals have speculated that Christians will be able to live for hundreds of years, as the patriarchs of the Old Testament always seemed to do. (There are some elaborate theories about the composition of the earth's atmosphere and the rays of the sun, if you're interested in the science behind this.) Because Satan hasn't actually been destroyed—that won't happen until the millennium is over—there is still sin in the world, but Christ won't put up with it. "He shall rule an age of peace with a rod of iron," Hagee warns.

9. *After a thousand years, Satan will be set loose again from hell. There'll be one more massive battle between God and Satan at Jerusalem. Satan will be permanently vanquished, the earth will be destroyed, and a new earth will descend from the heavens.*

Yet another apocalyptic drama might seem excessive, especially after the fireworks of the first one, but Hagee points out that the purpose of this millennial period is to demonstrate that people will still turn against God even when Christ rules over them in person. Only when Satan has been defeated for a second time, and the entire earth has been destroyed, can we expect a world without sin.

JOHN HAGEE APPEARS to believe all this with absolute confidence, which makes two questions seem particularly pressing. How could this message be remotely appealing to Jews? And should the rest of us feel unnerved that Hagee is meeting with Israeli and American leaders, and appearing on the news to offer advice about U.S. policy in the Middle East?

"JOHN HAGEE IS NOT a true friend of the Jewish people," says Rabbi Barry Block, who heads the Reform community in San Antonio. He assures me that he has a great deal of respect for Aryeh Scheinberg, and that the city's Jewish community is united on a lot of important issues. "The fact we don't always agree doesn't undermine our respect for each other," though John Hagee has become a sticking point. "He preaches hatred—he's anti-Muslim, anti-gay—and he advocates against positions that we hold dear." Block considers himself a supporter of Israel, and Hagee's game plan for the End Times rules him out as an ally. "His pro-Israel actions are based on his prophetic vision, but as Jews we don't come out well at the end of that story."

I hadn't expected Rabbi Block to be a fan of Hagee's, but I'm surprised at the extent of his criticism. "I don't have anything positive to say about Pastor Hagee," he concludes. But then he remembers the flurry of articles about CUFI and he thinks of a parting shot. "His new Christian version of AIPAC is positive, because it will show Americans that when the U.S. backs some of Israel's right-wing policies, it's because of their core religious right community, not the Protocols of the Elders of Zion or some Jewish conspiracy."

According to Barry Block, the stubborn opposition of the Reform community in San Antonio to many of Hagee's Christian Zionist activities has forced the pastor to team up with Houston's Jewish community instead. Rabbi Block has invested a lot of time in interfaith activities, and he's particularly appalled by Hagee's views of Islam. Aryeh Scheinberg sees things differently. To him, Hagee is a hero for his willingness to confront Islamists and to speak out against some of Islam's supposedly inherent limitations. "We go different ways in terms of our faith, in terms of our End of Days view of redemption," Scheinberg admitted to me. But he and Hagee share the view that "Islamofascism" threatens Israel, the United States, and "Western civilization."

But what about the inconvenient fact that Hagee believes militantly in a vengeful Christ, who will purge the world of unbelievers at the end of the Tribulation as surely as the Antichrist tormented brave Christians? The fact that, as Barry Block put it, things don't turn out so well for the Jews? When I put it to

Rabbi Scheinberg that you had to be willing to skip large chunks of *Jerusalem Countdown* if you were Jewish, he chuckles—"Well, I'm going to leave that up to the Good Lord!"—and suggests that Jews can respect the beliefs of prophecy enthusiasts without agreeing that the apocalypse is imminent. The more I push at this point, the more I realize that Scheinberg, in spite of his admiration for Hagee, doesn't feel in any way responsible for Hagee's views. "Ultimately what's important is how Jews think of Jews, and how we view ourselves."

You can hardly blame Rabbi Scheinberg for his pragmatism. If Hagee's ideas about politics are useful to Jewish conservatives in the here and now, but his ideas about the apocalypse will only be harmful if he's right about the Rapture and the Antichrist, why not roll the dice and embrace Christian Zionism? Why not agree to disagree with Hagee on the End Times but join with him in lobbying Congress on the need to support Israel unconditionally?

If you wanted to shoot down Barry Block's harsh assessment of Hagee—that he's not a true friend of the Jews, and that his theology leaves Jews high and dry when the vengeful Christ shows up in person—then you'd have a lot of ammunition in Hagee's own prophecy bestsellers. He's a tireless opponent of anti-Semitism, and he returns over and over to the tragedy of the Holocaust and the scandal of the Christian Church's silence. He argues that anti-Semitism may have prevented Jews from hearing the Christian message, and urges Christians to treat Jews with particular kindness.

Hagee regularly praises the contribution of Jews to the world at large. In his 1998 book, *Final Dawn over Jerusalem*, he lists a number of Hollywood stars, including Goldie Hawn, Dustin Hoffman, and Barbra Streisand, as evidence that God has fulfilled the promise made to Abraham in the Book of Genesis that Jews will bless all the nations of the earth with their talents.

Hagee's most daring suggestion about the Jews is that they may have a special exemption from rule number one of Christianity: you need to accept Jesus as your savior before you can be given eternal life. In his 1996 book, *The Beginning of the End*, Hagee argues that the Jews won't come around on the Jesus issue until the Tribulation period. Their hearts will be "warmed toward God" by Israel's miraculous escape from the Russian invasion, but it will be Christ's actual return—the arrival of the Son of God, accompanied by legions of angels and his vast wrath—which will finally bring Jews into the fold.

This is a controversial idea, since it sets up a different standard for Jews and Gentiles when it comes to salvation. Non-Jews are expected to recognize Christ on faith alone, either before the Rapture or during the terrible events of the Tribulation, but Jews can hold out right until Christ returns in person. The rationale for this is that God had punished the Jews for their disobedience in biblical times by blinding them to the Messiah's identity: they simply weren't able to recognize Christ when he came among them, and they're wearing the same God-given blinkers today. They'll eventually realize that Jesus is their redeemer only when they receive the supernatural revelation of his literal return to earth. It's not far from here to that *Jerusalem Post* headline: "Jews Can Get To Heaven."

While Hagee has taken heat from evangelical Christians on this point, he has reveled in his role as a warrior against Christian anti-Semitism. He points out that Christians have justified violence toward Jews since Christ's death by arguing that God has torn up his covenant with Israel. The Old and New Testaments contained many promises to the Jews, referring in detail to the nation of Israel, but then the Jews allowed Jesus to be crucified. Early Christians maintained that God's prophetic promises were then transferred to the new Christian Church, an idea known as "replacement theology."

Hagee hates replacement theology, and condemns it as the root cause of Christian anti-Semitism. But what really gets him steamed is the idea that prophecy might be figurative rather than literal. If "Israel" doesn't mean Israel but instead refers to the Church, then how can you be sure what anything means in Revelation or the Book of Daniel? This literalism is at the root of Hagee's obsession with all things Jewish, and he's willing to bend over backward in his theology to preserve the idea that prophecy has a special role for Jews.

Other evangelicals have landed themselves in trouble for suggesting that you can be saved without accepting Christ. In 2005, the wildly popular preacher Joel Osteen got into a tangle on CNN's *Larry King Live*. Osteen is the pastor of Lakewood in Houston, the largest megachurch in America. (Lakewood has so many members that it recently moved into the 18,000-seat basketball arena that was previously occupied by the Houston Rockets.) A soft-spoken fellow who largely steers clear of the apocalypse, Osteen was talking to Larry King about his new book, which combines Christian teaching with self-help techniques. Larry, who's Jewish, was encouraged by the book's touchy-feely tone. He asked sweetly if there might be a place in heaven for a Jew:

LARRY KING: What if you're Jewish or Muslim, you don't accept Christ at all?

JOEL OSTEEN: You know, I'm very careful about saying who would and wouldn't go to heaven. I don't know . . .

KING: If you believe you have to believe in Christ? They're wrong, aren't they?

OSTEEN: Well, I don't know if I believe they're wrong. I believe here's what the Bible teaches and from the Christian faith this is what I believe. But I just think that only God will judge a person's heart. I spent a lot of time in India with my father. I don't know all about their religion. But I know they love God. And I don't know. I've seen their sincerity. So I don't know. I know for me, and what the Bible teaches, I want to have a relationship with Jesus.

Having already admitted that he wasn't a "fire and brimstone" preacher, Osteen seemed to be walking away from the central tenet of Christianity. This didn't go unnoticed, and a legion of evangelicals went after Osteen for his performance. A few days later came the inevitable retraction: "I regret and sincerely apologize," Osteen said with a glum directness, "that I was unclear on the very thing in which I have dedicated my life."

You could certainly argue that John Hagee has the better excuse: if Osteen's wishy-washy approach has served to broaden his appeal, and maximize his book sales, Hagee's attacks on replacement theology and anti-Semitism may have done some good in a conservative Christian community that still struggles to do right by Judaism. (Witness the ugly debates surrounding Mel Gibson's movie *The Passion of the Christ*, or Mel's unfortunate remarks about Jews when he was arrested for drunk driving in the summer of 2006.) But one of the strange things about Hagee's love for the Jews, and his attacks on anti-Semitism, is that they're not grounded in an idea of tolerance and compassion for other viewpoints and faiths. What Hagee has done, by insisting that God will eventually redeem the Jews after blinding them to Jesus for two thousand years, is to make Jews into past and future Christians. The roots of Hagee's own faith lie in Judaism, since Jesus was himself a Jew, and the future of Christianity will see the reconciliation of Israel and Christians worldwide. On the tolerance and compassion fronts, Joel Osteen seems like a safer bet. In John Hagee's world, if you're not a Jew or a *real* Christian, you're in big trouble.

I'VE COME TO Cornerstone Church with an old friend who knows this part of the world very well. He's an Episcopalian, and he's slightly concerned that the Cornerstone crowd will sniff him out. (The Episcopalian Church has its fair share of people who are quite relaxed about women priests, gay marriage, and liberal ideas.) We're not getting any negative vibes as we reach the main entrance of Cornerstone, and we slalom our way past endless ranks of greeters who are trying to shake hands with the arriving congregation.

We walk through a pair of doors into the church proper. This massive hall is called the Sanctuary, but it's actually a cavernous auditorium with a deep stage, red theater curtains, thousands of seats, and a balcony. On one side of the stage is a large American flag; on the other, an Israeli Star of David. At the back of the Sanctuary are twelve embroidered pennants with Hebrew writing: these banners are intended to represent the Twelve Tribes of biblical Israel. Squeezed between the pennants and scattered all over the auditorium are television cameras. Cornerstone broadcasts its services live across Christian networks and the Internet.

It's a slick operation, and my Episcopalian friend briefly indulges the paranoid fear that he'll be spotted on TV by someone he knows. (I remind him that he doesn't have any friends who watch Christian TV, and he becomes a little calmer.) Just as he's starting to relax, we're assailed by an usher. Cornerstone has dozens of these—they're all men, and they're assigned to a particular section of the seating area. During the service itself, when the congregation is sitting and the ushers continue to stand, they look like prison guards. Our usher is named Robert. He's in his late sixties, and he casually asks where we're from. I tell him that I'm visiting from England, that I've heard about Pastor Hagee, and I'm keen to see him live. My friend seems to be channeling Jim Carrey in *Liar Liar* and blurts out unbidden that he's an Episcopalian. Robert removes an imaginary card from his coat pocket and scans it curiously: "Let's see if you're on the list," he says. He cracks a big smile, though I'm not sure if this entirely reassures the Episcopalian. Robert tells us that Pastor Hagee loves to meet visitors from out of town, and that we should be sure to catch up with him when the service ends.

As the Sanctuary starts to fill up, I'm impressed at the diversity of the congregation. I'd read in one of Hagee's books that he hates racial discrimination, and that he's particularly upset by the fact that so many American churches are effectively segregated along racial lines. I'd imagined that this was a token protest, intended perhaps to distract from the accusations of racial insensitivity that have occasionally been directed his way. In 1996, Hagee got into trouble by organizing a "slave sale" at Cornerstone to raise money for the private school attached to the church. Auctioning off members of the school's senior class, who had agreed to a day's hard work for the successful bidders, Hagee had announced with unseemly excitement that "slavery in America is returning to Cornerstone!" But the crowd at today's service has a lot of African American faces and even more Latinos. In the row directly in front of ours, a Latina is clutching a Cornerstone job application form and begins to fill it out just as the service starts.

If you've never been to an evangelical church, you'll struggle to get your bearings at Cornerstone. In the first place, the forces on display are vast: there's a gospel choir of more than a hundred people, a big band, and a roster of soloists who seem to specialize in every kind of music. Within the first twenty minutes, we've been treated to gospel numbers from the choir, and a long song about Zion belted out by a corpulent young man who looks a lot like Pastor Hagee. A soprano in a red dress sweeps through an aria about Christ, then a hillbilly quartet performs a catchy homage to a charismatic churchman who offers his services to a ne'er-do-well in a time of need.

> *Ain't it just my luck?*
> *Lost my wife and wrecked my truck.*
> *Preacher, I'll do anything you say!*

It's not quite 9:00 A.M., which only makes the experience seem more arresting.

John Hagee presides over all this, but he doesn't say a lot at first. He's a big man, dressed in a sober gray suit, with wire-rimmed glasses and slicked-back gray hair. He looks like a fat Donald Rumsfeld, and has something of Rumsfeld's aura as he sits in a chair—more like a throne, actually—and listens along with the rest of us to the music. Occasionally he waves, regally, at nothing in particular. On the throne next to his, the guy who sang the Zion song takes his place and I realize that he's Matt Hagee, the pastor's son. He's being groomed to take over the church when the time comes, assuming that the Rapture hasn't removed the entire Hagee clan before then.

(When Matt turns twenty-eight later that summer, his father subjects the Cornerstone congregation to a celebration of Stalinist proportions, including a "special video presentation" in which Hagee, Sr., finds the right words for the occasion: "This is my beloved son, in whom I am well pleased.")

During the occasional breaks in the music—which feels like a long warm-up act for the Hagee sermon that's coming—there are announcements for upcoming events, and an intense moment in which Hagee supervises the passing around of the collection plate. This takes me by surprise. Hagee has been quite chattily encouraging us to volunteer at the Cornerstone vacation Bible study school when he suddenly gets onto the subject of money. "How many of you today have come with your tithe or offering?"

The congregation stirs into life.

"Let me see it in your hand!" Hagee demands. "You are now determining God's ability to give to you!"

The pastor produces a verse from Luke's Gospel ("Give and it shall be given to you") to clinch this argument, and asks us to say Luke's words back to him just to be sure that we're all on the same page. Then he tells us to hold our money in the air again, while he prays to God that we'll get a good return on our investment.

The smallest bill I have is a twenty. I agonize over what to do with this. We've already befriended Robert, who's now approaching us with a basket in his hand and a gleam in his eye, and I don't see how I can hold on to my money. The Episcopalian gives me a look as if I'm about to firebomb an abortion clinic, but Robert's getting closer and I've already waved the money in the air on Hagee's cue. (In my defense: *everyone else* is waving money around.) I feel better for an instant, and then somehow much worse, when I see the woman in the row in front of ours—the one clutching the partially completed Cornerstone job application form—scour her purse and fish out her checkbook. After some deliberation, she signs over $85 to Cornerstone and hands the check to Robert. He offers her a smile that's at precisely the same wattage as the one he's given me. Robert ignores the Episcopalian, who sits on his hands glumly.

It wasn't my plan to go into Cornerstone undercover and pretend to be an evangelical, but now I'm caught between my English aversion to any kind of demonstrativeness, and an equally compelling (and equally English) reluctance to stand out in a crowd. There's nowhere to hide: Hagee asks all the visitors to get to their feet to receive the applause of the locals. You can hardly fail to seem like a giver or a holdout when you're asked to thrust your financial offering into the air; and there are so many people waving their arms around during the music that you can't look anonymous without doing the same. After several minutes of arm waving, it occurs to me that I look like someone's pointing a gun in my direction. Being caught up in the experience is something that can't easily be feigned.

When Hagee finally starts his sermon, I'm shocked by the ground he manages to cover. For the first ten minutes, he complains that Christians are marginalized in America and that Muslims get privileges and respect even though their faith inspires terrorism. "Radical Muslims attacked America on 9/11," Hagee tells us, "and they still have their sights set on the destruction of Israel and the United States of America. And yet the Koran is required reading in many universities and public schools—the same schools and universities that forbid reading of the Bible, and mock the teachings of the Bible in the classroom."

This doesn't seem very plausible, but Hagee steamrolls his way through a host of similar assertions: Muslims get to celebrate their religious holidays in American public schools, but Christian children are scolded for using the word "Christmas." Instead, Hagee spits, they have to celebrate a "winter holiday." (He's getting apoplectic about this in May, and he must be white-hot with rage when December rolls around.) Children are taught that "Heather has two mommies," while the nuclear family and Christian morals are disregarded. "Why are we teaching them witchcraft through Harry Potter?" Hagee inquires, before insisting that the audience choose between the liberal permissiveness of Dr. Spock and the timeless wisdom of Solomon. ("Spare the rod and spoil the child!") After one particularly withering attack on pornography, which the audience has applauded wildly, Hagee emits a loud, jarring shriek that sounds a lot like a macaw. There's some nervous laughter among the congregation, and I'm not sure if he's filled with the Holy Spirit or crowing at the hellfire that awaits those pornographers.

Hagee is only partly focused on the three or four thousand of us who are actually in Cornerstone Church. His real quarry lies beyond, in the audience watching on Christian television or via the Internet. It's these viewers who are surely sitting up as Hagee asks a pregnant question: "Do the people in the churches of America really know God?" America, it seems, "is being saturated with a counterfeit Christianity." Fake Christians and phony pastors are promoting an empty religion that doesn't make any real requests of its adherents, and doesn't outline any consequences for those who reject it. Hagee's having none of this, and rails against "cotton candy" preachers who "walk along the abortion issue, walk along the same-sex marriage issue," and who fail to register that abortion is "murder," and homosexuality is an "abomination." His angry questions shoot past us and into Christian living rooms across America: "Let me ask you, when was the last time you heard your preacher preach a sermon on sin? Your preacher sounds a lot more like Dr. Phil or Sigmund Freud than St. Paul."

The sermon oscillates between the shrewd and the hysterical; Hagee occasionally mixes up his targets, or froths with such abandon that you begin to fear him more than his wrathful God:

> Cotton candy preachers don't mind sinners saying, "I didn't get enough cookies when I was in the Boy Scouts, therefore I've grown up to become a psychopathic killer. And that's my problem." But your real problem is that you've got the DEVIL in you! THAT'S the problem!

The performance builds to a climax that leaves you with some coherent ideas about God and America. Hagee seems to have no faith in many of his fellow Christians, and suggests that the 160 million church members in the United States are mostly "counterfeit" believers. He argues that the overwhelming evidence of "deception" in contemporary moral and religious teachings—from sinister public school teachers who tell eight-year-olds to celebrate lesbianism, to the phony Christians who appoint gay bishops or who try to put pressure on Israel—demonstrates that the End Times are at hand. Jesus prophesied that deception would be one of the signs that humanity had entered its last days: "We're there!" Hagee announces, before adding a rhetorical flourish: "There are many false prophets who are going to deceive—many, not a few!" He pauses for a second. "Many, as in MOST!"

The apocalyptic motifs work quite differently in the sermon than in Hagee's books. Here, he warns us that we could be taking our last breath—that Christ could come back to earth *this minute*—and that the imminence of the Rapture should compel us to beg God for forgiveness. Hence the theater at the end of his sermon, when he calls upon anyone in the congregation with unconfessed sins to come forward. To my surprise, some people bound up right away (as if they did this every week) and happily head for the area in front of the stage where Hagee towers over them. "Dozens of people now raising their hands," Hagee whispers into his microphone for the viewers at home.

The choir begins softly singing "There's Room at the Cross," and Hagee allows a few minutes for people's sins to catch up with them. "This is the greatest decision you'll ever make in your life," he begins, before eventually making it clear that if we don't head to the front *right now*, then he'll be blameless if we fail to get into heaven. "Don't run to me on the day of judgment and say, 'If you'd made that a little clearer, I'd have got it.' It's clear." He looks around the audience. There are perhaps a hundred people now squeezed up against the stage. "Anyone else? Just before we close? God bless you."

There's a bathos about all this, in spite of the undeniable sincerity that's driving the sinners to pray at Hagee's feet. This becomes clear as the sinners are led away by one of his helpers to a "counseling room," where they'll be advised on their next step toward accepting Christ. (As they're leaving, Hagee addresses the rest of us like a game show host: "Give them a warm hand as they go!") But it's hard to deny the power of Hagee's performance. In his Cornerstone services, he's created a highly efficient machine for winning souls, promoting conservative values, and insisting that the apocalypse is just around the corner. Weirdly, he seems to have succeeded in this mostly by attacking other Christians, and portraying Cornerstone and its patrons as the embattled minority amid an America of counterfeit believers.

I WENT TO MEET Pastor Hagee afterward. Taking directions from Robert, the helpful usher, I made my way to the guest reception that Hagee had announced during the service. Once again, outstretched hands were everywhere: a vanguard of Cornerstone officials had spread across the large reception room before the arrival of the visitors, and they circulated forms that would help the pastor keep in touch with us from afar. The operation was so well drilled that, if you agreed to fill out a card, Hagee's staff would telephone or write to you if the pastor held an event anywhere within 150 miles of where you live. I didn't return my card, but I have no doubt that this is true.

When Hagee showed up, he took to a dais and asked us all where we'd come from. Most of the visitors were from other parts of Texas; a few were from Oklahoma, Missouri, and California. When Hagee finally got to me, I told him that I'd come from London and he seemed distinctly unimpressed. One of his handlers had promised that I'd win the ribbon awarded each week for the most far-flung attendee, but Hagee seemed to realize instantly that I wasn't a real pilgrim. I waited to meet him when he'd finished talking, and eventually I got my audience. I told Pastor Hagee that I'd love to chat with him about his career, and that I'd call his office on Monday for an interview, but he quickly moved past me to the folks clutching multiple copies of the *Hagee Study Bible* and *Jerusalem Countdown*. (I'd left mine in the car.) So I wandered back to the parking lot and rejoined the traffic on the freeway that runs right past Cornerstone. As I drove away from the church, the cars were already arriving for the 11:00 A.M. service. Men wearing bright orange bibs directed the long lines of traffic, and an armed guard patrolled the parking lot as another set of families spilled from their SUVs toward the Sanctuary.

Before I left San Antonio, I stopped by the local mosque to find out what the city's Muslims thought of their intemperate neighbor. I was expecting to find a community that was much more embattled than Cornerstone. In the summer of 2005, the custodian at the Islamic Center on the southwest side of the city arrived one morning to find a metal briefcase outside the main doors. He called 911, and morning prayers were canceled as the police investigated the mysterious package. It turned out to be several hundred dollars in cash, which had been left by an anonymous donor.

There wasn't any security on the day I visited the Islamic Center. I wandered in, was greeted by a mosque official who'd learned English in Kuwait via a Cambridge correspondence course, and I was quickly introduced to the imam. He was happy to talk about Hagee. I told him about some of the more provocative things in *Jerusalem Countdown*, and about the attacks on Islam in Hagee's sermon, but he seemed positively serene. "He must tell people what he thinks to be the truth," he told me. "And I must do the same. And then people can decide for themselves what is the truth."

2

In Search of a Perfect Red Heifer

When John Hagee takes to the stage at the Washington Hilton in July 2006, he looks out on a ballroom filled with cheering evangelicals. Christians United for Israel is holding its first annual Washington-Israel Summit, and nearly 3,500 delegates from every state have traveled to the capital. Tonight is the "talking points banquet," during which the delegates will be given their marching orders by the executive director of CUFI, David Brog. Tomorrow, thousands of evangelicals will converge on Capitol Hill to bring the message directly to Congress. A Christian TV network is carrying the banquet live, and John Hagee is in his element. As he begins his speech, he's framed by an enormous Israeli flag draped behind the platform. "Every person here tonight knows that he is here through divine appointment," he says, and the crowd goes wild. "If you clap like this all night, it's gonna be a long party."

He's right about the second part. The CUFI organizers have recruited an impressive roster of guests and speakers. Jerry

Falwell is here. So is Pat Boone, the 1950s rock and roll legend, who's now a born-again Christian and a tireless foe of the Dixie Chicks. The blessing comes from Bishop Keith Butler, an African-American conservative minister from Michigan who is waging an unlikely battle to win a seat in the U.S. Senate. The Israeli ambassador, Daniel Ayalon, assures the crowd that the government of Israel appreciates their support. Gary Bauer, the former Reagan aide, presents the founding of CUFI as a pivotal moment in American history. Rabbi Scheinberg attests to the Jewish community's love for Hagee. Ken Mehlman, the chairman of the Republican National Committee, has a John F. Kennedy moment as he announces that "today we are all Israelis." Two senators—Sam Brownback of Kansas and Rick Santorum of Pennsylvania—tell the crowd that their efforts are making a difference in Congress. And the former chief of staff of the Israeli army, General Moshe Ya'alon, outlines the military threat to Israel, and suggests that the Arabs have proved themselves to be terminally unreliable partners in peace.

The backdrop to all this is a week of meltdown in the Middle East. Members of Hamas dug a tunnel under the Gaza-Israel border in late June 2006 and kidnapped an Israeli soldier; Israel bombarded and eventually invaded Gaza to try to retrieve him. Then Hezbollah, the radical Shia group, stole across Israel's northern border and kidnapped three more Israeli soldiers, demanding the release of Hezbollah prisoners in Israel. Even though the military response in Gaza had failed to locate the missing soldier, the new Israeli prime minister, Ehud Olmert, launched a sweeping attack on Lebanon as well. Hezbollah fired rockets into Israel, and killed nearly a dozen civilians in the city of Haifa. And so it went, with Israel hitting back with even greater force, and no end to the conflict in sight. By the night of the CUFI summit, more than twenty Israelis are dead, and the residents of northern towns and cities are dodging the sporadic, capricious rockets of Hezbollah. Lebanon, meanwhile, is in a state of chaos: roads and bridges have been destroyed, nearly half a million Lebanese have fled from their homes, and perhaps three hundred people (the vast majority, civilians) have been killed.

In Europe, and much of the world outside the United States, the talk is of a disproportionate response from Israel. In Congress, meanwhile, legislators have passed a resolution offering staunch support for Israel. Congressional resolutions aren't the be-all and end-all of American politics—the House of Representatives recently agreed to "congratulate Italy on winning the 2006 FIFA World Cup" and to recognize "the extraordinary leadership of coach Marcello Lippi and captain Fabio Cannavaro." But the sheer extent of bipartisan support for the pro-Israel motion is striking, especially given the anxieties around the world about the war in Lebanon. The Senate resolution has sixty-one co-sponsors—people who are willing not only to vote for the motion but to attach their name to the draft. Among these sponsors are the Democratic Party's biggest names: Hillary Clinton, Ted Kennedy, John Kerry, Barack Obama. The story in the House of Representatives is the same: the motion there is sponsored by Nancy Pelosi, the Democratic leader who's regularly derided by Republicans for being a far-out San Francisco liberal.

Given that the Democrats have lined up with Republicans to defend Israel even at this delicate moment, it's hard to see what the CUFI summit can achieve. Could the U.S. government be any more pro-Israel than it already is? Gradually, though, the speeches in the ballroom reveal a more extreme agenda that will inform tomorrow's lobbying. The speakers insist that the Israeli withdrawal from Gaza in September 2005 was a big mistake. The Arabs haven't shown any gratitude, they've continued their war against Israel, and they've proved that they're not interested in a land-for-peace deal. Iran and Syria are behind the new crisis in Lebanon. Iran is led by a madman in the mold of Adolf Hitler who must be faced down, and the United States cannot allow Iran to acquire nuclear weapons. America faces a religious war in which "radical Islam" or "Islamofascism" is trying to conquer the world.

There are some strange moments in all this. A number of speakers imply that the Israeli attacks on Lebanon are an effort to liberate the majority of Lebanese from Hezbollah. Meanwhile, Senator Santorum keeps insisting that the "war on terror" is a misnomer. "Terror is not the enemy," he says, "the enemy are Islamic fascists." Someone in the crowd shouts "Yeah!" A few people start to whoop, and the audience breaks into applause. I'm confused. Wasn't it President Bush who came up with that phrase? Santorum tells the audience that the "war on terror" is a conspiracy to deny the real, religious nature of America's struggle. "Get that phrase out of your lexicon. Never use it." He concedes that Islamic fascism is a "mosaic," but he hasn't neglected his talking points for the evening: "The biggest piece of this mosaic, the one that reaches out and touches all the others, is Iran. We must confront Iran."

Iran is the subject of *Jerusalem Countdown*, and John Hagee has been forecasting an End Times confrontation with Mahmoud Ahmadinejad since the book was published in January. In the past week, Hagee and other apocalyptic Christians have been popping up on news programs speculating on whether this latest Middle East battle might trigger the End Times sequence. Rick Santorum, though, has different ideas.

"Iran is led by a group of mullahs that are messianic in their belief, in their Shia belief. They believe in the return of the hidden or twelfth imam, and they believe it is their obligation to bring about the end of such times by the destruction of the State of Israel and the West. That is the reality of who we fight in Iran."

No one applauds this, and perhaps some of the delegates are a little embarrassed by the senator's chutzpah. It's the *Iranians* who are leading us to doomsday?

As the banquet enters its third hour, the organizers try to keep the audience happy with musical interludes. Pat Boone is just here for the speeches, so the Cornerstone choir and orchestra are left to entertain the crowd. They've brought their Hebrew-language repertoire from San Antonio, and Matt Hagee is also here to sing his song of Zion. (Matt, in what must be a family joke, has been appointed regional director of CUFI for New England, the smallest delegation.) Then everyone sits up for the late appearance of Tom DeLay. Formerly leader of the Republicans in the House of Representatives, DeLay has been lying low since being indicted in a political fund-raising scandal. He seems extremely chipper, and throws his support behind Israel and the CUFI effort in Washington.

When John Hagee returns to the stage, four hours after he kicked off the banquet, the delegates are exhausted. In the middle of the speeches, the air conditioning has broken down, and the room is unbearably warm. He pleads with them to stick around in the giant hotel ballroom to meet with their regional coordinators and to strategize for their meetings the next day. David Brog, CUFI's executive director, urges the delegates to "be nice" when they meet with their representatives, and to stick to the three talking points ("and only these three!") that CUFI wants them to focus on.

Israel's actions in Lebanon and Gaza. Please remember: Israel withdrew from southern Lebanon. Israel withdrew from Gaza. The response to their withdrawal was aggression! Support Israel in what it needs to do in Lebanon and Gaza, for as long as Israel deems necessary. Do not pressure Israel to withdraw from territory that it deems necessary to its security.

We're going to talk about blocking aid to the Hamas-led government. It mustn't receive one dollar in U.S. aid. President Bush has cut off aid to Hamas, but we need to make this law so that anyone who comes after will likewise cut off aid to Hamas.

Preventing a nuclear Iran. There is a bill in the House called the Iran Freedom Support Act; it's passed the House so thank your member for supporting it. There's yet to be action in the Senate. Ask your senators to support renewal of the Iran-Libya Sanctions Act.

Brog tells the delegates to push Congress beyond merely supporting Israel. Instead, American politicians should give Israel a free hand to deal with its neighbors, they should abandon their faith in land-for-peace as the basis for diplomacy in the region, and they should prepare Americans for a conflict with Iran over nuclear weapons. Although this agenda sounds ambitious, Brog reminds the delegates that both the Senate and House have already demonstrated their firm support for Israel during its latest war in Lebanon. "It's all about building a relationship," he says brightly.

AS DAVID BROG COMPLETES the briefing, it's clear that the delegates are not supposed to bring up the timing of the apocalypse with their elected representatives. Brog has already fended off questions from an NPR reporter on this subject: "I think there's no greater fallacy than the one that claims Christians support Israel simply to speed the Second Coming." The apocalyptic backdrop to John Hagee's pro-Israel crusade emerges only fleetingly through the evening. The regional directors are asked to come up to the stage and lead a cheerleading session for their particular delegation, and these lieutenants allude obliquely to the importance of Israel in God's plan for the future. One of the directors is John Hagee's publisher, Stephen Strang, and he can't resist mentioning *Jerusalem Countdown* to warm applause from the crowd. The delegates are clearly fans of Hagee's books, but I wonder if Rick Santorum has seen Hagee's *Attack on America: New York, Jerusalem, and the Role of Terrorism in the Last Days*? Has Senator Brownback read *Final Dawn over Jerusalem*? If they have, would they be more or less likely to take to the stage alongside the pastor?

My impression from talking to people in San Antonio is that many of Hagee's critics haven't spent much time with his books. Barry Block, the Reform rabbi who'd been particularly outspoken in his criticism, admitted that he hadn't read *Jerusalem Countdown*. Even Rabbi Scheinberg, Hagee's emissary to the Jewish community, seemed sketchy on the pastor's new bestseller: "I've read segments of it—significant segments," he told me.

John Hagee has written more than a dozen books, mostly on prophetic themes. In 2000, he even started writing a series of apocalyptic novels directed at readers of the *Left Behind* series, though these didn't prove as popular as his "nonfiction" work. Since Hagee has produced five or six books like *Jerusalem Countdown* in the past decade alone, I thought I should read them all and try to get a sense of his thinking. In particular, I was interested in a question that had bothered me since I first saw *Jerusalem Countdown* in that New York bookstore. Was John Hagee simply interpreting current affairs for his readers, or was he encouraging evangelical Christians to get involved in politics and to hasten the apocalypse?

There's a clear formula in Hagee's prophecy writing. He starts with a hot-button topic from international affairs, something that will make for a juicy title or a striking image on the book jacket, and then explains the prophetic significance of what's going on in the world. With extraordinary persistence, he reverts to the scheme that I outlined in the last chapter: Russia will attack Israel, God will protect the Israelis and vanquish the Russians, the faithful will be Raptured, the Antichrist will emerge and take over the world, and after the seven years of Tribulation, Christ himself will destroy his enemies at Armageddon and establish his earthly kingdom for a thousand years.

What makes these books interesting is that, invariably, they begin with a totally straight section on current affairs. Hagee writes about diplomatic negotiations, the technical specifications of nuclear weapons, or the details of Middle Eastern politics as if he were a journalist for the *Wall Street Journal* or a conservative magazine like the *National Review*. Only after you're lured in by this ostensibly reasonable and secular preamble does he hit you with the apocalyptic stuff.

Take his 1996 book, *The Beginning of the End: Yitzhak Rabin and the Coming Antichrist*. This appeared soon after the assassination of the Israeli prime minister in November 1995, and seems at first to be a tribute to his peace efforts. The back cover notes that Rabin was "cruelly and coldheartedly struck down by an assassin's bullet," and that the promise of peace is "a prophecy that the Bible makes for the last days." What you don't find out, until you read the book itself, is that Hagee sees Middle East peace as a project of the Antichrist rather than an effort that the world should unite behind. In Hagee's view, there can be no lasting peace in the Middle East until Christ arrives in person.

In fact, any signs of a thaw between Israelis and Palestinians merely indicate that the Antichrist is on his way, since he will use his miraculous powers of diplomacy to bring a temporary end to the Middle East crisis and to smooth his own path to world domination. "Israel will unite and peace will prevail," Hagee promises, "when the country accepts the false man of peace who steps out onto the world's stage." At this point, true Christians will recognize the Prince of Darkness (if they haven't already been whisked away in the Rapture) and will distance themselves from the satanic peace process.

Reading *The Beginning of the End* is a disorienting experience, not least because it makes you sympathize more with the assassin than with his victim. Rabin was shot by a right-wing religious extremist, Yigal Amir, who believed that the prime minister had betrayed his country by handing over parts of the Occupied Territories to the Palestinians. Amir, like John Hagee, was convinced that Israel had a biblical right to this land. Hagee stresses that Amir had no criminal record, that he came from an upstanding family, and that he'd worked for the Israeli government overseas. He makes strenuous efforts to understand Amir's position, and then moves into a discussion of the gulf between religious Israelis like Amir—who believe that Israel has "a holy deed to the land"—and the secular majority, which is trying to build "an economy based on technology and tourism" and which places "more faith in man than in the God of their fathers." What's to like about Rabin if he represents this secular and material generation? Hagee's only explicit reservation about his killer is that Amir may have deterred other Israelis from returning to the faith of their fathers. Beyond this, there's a good deal in *The Beginning of the End* that justifies Amir's motives, if not his method.

Hagee, like a lot of other prophecy interpreters, was enthralled by the Middle East peace process in the 1990s. The sight of Rabin and Yasser Arafat shaking hands on the White House lawn in 1993 prompted a wave of speculation about the Antichrist's identity among prophecy enthusiasts. Perhaps it was President Clinton himself, with his arms spread wide in that famous photo of the Palestinian and Israeli antagonists. Even after Rabin's assassination, Hagee believed that the peace process would culminate in a comprehensive settlement and the rise of the Antichrist.

Things didn't turn out that way. In the spring of 1996, before *The Beginning of the End* hit the bookstores, Rabin's successor, the supposedly dovish Shimon Peres, launched his own war against Lebanon. The Israeli public believed that he hadn't gone far enough against Hezbollah, and he was replaced by the hardliner Benjamin Netanyahu. Bill Clinton, meanwhile, fell into the secretarial honey pot and endured a painstakingly graphic public examination that hardly suited a son of Satan. The Antichrist would surely have been more careful with the intern, or would have covered up his dastardly actions more effectively than Clinton managed Monica Lewinsky. Can you be too grubby to qualify as the Prince of Darkness? Clinton's skills of deception were made to seem wanting as Congress and the media laid bare his indiscretions.

And so John Hagee struggled to see either a peace deal or an Antichrist contender in the messy standoff between Israelis and Palestinians, and by the end of 2000 he was looking for another prophetic angle on current events. His new book, *The Battle for Jerusalem*, was completed just as George W. Bush and Al Gore were locked in their electoral stalemate in Florida. Hagee seized on this unusual situation to fashion a new argument about the Antichrist's emergence: perhaps the political confusion in America would create an opportunity for a "charismatic strong leader" to take over the world. That leader could hardly come from the United States, where the bitterly contested election would probably result in a weakened and unpopular president. Surely the European Union was more likely to yield a figure with global appeal. Or perhaps the United Nations.

If you read *The Battle for Jerusalem* today, Hagee's efforts to create apocalyptic tension will seem quaint. The Peruvian president has resigned, he informs us. There's an impeachment scandal in the Philippines! These events don't seem like the harbingers of the Antichrist, and the failure of events in the Middle East to match up with Hagee's predictions makes you feel almost sorry for the pastor.

But then came 9/11. Hagee's apocalyptic plotting was revitalized by Al Qaeda, and before the end of 2001 he had issued an updated version of *The Battle for Jerusalem* with a new title and cover: *Attack on America* makes no reference to the earlier version, even though the book is identical save for a new introduction. (And the deletion of that chapter on instability in Peru and the Philippines.) The new cover features a close-up of the World Trade Center. "The world as we know it ended Tuesday September 11," says Hagee in the introduction. In fact, 9/11 simply gave him a new way to present the familiar apocalyptic scheme.

What's interesting about this post–9/11 perspective, though, is that John Hagee finds himself torn between old-fashioned American patriotism and the theological fatalism of his prophecy beliefs. He tells us that he found out about the attacks while he was conducting a prayer service at Cornerstone. He rushed to his television and instantly realized that "the Third World War had begun and that it would escalate from this day until the Battle of Armageddon."

But does this mean that the United States is destined to lose the war on terror? Is it unpatriotic to follow apocalyptic logic to its dark conclusion?

Hagee can't quite give up on America. "This is not a time to 'prove' who ordered this bloody attack," Hagee chides politicians in Washington. "We don't need lawyers at a world tribunal in the Hague. We need warriors! America will either take bold, aggressive action and win, or we will continue to make excuses and lose." But if God has decided to start the countdown toward Armageddon, what difference will it make if American policymakers get tough with the Taliban, or set up an extralegal prison camp at Guantánamo Bay?

Shouldn't apocalyptic Christians *want* America to lose?

Hagee offers three explanations for the 9/11 attacks, and they don't sit easily with one another. In the first place, he argues that God is pulling the strings and that the End Times are at hand. But he's also working out a conservative machismo that makes him sound like Bill O'Reilly or Glenn Beck. "Why did this attack happen? It happened because our enemies believe America lacks the will to win." Hagee reminisces about the wars in Korea and Vietnam, and concludes that America would have won these conflicts (and would already have defeated Al Qaeda) if politicians had been "committed to victory."

Weak-wristed liberals bear the blame for a dovish foreign policy, but Hagee also has their domestic policy in his sights: "Why did this attack happen? It happened because the United States has an open border policy that makes it impossible to tell who is in our country and for what reason." For a group of people who expect to be Raptured from this world in the near future, apocalyptic Christians are remarkably hostile toward immigrants. Hagee's shot in *Attack on America* seems especially low: "Our political leaders for more than a decade have been so fearful of offending one ethnic group or another that we have put all Americans at risk."

A lax immigration policy isn't the nation's only problem. "America has mocked God," Hagee notes, before producing a long list of moral crimes that might explain why God would allow terrorists to attack the United States. "We, as a nation, have accepted Satanism into the U.S. military with the full knowledge and approval of the U.S. Congress." (This goes unexplained.) "The Virgin Mary, the mother of God, was painted as a work of 'art' funded by tax dollars and presented to the citizens of New York City covered in elephant dung." (This is a reference to Chris Ofili, the British artist who incurred the wrath of Mayor Rudy Giuliani when he exhibited his dung Madonna in Brooklyn in 1999.) Hagee rails against secular humanism, drugs, alcohol, materialism, and pornography, then argues that the nation deserves punishment for its wrongdoing. "America has committed every sin of Sodom and Gomorrah, and just as God's judgment came to Sodom and Gomorrah, it is now being poured out upon America." Unless America is willing to repent, then 9/11 will simply be the beginning of the nation's woes. "Will this happen again?" Hagee asks. "Absolutely!"

JOHN HAGEE'S POLITICAL VIEWS, which overlap with those of many secular right-wingers, are occasionally punctuated by truly bizarre diversions that remind you of his religious obsession. Like many prophecy enthusiasts, Hagee believes that the Temple in Jerusalem—which was destroyed by the Romans in the first century—will be rebuilt in the End Times. Temple worshippers must be spiritually clean before entering the Temple, and so biblical purification rituals must be observed in the rebuilt Temple before Christ can return. According to the Book of Numbers, believers can only be purified by the ashes of a red heifer. In fact, the cow has to be *perfectly* red: "without spot, wherein is no blemish, and upon which never came yoke."

Finding a perfect red heifer might seem like an arcane pursuit for a successful televangelist, and an unlikely diversion in a book about 9/11. But John Hagee writes excitedly about the search for the favored cow in *Attack on America* and in his other prophecy books. He is particularly enthusiastic about the work of Mississippi cattle rancher Clyde Lott, who has been trying for more than a decade to produce animals in the United States that could be flown to Israel. (As soon as their status as perfectly red has been confirmed by rabbinical authorities.) Lott's best shot was a calf called Melody who, alas, "developed a few white hairs" before she could be declared kosher. This keeps happening to Lott, and Hagee has been let down on a number of occasions by last-minute glitches like the one that afflicted Melody. In 2000, he bought his own South Texas ranch and entered into a mysterious partnership with the grandly named Texas Israel Agricultural Research Foundation. Perhaps his own operation can uncover the cow that will hasten Christ's arrival.

Heifers and Hezbollah make strange bedfellows, and a reader of Hagee's books could be forgiven for asking why the pastor turns out these repetitive bestsellers. (Save for the crude argument that they boost his income.) Here's what he says about this in *The Beginning of the End*: "My single purpose in writing this book is to prepare you for the future and coming of Antichrist." This works on two levels. If you're smart, you can read a Hagee book today and embrace Christ completely. If you do this, then you're in with a chance of the Rapture and you can escape the Tribulation. This is definitely the best option, and Hagee speaks about the experience of being Raptured in ecstatic terms:

I'll know Jesus has reappeared when my glorified body sails through the heavens past the Milky Way into the presence of God. I'll know I'm with the real Jesus when I stand in his glorious presence with my brand-new, disease-proof, never-dying, fatigue-free body that looks better, feels better, and is better than Arnold Schwarzenegger's.

Hagee is sixty-six years old, and he doesn't look much like Arnold Schwarzenegger. Embracing Christ is obviously the way to go if you can get hold of a Hagee book in time.

If you disregard the message of *The Coming Antichrist* or *Attack on America*, all is not lost. John Hagee agrees with the *Left Behind* authors that you may get a second chance at salvation if you miss the Rapture, since new converts to Christ will band together to fight the Antichrist during the Tribulation period. This is a controversial idea even for some apocalyptic Christians, who see little reason for hope in Bible prophecy before Jesus comes back in person to obliterate his enemies. Hagee is much more upbeat: "If this book outlives my time on earth, and I honestly believe it will, let me assure you that it is not too late to recognize Jesus Christ as the son of God, the promised Messiah."

Beyond preparing people for the Rapture or the Tribulation, Hagee's books have a definite political edge. But perhaps it's not quite as direct or as obvious as the titles or covers of the books might lead you to imagine. If you bought *The Beginning of the End* or *Attack on America* for a simple answer—What's the significance of Rabin's death? Why was America attacked on September 11?—you'll be disappointed by the contents. While Hagee begins with a discussion of Middle East politics or American military strategy, he's soon offering paeans to biblical Israel or trying to fit the place-names of the Book of Ezekiel onto the landscape of southern Russia. Sooner or later, every Hagee book goes down the rabbit hole of prophetic speculation, and the thing that you were chasing when you picked up the book—the image of the burning World Trade Center, say, or Rabin's assassination—has vanished.

Hagee's books are most successful in establishing an apocalyptic anxiety among readers, and advancing a set of political
prejudices that shape the way in which American evangelicals
view the rest of the world. The most immediate of these concerns
Israel. Hagee is convinced that "lasting peace will not come to
Jerusalem until Messiah comes." There's no point in talking to
Palestinians, and even secular Israelis should be shunned if they
seem eager to embrace their neighbors. Hagee is a fundamentalist on the issue of territorial compromise. God gave Israel a land
grant that encompasses the Occupied Territories. This makes
Hagee an unapologetic supporter not only of right-wing Israeli
leaders like Benjamin Netanyahu but of the Israeli settlers whose
expanding presence in the Palestinian territories is at the heart of
the conflict. During the Night to Honor Israel in October 2006,
John Hagee presented an enormous check for $500,000 to Ron
Nachman, the mayor of Ariel, one of the largest settlements in
the West Bank. In the left-hand corner, where you're supposed to
record the purpose of the check, John Hagee had written in very
large letters, "THE LAND."

Beyond reminding his readers of the inviolable land grant
from God to the Jews, Hagee insists that any successes in the
peace process only confirm that the Antichrist is making head-
way. This allows him to pour scorn on the possibility of peace,
and to cast aspersions on those diplomats who seem to be making
progress in that direction. You can easily find this prophetic logic
in Hagee's books, but it's not something that he aired in front of
the VIPs and congressional representatives at the CUFI summit
in Washington. Sounding like any other American conservative,
Hagee did not subject the Israeli ambassador to a lecture about
the coming Antichrist, and yet the End Times are central to his
support for Israel.

For John Hagee, Bible prophecy has made Israel into a heroic
nation that deserves uncritical support. The same prophecies
have also created a number of bogeymen, and Hagee encourages

his followers to share his suspicions about them. His insistence on the literal truth of Ezekiel—and his rickety reading of Gog and Magog—has led Hagee to see Russia as a natural enemy of Israel and America. The Russians, he insists, will be dragged by God into attacking Israel and igniting "Ezekiel's war."

Before 1991, prophecy interpreters found it easy to stir up hatred toward the Soviet Union, and the priorities of the Cold War and the End Times were neatly aligned. For the past decade and a half, writers like Hagee have had a harder time of it. In 1996, he claimed that Russia was still sore about its loss of superpower status, and wanted to control the Middle East to regain its pride and its place in the world. By 2001, after the Russian government's disastrous handling of the independence movement in Chechnya, Hagee was warning that a homegrown Muslim threat could explain a Russian attack on Israel. (He also suggested that God had chosen Russia as the cosmic fall guy in the doomed attack on Israel to punish the Russians for their godless embrace of communism, and their persistent anti-Semitism.) Finally, in 2006, Hagee predicted an alliance between Russia and Iran that would lead to a joint operation against the Jewish state; this time, it was the supposed mineral deposits beneath the Dead Sea that would inspire Russia's leaders to pursue such a rash invasion: "The wealth of the Dead Sea has the Russian bear salivating at the mouth," he concluded.

I'm not sure that Hagee knows much about Russia, and I imagine that his audience can simply build on the long hostility of the Cold War in visualizing a Russian threat. Russian-American relations may be robust enough to survive this evangelical paranoia, but the intention of Hagee's predictions is clear: he wants to turn back the clock of the past twenty years, and to isolate Russia from the international community.

Another End Times villain is the United Nations, which comes in for a bashing not only because it often reaches a different conclusion about world events from the United States but because the very idea of a world government is indelibly associated in the mind of apocalyptic Christians with the devilish scheme of the Antichrist. In recent years, the UN has seemed more feeble than Russia, and an unlikely vessel for Satan's hopes. But Hagee is in the watchtower, scanning events for any sign of the world government, world religion, and world economy that the Antichrist will soon exploit.

The UN, he claims, foiled the American effort during the Korean War, tying the hands of the United States and preventing the courageous Douglas MacArthur from winning the conflict outright. (MacArthur was eventually removed from command by Harry Truman, soon after the general had drawn up plans for the use of nuclear weapons on the North Koreans.) The UN was also to blame, indirectly, for America's other great frustration in Southeast Asia. The seductive ideas of international law, which were peddled by UN officials and proclamations, had so overtaken American leaders by the 1960s that they were forced to fight the Vietnam War with one hand tied behind their back. Even in the 1990s, the UN drew the United States into the wars in the Balkans with one-world thinking. "Quietly, and with great subtlety," Hagee declared in 1996, "the road is being paved for the one world government of the Antichrist."

One could hardly accuse George W. Bush of pursuing a one-world agenda, or having much time for the United Nations. In 2005, he appointed a UN ambassador, John Bolton, who had once remarked that if the UN Secretariat building "lost ten stories, it wouldn't make a bit of difference." Hagee remained vigilant even as the Bush administration charted its own course. "The UN deeply resents the U.S. for not bowing to its global agenda," he wrote in *Jerusalem Countdown*. This meant that the United Nations would be entirely inappropriate for the job of monitoring Iran's compliance with arms control agreements, or organizing an international response to Iran's supposed nuclear program.

But the most unnerving of Hagee's prejudices concerns Islam.

Hagee has won the admiration of many Christians—and even conservative Jews—for his "courageous stands against Islam," as Rabbi Scheinberg of San Antonio put it to me. Even before September 11, Hagee liked to argue that Islam had a "triumphalist" ideology that demanded the overthrow of Israel. He took the 2001 attacks as a confirmation of this, and then began to dismantle the popular assumption that Muslims, like Christians and Jews, share a common religious heritage: "Do not be confused into thinking that Allah is just another name for the same God worshipped by Christians and Jews," he cautioned. By 2006, theology had become the root cause of the Israeli-Palestinian conflict, rather than land or history; the God of Islam was now "totally different from the God we know"; and American Christians should steel themselves for a "religious war" in which tolerance and mutual respect would only cloud the battlefield: "We can sit around making diversity quilts and thinking happy thoughts, or we can, with charity, commit ourselves to soberly assess the historical and present-day reality of the absolute commitment of Islam to violence, to murder, and to terror toward anyone who rejects their faith."

I thought about that line during the CUFI banquet in Washington, when the only Democratic member of Congress to address the crowd—the representative from Las Vegas, Shelley Berkley—reached for a comforting line on diversity in America even as she pledged her support for Israel. "What's great about America," she told the delegates, "is that I can be a Jewish woman from a town like Las Vegas, coming before a group of Christians wearing a sweater made by a Muslim woman." This was the only positive thing that anyone said about Islam or Muslims all night. Perhaps Berkley was surprised when the delegates didn't greet her words with a cheer, but this is a crowd that has been groomed by Hagee and others to see Islam itself as the problem.

Which brings us to *Jerusalem Countdown* and John Hagee's new role as a cheerleader for war with Iran. "The Jerusalem Countdown has begun," he writes on page two. "It is a countdown that will usher in the end of this world." In some ways, this book is like all the others, and it has the same strange mix of policy and prophecy. Detailed discussions of nuclear proliferation sit side by side with chapters on God's promises to Israel and the flawed logic of replacement theology. Hagee spills the beans on secret conversations he's had with Israeli leaders (mostly Benjamin Netanyahu) relating to the location and defenses of Iranian nuclear research sites, and then considers what Revelation has to say about China's role in the End Times. This is surely the only book to include a section on "The Six Step Procedure for Making a Nuclear Bomb" and a discussion of "The Parallels Between Moses and Jesus."

What makes *Jerusalem Countdown* different from its predecessors is not only its commercial appeal but its relentless focus on the need to attack Iran. If Hagee's previous books have tended to blur the question of political action, *Jerusalem Countdown* sticks to its talking points with the practiced discipline of a CUFI delegate: Iran's nuclear program is real; Iran obtained the ability to launch a nuclear attack sometime around the middle of 2006; President Ahmadinejad is determined to use nuclear weapons against Israel and the United States.

Hagee presents the obvious policy conclusion: American policymakers should launch a preemptive strike on the suspected Iranian nuclear sites, perhaps in conjunction with Israel. You don't need to be a prophecy enthusiast to devise a plan like this: the same logic was applied to Saddam Hussein's Iraq before the 2003 invasion. But another preemptive attack on another Middle Eastern nation turns out to be the least arresting part of the Hagee vision. He predicts, with remarkable composure, that this preemptive U.S.–Israeli attack on Iran may force Ahmadinejad into the arms of Vladimir Putin, who would then team up for an all-out attack on Israel. This would bring on the war predicted in Ezekiel 38 and 39, and would usher in the Tribulation. On the other side of an American attack on Tehran lies the Rapture and the End Times. The United States won't be able to contain the evil unleashed by its preemptive strke on Iran, but at least Christ can be relied upon to vanquish his enemies at Armageddon.

Again, I wonder how many people have actually read *Jerusalem Countdown*. Do the guest bookers at Fox News think about all this before they invite John Hagee to discuss Iran's nuclear ambitions? In his appearances on Fox, Hagee has seemed like any other right-wing pundit: Americans should support a preemptive attack on Iran as a form of self-defense against Ahmadinejad's nuclear ambitions. But Fox viewers don't get the full picture, especially since Hagee isn't grilled on his unsettling conviction that an attack on Iran may help to trigger Ezekiel's war.

John Hagee is not a very systematic thinker. A book like *Jerusalem Countdown* doesn't so much persuade you with its logic as overwhelm you with its grim relentlessness. This isn't to deny its power and potential to convince readers of the core arguments: Iran is a dangerous enemy; Islam is an intolerant religion bent on confrontation with "Western civilization"; God wants the United States to support Israel; the last days are imminent. These different arguments don't always add up neatly. In *Jerusalem Countdown*, Hagee imagines the United States as God's instrument for attacking Iran, but also envisages national disasters for America if it fails to support Israel as fully as it should. "This is not a time to provoke God," he warns, "and defy Him to pour out His judgment on our nation for being a principal force in the division of the land of Israel." The plan to attack Iran, though, seems like a more coherent aim than anything Hagee has previously mapped onto prophecy.

The ultimate irony of this apocalyptic assault on Iran is that Hagee, like Rick Santorum, paints the Iranians as messianic fruitcakes. In *Jerusalem Countdown* he quotes from an Iranian exile who had defined the threat of President Ahmadinejad in theological terms: the danger facing Iran and the world, the exile suggested, was that the Iranian leadership was "knotting religious beliefs with the nuclear issue." Perhaps Hagee doesn't see this as ironic: after all, the Christian apocalypse is based on scriptural truth, whereas the Islamic equivalent is a twisted fanaticism. Those of us who aren't persuaded by apocalyptic thinking of any stripe—Christian or Islamic—may not be reassured by this, especially given Hagee's extraordinary access to Washington's elites. The politicians who turned up at the CUFI banquet and welcomed Hagee's delegates to their Capitol offices are being nudged by a worldview that's alternately bleak and terrifying. As you watch John Hagee shake hands with ambassadors and senators, and lead thousands of his followers through the Capitol, his view of the End Times seems at least as urgent and all-consuming as any Iranian equivalent.

ON THE SUNDAY AFTER the CUFI summit in Washington, John Hagee was back in San Antonio, preaching to a packed Cornerstone Church and filling in his congregation on what had happened during the week. He read a message of support that he'd received from President Bush just before the Washington banquet, which must have seemed frustratingly fuzzy to many Hagee devotees. Bush made the tenuous claim that the United States and Israel were "dedicated to improving the lives of people across the Middle East," adding that both nations "share the belief that the Almighty watches over the affairs of men, and values every life." (I wondered if Hagee was thinking about diversity quilts and "happy thoughts" when he read the first part of this to the crowd.) Bush also seemed oblivious to the imminence of the End Times when expressing his hope that CUFI would "build a better world for our children and our grandchildren."

Hagee seemed happier when telling his Cornerstone congregation about the press conference that had taken place on the morning after the banquet. This was the "most exciting part" of the entire trip, he claimed. "When you're standing in front of the Washington press corps—cynics, or liberals—you know it's going to be the shoot-out at the OK Corral." The congregation roared with laughter, and then listened enthusiastically to Hagee's account of his battle with a particularly stubborn reporter from the Reuters news agency. "Pastor Hagee, in your book you said we're facing the end of the world, in which all the Jewish people get killed." Hagee tells the crowd that it took him a moment to get his "German disposition under control," then he marched toward the Reuters man, seized the book ("He looked like I was going to slap him!"), and told the reporter that he'd misread it. Having punted the other hostile questions, including two more attempts from the hapless Reuters journalist to unsettle Hagee, the pastor had carried the day. "The press conference ended," he told the Cornerstone crowd. "Score: Christians 10, Media nothing." That got the biggest cheer of all.

3

Of Horns, Little Horns, and Antichrists

I t's easy to imagine Bible prophecy as a playpen for lunatics. Most Americans vividly remember David Koresh, the "wacko from Waco," who led his Texas cult into a fiery confrontation with the FBI in 1993. Back in the 1970s, Jim Jones of Indiana moved his followers to Guyana to escape from the IRS, preaching apocalyptic ideas with such fervor that, when federal investigators finally closed in, he persuaded more than nine hundred people to join him in a fatal cocktail of Kool-Aid and cyanide.

The temptation, when considering these notorious cult leaders or the avid audience for the *Left Behind* novels, is to dismiss End Times thinking as deranged. Most nonevangelical Christians (and even some who are born-again) tend to skip over the prophetic books of the Bible, even as they invest the rest of scripture with divine authority.

But apocalyptic ideas have fascinated believers for more than two thousand years, engaging some of the greatest minds as well as those on society's fringes. Saint Augustine, perhaps the most influential thinker in the early Christian Church, gave a good deal of thought to these matters. Martin Luther, who triggered the Protestant rebellion against the Catholic Church in the 1520s, told everyone who would listen that the Pope was the Antichrist. Jonathan Edwards, the most celebrated theologian in American history, informed his fellow colonists that the religious revivals of the 1740s (which were later known as the "Great Awakening") were the first sign of the millennium promised in the Bible. Even Isaac Newton struggled to resist the lure of the apocalypse. In addition to his numerous breakthroughs in the fields of mathematics and physics, Newton believed that he could bring a scientific method to the study of Revelation—and perhaps even determine the date of Christ's return.

What gripped these men was the tantalizing idea that the future could be read in the verses of scripture; that the tangled and obscure descriptions of Ezekiel, or the flamboyant visions of Daniel, might have some relevance to their own moment in time. Given the obsession of many of the prophets with numbers, the parades of dates and intervals that mark out the sequence of the End Times, some interpreters thought they could reconcile prophecy with history to identify the road ahead. If the Bible—the essential text of every Christian—had laid out the future of the world in this kind of detail, surely it would be foolish to ignore these passages and to refuse the challenge of sketching God's plan for the world.

THERE'S NOTHING especially Christian about prophecy. Jewish prophets were active long before Christ's birth. The first major prophecy writer was Ezekiel, who lived in the sixth century before Christ. A neighboring king, Nebuchadnezzar of Babylon, attacked Jerusalem in 597 BC and again in 586, destroying the great Temple which was at the center of the Jewish faith. Nebuchadnezzar captured thousands of Jewish leaders and notables, along with their servants and their families, and transported them back to Babylon. These were difficult times for the Jewish people, but Ezekiel—one of the hostages—had a vision that suggested better things in the future. He predicted the return of the Jews to Israel, and the rebuilding of the Temple. He also predicted another foreign invasion of the Jewish homeland—launched by a mysterious cabal of Gog, Magog, Meshech, and Tubal, as well as the less cryptic Persia, Egypt, and Ethiopia—but assured his fellow Jews that the onslaught would be repelled by divine intervention. His prophecy had a happy ending: the Jews would be returned not only to their land but to their God as well.

Your feelings about this story will depend on your religious perspective. If you believe that the Bible is the revealed word of God, and that Ezekiel's prophesying of war and the ultimate redemption of Israel has a literal and sacred truth, then you won't be very interested in psychology or history. If, on the other hand, you're prepared to think about the Bible as a document of its times, then you might conclude (with many scholars) that this story was a kind of literary reassurance for Jews. The Babylonian captivity was a dark moment, and Ezekiel's prediction offered hope that these troubles would eventually pass.

Another great Jewish prophecy, the Book of Daniel, also has a Babylonian connection. King Nebuchadnezzar had been tormented by a terrible dream, which he'd promptly forgotten but which still upset him. In a kind of psychoanalytical crisis, he gathered his advisers and demanded not only an interpreter of dreams but a psychic who could tell him what he'd dreamed in the first place. The advisers told the king, not unreasonably, that this was a tall order, but Nebuchadnezzar dismissed their objections and decreed that all the wise men of Babylon—including the Jews who'd been kidnapped from Israel—should be put to death for their failings.

Daniel, like Ezekiel, was a Jewish captive in Babylon, and when he heard about the king's ultimatum he asked God for help.

Daniel was miraculously rewarded with exactly the same dream that Nebuchadnezzar had forgotten. This vision still fascinates today's prophecy enthusiasts, and is regularly deciphered in apocalyptic books and TV shows. Daniel first saw a giant statue made of different materials: the head was gold, the torso was made of silver, the midriff of brass, the legs of iron, and the feet were a mixture of iron and clay. When he'd sized up this curious statue, Daniel saw a stone fall from the air and destroy it. Then the rubble rose up into a huge mountain.

This strikes me as quite a perplexing dream, but Daniel was already renowned for interpreting visions (he'd been trying out this skill on his captors) and he had no trouble unraveling this one. The statue referred to the four great empires that would dominate the history of the world. The stone referred to their inevitable destruction, and the mountain indicated that earthly empires would eventually be replaced by an eternal kingdom in which God would rule directly.

Given that Nebuchadnezzar's empire would be the first to go—his dominions were the head of gold at the top of the statue, insisted Daniel—the king seems to have been surprisingly cheerful about his prisoner's prediction. He made Daniel his official dream consultant. Daniel continued to write down his own dreams, though he didn't always elaborate fully on what they meant. Another vision in the book, which Daniel related to Nebuchadnezzar's successor as Babylonian leader, featured four beasts rising up from the sea in menacing fashion. The fourth beast had ten horns, including a mini-horn which sported human eyes and "a mouth speaking great things." These beasts, like the kingdoms of Daniel's earlier vision, were eventually vanquished by God, but only after a good deal of specific and perplexing detail had been given about the mystical fourth beast and its talking horn.

(Like the statue of the earthly empires, this stuff about beasts and horns is also an ongoing concern for today's prophecy enthusiasts, so bear with me here.)

At one point, the talking mini-horn attacked three of the other full-grown horns, a battle which might seem one-sided given the size of the big horns but which resulted in an easy victory for the "mouth speaking great things." Then the horn started to "make war with the saints," at which point Daniel mercifully interceded and reassured the reader that this fourth beast (with the warring horns, and the garrulous mini-horn) was the fourth kingdom that he'd glimpsed at the base of that statue in the earlier dream.

There's a good deal more of this, but I hope it's already clear that Daniel is a weird book. It's also a fascinating and seductive one, since these verses combine sweeping claims about world history with obsessively specific detail. If Daniel really did glimpse the future, as Nebuchadnezzar and generations of Jews and Christians have believed, wouldn't you like to know which nation the fourth beast represents? And which horn is likely to feature the talking mini-horn? (I'd also like to know the identity of the unfortunate horns that fall victim to the mini-horn's attack. In fact, I'm interested in all the horns.) Like one of the Sphinx's riddles, or a particularly fiendish crossword clue, Daniel's prophecies demand compulsive effort to uncover a solution. To make things worse, the devil is in the details.

I feel like a killjoy for suggesting a more prosaic way to understand the Book of Daniel: as a document of its times, written for a specific audience and purpose. Since the very early origins of the Christian Church, when the Book of Daniel was folded into the Old Testament, scholars have argued that large portions of the book weren't really written in the sixth century before Christ, with Daniel jotting down his thoughts between bouts of intensive dreaming and interpretation for his Babylonian captors. Instead, they were cooked up more than four hundred years later when yet another foreign invader, Antiochus IV of Syria, looked to impose his own ideas and practices on the Jewish people. Antiochus's dynasty had been founded by one of Alexander the Great's generals, so it was a Greek culture that came to Jerusalem when he seized the city around 168 BC. He forbade Jewish religious practice, and dragged a statue of Zeus into the Temple. Worst of all, he persuaded a small Jewish elite to go along with his program, replacing their own traditions and observances with pagan worship, pork eating, and other defiling practices.

The Book of Daniel became a literary apocalypse with a political edge: the author, alarmed at yet another foreign invader, followed Ezekiel's example by narrating stories of imperial decline and Jewish persistence. In a clever touch, he invested his stories with authority by suggesting that they'd come from the sixth century rather than from his own pen. These Jewish apocalypses were a kind of cultural armor to be donned in times of invasion or external interference. The visions of Ezekiel and Daniel clearly stated that the God of the Jews would be around for the long haul, and would outlive the mighty empires of Babylon and Greece. Meanwhile, the details in Daniel were probably intended as a code for second-century Jews to interpret against history and the events of their own time. The little horn with the big mouth was Antiochus himself. The writer of the Book of Daniel couldn't say this directly without getting into trouble, so he covered his tracks by setting his story in the time of Nebuchadnezzar, and putting his reassuring visions into the mouth of a Jewish exile who'd been dead for more than four centuries.

THIS PATTERN in Jewish prophecy writing continued even after Christ's death. In the first century AD, the Romans had replaced the Greeks as the imperial rulers of the Middle East, and the Jews were again on the ropes. After revolting against Roman rule in AD 66, the Jews were vanquished in the Roman assault on Jerusalem four years later. The Temple was destroyed, and Jews entered a long exile from Israel, which ended with the formation of the modern Jewish state in 1948. The prophetic books of Ezra and Baruch came out of this moment, predicting the fall of empires once more and replacing Greece with Rome as the bad guy in the historical scheme.

This sense of crisis—that the walls were closing in, and God's people required supernatural reassurance about their fate—also defined the prophecies of the New Testament, which were written in the first and second centuries after Christ. The Christian Church, in its earliest days, was extremely unpopular with a series of Roman emperors. In their letters to other Christians throughout the Middle East, the apostles spoke of a time of great trouble, followed by the return of Christ and the establishment of his kingdom on earth. St. Paul, who was beheaded in AD 64, came up with the idea of the Rapture in his second letter to the Thessalonians. When you consider the fate of many Christians in the first century at the hands of the Romans—beheading was one of the better ways to go, relatively speaking—the idea of a teleport to heaven seems very appealing.

Even the Gospels got in on the act, with Christ himself predicting dark times before his second coming. Modern prophecy enthusiasts are particularly drawn to Matthew 24 and 25, in which Christ goes to the Mount of Olives a little before his arrest and holds a kind of apocalyptic Q&A with his disciples. (This scriptural passage is known in prophecy circles as the "Olivet Discourse.") Jesus reads off a long list of signs that will indicate that his return is imminent, and they're extremely unnerving. First, an abundance of false prophets and false Christs will try to deceive faithful believers. There will also be wars, "rumors of wars," and a host of unpleasant developments: diseases, earthquakes, meteorite strikes, and so on. The Jewish Temple in Jerusalem will be desecrated, and Christians will be afflicted throughout the world. The sun and the moon will darken, the stars will fall from the skies, and a "great tribulation" will engulf the entire world. Then, and only then, will Christ reappear.

Did Jesus actually say these words? And, if he did, was he obliquely referring to Mahmoud Ahmadinejad or the Indian

Ocean tsunami of December 2004? Again, this depends on your point of view. For many nonevangelicals, and even some fundamentalist Christians, Jesus was trying to steel his followers for Roman persecution in the years after his death. Christ still qualifies as a prophet, since he foresaw the struggles that the early Church would face. Jews and Christians suffered mightily at the hands of the Romans in the first and second centuries, and the Temple in Jerusalem was ransacked and destroyed within four decades of the Crucifixion. Christ was trying to comfort early Christians, in the same way that Ezekiel and Daniel had reassured Jews: the worse things became for his followers, the closer they got to the messiah's return.

This inverse relationship between earthly peace and the second coming of Jesus is at the heart of the Book of Revelation, the most famous apocalyptic text in the Bible. Revelation was written by a prophet named John, who may or may not have been the same person who wrote one of the Gospels. We think that the vision was set down toward the end of the first century on the Mediterranean island of Patmos, where John was exiled by the Romans for his beliefs. Though we're still not sure exactly when John was writing, scholars have traditionally argued that the dark visions of Revelation were composed during the final years of the Emperor Domitian. As Roman emperors went, Domitian was particularly nasty. He was appalled by the spread of Christianity in the eastern Mediterranean, and determined to stamp out the new faith by reminding subjects that they should be worshipping their emperor rather than a renegade Jew.

Revelation is notoriously difficult, filled with wild images and abstruse terminology. John sees a book in heaven with seven seals; as the seals are opened, each produces a new vision that's also perplexing. The first four seals produce horses and riders (the four horsemen of the apocalypse); the sixth produces a great earthquake, and so on. After the seals are opened, seven trumpets sound terrible calamities on earth. Then a Beast with seven heads and ten horns emerges from the sea, following Daniel's vision, and takes over the world with the aid of his false prophet. The Beast—known to later writers as the Antichrist—doesn't seem to be the devil per se, but a satanically inspired figure who's doing the devil's bidding.

If you've ever seen a movie or read a book about the apocalypse, you'll recognize John's influence. He came up with the idea that 666 is the number of the Beast. He also sketched the elaborate efforts by the Antichrist to control every aspect of global commerce, insisting that all human beings accept his "mark" on their forehead or their right hand if they want to buy or sell anything. (John implies that people will be imprinted with either the Beast's name or with 666 itself, like little Damien in *The Omen*.) After the emergence of the Antichrist, John watches as seven vials are poured out; these are God's wrath against the Beast, and the sixth one "dries up Euphrates" (presumably the Iraqi river) and paves the way for the gathering of the "armies of the east" at Armageddon for a final conflict. A woman appears on a red beast with seven heads and ten horns. Not entirely helpfully, her name is written on her forehead: "Mystery: Babylon the Great, the Mother of Harlots, and Abominations of the Earth."

At this point, just as the horns are back and things seem to be sliding once more toward the unintelligible, one of the angels who's been overseeing John's vision helps him to make sense of what he's seeing. The beast, the heads, and the horns are all symbolic: John's vision is related to the kings and nations that will be caught up in the events of the last days, and will come under the sway of the Antichrist. With this on board, John moves to the breathless conclusion of the Beast's reign. God utterly destroys the Antichrist's capital at Babylon. Christ himself returns to earth, astride a white horse and dressed for battle. He casts the Beast and the false prophet into "a lake of fire," and throws Satan (who's lurking in the wings during all this) into a "bottomless pit." This is the "furious Christ" that John Hagee warned about, and he's taking no prisoners as he surveys those who continue to reject his message: "The remnant were slain with the sword of him that sat upon the horse, which sword proceeded out of his mouth: and all the fowls were filled with their flesh."

After the carnage, Christ takes up residence on earth for a thousand years, bringing back to life those Christians who have been killed by the Beast during his rise to power. Rather oddly, John says almost nothing about the millennium. There are three verses in the entire book on this topic; the other 401 are dominated by stories of woe and upheaval.

After the thousand years of peace have elapsed, for reasons that aren't entirely clear, Satan "must be loosed [for] a little season." The devil somehow sneaks out of the bottomless pit, finds some new followers in the mysterious nations of Gog and Magog, and lays siege to Jerusalem one last time; at which point, in one of the great anticlimaxes of Western literature, fire comes down from heaven and incinerates the invaders with no fuss whatever. (This reminds me of the scene in *Raiders of the Lost Ark* in which Harrison Ford wearily shoots the Egyptian master swordsman with his pistol.) Satan is vanquished with ease, he's cast into the lake of fire alongside the false prophet and the Beast, and then every human being who has ever lived is resurrected by God for the last judgment. When humanity has been divided up, and everyone knows whether they're going to be rewarded with perpetual bliss or perpetual residency at the lake of fire with Satan, the earth itself is destroyed, then remade, and a "new Jerusalem" descends from the heavens as the capital of God's everlasting kingdom. This is the end of history, and the beginning of eternity.

THE BOOK OF REVELATION was very appealing to embattled Christians, but its unapologetic attack on earthly powers became more problematic as the Church began to establish itself across Europe. In the two centuries after John wrote down his visions, Christianity transcended its beginnings as a marginal and dangerous cult. The Emperor Constantine decreed in AD 313 that the Christian faith should become the official religion of the Roman Empire. The first apostles had been succeeded by bishops and bureaucrats and, in the space of two hundred years, Christianity had gone mainstream.

The apocalypse seemed less appealing now that the tables had been turned, and many early Christians omitted John's Revelation as they compiled the first versions of the New Testament. Even when the new Christian empire fell on hard times—after the Goths had sacked Rome in AD 410, for example—political and religious leaders were reluctant to fall back on apocalyptic explanations. The greatest theologian of early Christianity, Augustine of Hippo (354–430), suggested just a few years after Rome had been overrun that the millennium was already in progress. But he refused to say when it had begun, or when Christ would return in person. He poured cold water on the idea that the Jews would literally return to Israel, and he admitted that the prophetic books of the Bible were a bewildering mix of the literal and the figural. Prophecy would be realized, Augustine reassured Christians, "but how, or in what order, human understanding cannot perfectly teach us, but only the experience of the events themselves."

In the centuries after Augustine, apocalyptic thinking was a fault line between "official" Christianity and the experiences and hopes of ordinary believers. In medieval Europe, countless people were trapped in poverty and forced to endure the hardships of feudalism. As the Church became more prosperous and powerful, many poorer people felt that it was unresponsive to their needs. The proliferation of monasteries from the sixth century onward tended to isolate the purest, most pious Christians from the population at large; meanwhile, the attempts of Church leaders to professionalize the clergy, and to create local priests and grassroots ministries, only led poorer people to conclude that the

Church was corrupt. (The quality of these local priests was notoriously variable.) The apocalypse, and its promise of redemption through suffering, offered an escape route of sorts. It also encouraged believers to look out for false Christians in the End Times, and undermined their confidence in the Church hierarchy and in the nobles who presided over them. From the perspective of Europe's rulers, this was hardly a firm foundation for Christianity or for any kind of government.

So why didn't the religious and political elite simply outlaw apocalyptic belief in medieval Europe? To some extent, they did. Wandering preachers who stirred up enthusiasm for the End Times were jailed or executed, especially if they succumbed to the adulation of their followers and proclaimed themselves to be Jesus Christ. A number of confidence men popped up in France, Germany, Holland, and elsewhere in the Middle Ages, riding waves of apocalyptic enthusiasm toward personal wealth or political power. (The most infamous of all, a French serf called Bertrand, managed to be crowned Emperor of Constantinople and Thessalonica in 1225, though he was exposed by the King of France and hanged for his impudence just a few months later.) In addition to tricksters like these, the rulers of the Middle Ages had to contend with pious and sincere preachers who trained the apocalyptic message on the injustices of the day. These preachers spawned a number of radical sects that were determined to shake up society, and to inaugurate a new order based on very different principles.

But the intellectuals and leaders at the apex of medieval society couldn't quite give up on apocalyptic ideas. Scholars found it hard to resist the temptation to return to the scriptures in search of clues about how the world would end, or when Christ would return. The celebrated Italian abbot, Joachim of Fiore, produced a new interpretation of Revelation at the end of the twelfth century, and reignited interest in the academic study of prophecy. (In the following century, debates on this topic were conducted at the universities of Oxford and Paris.) Joachim rejected Augustine's suggestion that Christians were already living in the millennium, and promised that there would be a wonderful era of peace between the Second Coming and the eventual end of history.

Meanwhile, popes, religious leaders, and local rulers tapped into apocalyptic thinking to justify wars and crusades against their enemies. Since the rise of Islam in the seventh century, European Christians had protested against the defilement of the Holy Land by its Muslim conquerors. The Crusades to recapture Jerusalem—launched between 1097 and 1270—were fueled by propaganda that assured ordinary believers that the last days were imminent. Joachim of Fiore even became a guru of sorts to leaders across Europe who sought his opinion on apocalyptic matters.

Ironically, given the current enthusiasm among prophecy believers for all things Jewish, the kings, emperors, and popes who waged the Crusades tested their apocalyptic rhetoric by calling for Christians to eliminate the Jews who lived in European towns and cities. Arguing that nonbelievers had to be eliminated before the millennium could begin, priests and Christian writers stressed that the Jews had rejected Christ, or that the Antichrist would himself be Jewish, or that Jews would willingly follow the Antichrist in the last days. All these accusations were used to encourage pogroms, which served as a kind of warm-up (and recruiting drive) for the more ambitious plan to travel to the Middle East and kill Muslims.

Some Christians refused to go along with this, and tried to protect Jews for reasons that John Hagee might relate to: before the End Times could begin, God's former chosen people had to be converted to Christianity. But in the main, the apocalyptic rationale for the Crusades intensified the culture clash between Islam and Christianity and undermined relations between Christians and Jews in Europe. It may therefore have been especially appealing to rulers who looked for a way to unite their Christian subjects in the midst of poverty and social tension. Still, the vagueness of prophecy made it a dangerous tool for preserving the status quo. Richard the Lionheart, bound for Jerusalem on the Third Crusade in 1190, took a diversion to Messina to consult in person with Joachim of Fiore on the prophetic meaning of his mission to the Holy Land. Richard must have been excited to hear Joachim's verdict that the Antichrist had already been born but perplexed to learn that, in the opinion of the abbot, he was living in Rome and would soon be appointed pope.

WHEN MARTIN LUTHER plotted his break from the Catholic Church around 1520, he was initially wary of apocalyptic thinking. Partly this reflected his sense that the new Protestant faith should be easy to follow: John's visions would hardly fall into that category. Luther also wanted to avoid the religious enthusiasm which was already distorting other protest movements against the Catholic Church. In his native Germany, Luther knew about the Anabaptists (literally, the "born again" believers) who had begun to rail against the established orders of power and property, and to interpret their own clashes with authority as evidence that the last days were imminent. In response, Luther and the other major leader of the Reformation, Jean Calvin of Geneva, were quite hard on the Book of Revelation. Luther declared in 1522 that John's vision was "neither apostolic nor prophetic"; Calvin, who wrote voluminously on the rest of the Bible, pointedly omitted Revelation from his scriptural commentaries.

Luther eventually came round on the apocalypse, though his motives were material rather than spiritual. By the 1530s, with religious warfare breaking out across Europe, he saw the political advantages of reviving Joachim of Fiore's old suggestion that the head of the Catholic Church was the Antichrist. After all, the pope was the most powerful figure in a religion which dominated and deceived all of Europe. When Luther died in 1546, this identification of the pope with the Antichrist had become widely accepted in the new Reformed Church. As a Protestant, you didn't need to debate the identity of the Antichrist or speculate on the moment of his emergence: he sat in Rome, in full view, and provided daily inspiration in the Protestant wars against Catholicism throughout Europe.

Apocalyptic thinking flourished in the sixteenth and seventeenth centuries, feeding off the brutal wars of religion that enveloped Europe. But applying the apocalypse to politics was a dangerous business. England was an especially receptive place for Bible prophecy after the Reformation. Even as the nation pivoted between Catholicism and Protestantism during the sixteenth century, popular writers fused prophecy with English nationalism and convinced many readers that the End Times were at hand. By the 1620s, apocalyptic anticipation was widespread in England, and many theologians and writers speculated about the timing and the details of the various prophecies. The most famous of these was Joseph Mede, a Cambridge scholar who distinguished himself in his teaching and research. John Milton was one of his undergraduates, and he became the most famous prophecy scholar of his day.

Mede was a man of diverse interests—history, botany, astrology. He could sometimes be found at the human dissections conducted in the laboratories of a neighboring college. In 1627, he published (in Latin) his *Key of the Revelation*, which among other things offered a brilliant explanation of how the prophecies of Daniel and the Book of Revelation were connected to each other. Mede also rejected the idea of Augustine and other scholars that the millennium had already begun, or had taken place in the past, insisting that the happy era was still ahead. The *Key of the Revelation* was well received in scholarly circles, and soon Mede was answering letters from across Europe on the details of Bible prophecy. When he died in 1638, Mede had achieved fame well beyond his immediate Cambridge circle. He'd also managed, quite inadvertently, to fuel the more general apocalyptic fervor in English society.

Mede's death coincided with an extraordinarily tumultuous moment in English history. Since taking the throne in 1625, Charles I had alienated many of his subjects by ruling without Parliament and tilting toward the Catholic Church. Some of his disgruntled subjects moved to America, and founded the New England colonies as a refuge from Charles's high-handed rule. Others remained in England to bide their time, eventually seizing on a Scottish rebellion in 1640 to reassemble Parliament and challenge the king's authority. By the middle of the 1640s, the English Civil War was under way; in 1649, Parliament's armies defeated Charles and beheaded their former king. England briefly became a commonwealth, first under the direction of Parliament and then, after 1653, under the supreme military leader of the day, Oliver Cromwell. When Cromwell died five years later, he left a power vacuum that was only filled by the return of Charles II in 1660. These were turbulent times, and they were marked by endless speculation about Bible prophecy.

In the lowest ranks of society, apocalyptic ideas helped ordinary people to imagine the redistribution of property and the need for political revolution. If the world was entering its last era, they reasoned, society could be completely transformed. The same confidence about the imminent return of Christ was experienced not only by the poor but by preachers, government officials, army officers, and by members of Parliament who rose to challenge Charles I. In 1643, with Parliament again in session but hostile to the king, MPs commissioned an English translation of Joseph Mede's *Key of the Revelation*. For the next decade, Parliament issued or sponsored a number of publications with apocalyptic themes.

At the extreme end of the scale were the Fifth Monarchy men, a group of religious radicals (many of them veterans of the army which defeated Charles in 1649) who believed that the execution of the king was the first step in an even more dramatic sequence: the other kingdoms of the world were on the verge of collapse, and Jesus Christ would soon return. The Fifth Monarchists took their name from the visions of Daniel and John, each of whom had predicted the destruction of four earthly empires or kingdoms before the emergence of God's kingdom on earth—the Fifth Monarchy of Jesus Christ. They couldn't agree on when Christ would actually appear in person, but they were firmly committed to the idea that a godly government, the millennium of Bible prophecy, was at hand. They had a religious duty to bring this into being.

In the middle of all this was Oliver Cromwell, who believed passionately that God directed earthly events. What he wasn't so sure about was the relationship between current affairs and the bewitching tales of Bible prophecy. Cromwell had ambitious ideas about England's role in transforming Europe and advancing God's cause, but he tended to get dispirited when events went against him, as if God was sending him a message that he was on the wrong track. Worse, he couldn't quite persuade himself that he should impose his religious ideas on everyone else in England. Cromwell was a believer, albeit a tortured one, in religious toleration, at least among the numerous Protestant denominations and sects that had been squabbling for decades. (In Catholic Ireland, to which Cromwell turned immediately after the execution of Charles I, it was a different story.)

Although Cromwell originally hoped that a purified, righteous Parliament would be able to govern the nation—a hope that was shared by the Fifth Monarchists—he became frustrated by political infighting and began to rule directly in 1653. Assuming the title of Lord Protector, he struggled to sustain the sublime confidence in God's will that the Fifth Monarchists seemed to have in abundance. On the rare occasion when he found a channel for his apocalyptic convictions, the results were disastrous.

In 1655, Cromwell launched an ambitious effort to displace the Spanish from Hispaniola, the Caribbean island which is divided today between Haiti and the Dominican Republic. Hispaniola had symbolic value—it was the location of Columbus's famous American landing in 1492—but also strategic significance. It was a stepping-stone to the rest of Spanish America, a vast expanse that sprawled from Mexico to Chile. Cromwell had convinced himself that God wanted to force Spain out of America. According to one contemporary source, Cromwell also believed that a successful campaign in the Caribbean might advance the drama of the Book of Revelation.

A few years before the Hispaniola invasion, Cromwell wrote to the leading prophecy expert in the New England colonies, John Cotton, to seek guidance on this question. If he attacked the Spanish in the Caribbean, Cromwell inquired, would this help to "dry up Euphrates," the vision that John had glimpsed at the pouring of the sixth vial of God's wrath? (Cotton, in a sticky situation here, rather suspected that it might.) Since the original letters are lost, it's difficult to speculate on exactly what was going through Cromwell's head at this moment. He may simply have meant that an English Hispaniola would be a beachhead to the conquest of the rest of Spanish America. Or perhaps he imagined that the spectacular seizure of Hispaniola from Spain could hasten Christ's return.

Cromwell pushed ahead with his plan. Thirty-eight ships sailed from England in December 1654, carrying an invasion force of ten thousand men. The English troops were confident: the Spanish garrison on Hispaniola was modest, and Spain's leaders were not expecting an attack inspired partly by the Apocalypse of St. John. But the operation suffered from spectacularly bad planning. (For example, the troops forgot to bring any receptacles for holding water.) After a forlorn trudge through rain and tropical forests, enduring Spanish ambushes and roaring cataracts of floodwater, the disconsolate survivors were gathered up by the fleet and transported to the much smaller Spanish island of Jamaica, which they seized as a consolation prize. Everyone dreaded the voyage home, and the Lord Protector's wrath.

Cromwell was mortified at the news of his failure, and after throwing his commanders into the Tower of London, he withdrew into dark brooding over what had gone wrong. His political opponents had already decried his seizure of absolute power in 1653. Now one of them observed acidly that there had been a "great silence in heaven" since he'd seized power. Cromwell never regained his confidence in God's plan for England and the world. He died in 1658, and his son, Richard, struggled to unite the nation behind a new line of Lord Protectors.

The Fifth Monarchists made striking progress as Cromwell's star descended. By the summer of 1659, they had assumed trusted positions in the army, in the government presses, and in Parliament itself. But their own zeal worked against them once again, and they became frustrated at the refusal of Parliament to reform Church laws and to adopt their own proposals for a millennial government. With Parliament hopelessly divided, and a new monarch waiting in France for the signal to return to London, the Fifth Monarchists could do little to push through their ideas or to revive the English Revolution. When Charles II returned to London in 1660 to take his father's throne, he moved quickly to crush his remaining apocalyptic opponents.

Taking heart from the now familiar logic that, as things got worse, Christ's return became more imminent, the Fifth Monarchists staged a bloody last stand in the streets of London. In January 1661, more than fifty apocalyptic holdouts attacked one of the king's regiments, creating chaos in the city and killing nearly two dozen soldiers. The cause of the Fifth Monarchy continued to inspire some English radicals outside the capital but, for many onlookers, the bloody end of the movement in London only confirmed the excesses of the past two decades. Apocalyptic ideas were grouped with the execution of the king and the rise of Cromwell as a symptom of the nation's temporary insanity, and Bible prophecy was indelibly marked as dangerous and irresponsible.

Prophecy didn't disappear from English life altogether. At the end of the seventeenth century, Isaac Newton quietly speculated on the apocalyptic calendar, and searched the Bible to determine when the Jews would be restored to Israel. In one calculation, he suggested that their return would begin around 1895; an impressive estimate, given the founding of the Zionist movement in Europe at almost precisely this moment. (Less impressively, the same calculation suggested that Christ would return in 1944.) But the apocalyptic hopes of many English observers, and of European Protestants in general, had waned significantly by 1700. European intellectuals lionized Isaac Newton for his achievements in mathematics and physics rather than for his speculations about prophecy, and the apocalypse seemed increasingly out of place in the new age of observation, measurement, and science that became known as the Enlightenment.

IN OUR OWN TIME, Europeans who insist on a literal interpretation of prophecy have seemed like fish out of water. In 1988, Reverend Ian Paisley waited patiently for Pope John Paul II to address the European Parliament in Strasbourg, France. Paisley, a radical Protestant politician from Northern Ireland, was a member of the Parliament and a committed opponent of the Catholic Church. Before the pope's arrival in the chamber, he'd given notice to his fellow legislators that he could not countenance a visit from the Whore of Babylon. A few seconds after John Paul began to speak, Paisley rose from his seat and unfurled a red banner, on which he'd daubed in black paint:

Pope John Paul II ANTICHRIST

"I renounce you as the Antichrist," Paisley shouted from his chair, while the pope leaned back from the microphone and struggled to suppress a smile. "I refuse you as Christ's enemy and

Antichrist with all your false doctrine!" Paisley was bundled from the chamber and ridiculed by the media. It's hard to know what would have irked Paisley more: that the pope was invited to visit, or that no one seemed to heed his warnings.

The Vatican, meanwhile, has distanced itself from the idea that St. John glimpsed a terrifying future in his visions on Patmos. In August 2006, Pope Benedict told nearly seven thousand visitors to Rome—including many from the United States—that John had been given these visions "to reassure the Christians of Asia amid the persecutions and trials of the end of the first century." Benedict rejected the idea that Revelation promised an "imminent catastrophe," suggesting instead that Catholics should read it as a metaphor, or as a reflection on the turbulent era in which it was written.

The Catholic Church still believes in saints and miracles, but prophecy isn't fashionable anymore. Perhaps there's a sinister explanation for this—if the pope really is the Antichrist, wouldn't you expect him to say that the Book of Revelation isn't literally true? More likely, Benedict's speech simply confirms that most Europeans—even devout Christians—no longer give much thought to the End Times. Prophecy played a major role in European culture before the eighteenth century, and occasionally spilled over into politics, but it doesn't have much contemporary appeal. In America, on the other hand, the idea that the end of the world is nigh is more popular than it's ever been.

4

Riding the White Elephant

After my visit to San Antonio, I've driven north to try to find out why John Hagee's message about the End Times is so appealing to many Americans. Texas is a good place to ask this question. There are a lot of evangelical Christians here, and it's also the home of Dallas Theological Seminary, the leading center for the study of Bible prophecy in the United States. DTS was founded in 1924 to train conservative theologians, but it won a reputation as a prophecy powerhouse after the appointment of its second president, John F. Walvoord, in 1953. Students were drawn to experts like Walvoord and his fabulously named colleague, J. Dwight Pentecost, and DTS produced numerous graduates who went on to generate a new wave of prophecy enthusiasm in America. Its most famous alumnus is Hal Lindsey, who received his degree from Dallas in the mid-1960s before writing the first prophecy blockbuster, *The Late Great Planet Earth*, in 1970.

In recent years, there's been a conscious effort among prophecy enthusiasts to beef up their scholarly credentials. Tim LaHaye founded a research center for Bible prophecy back in 1992, teaming up with Liberty University in Virginia (prop. Jerry Falwell). The center promotes "the any-moment possibility of the Rapture," distributes papers on prophecy, and hosts the occasional conference. (John Hagee is the preferred after-dinner speaker at these events.)

Originally, I'd hoped to meet with Tommy Ice, a DTS alumnus who's been the director of Tim LaHaye's research center since 1993. Tommy sent me a couple of very friendly e-mails, and he said that we should meet up in person during a trip he was making to England. He also told me why prophecy believers need a research center in the first place: even as the *Left Behind* books have broken all records for Christian merchandise, some evangelical Christians still don't believe that the world is about to end.

Before our meeting, Tommy sent me some MP3s of a debate he'd just done with Gary DeMar, a purveyor of "Dominion Theology" who dismisses the idea of the Rapture and the Tribulation. DeMar, like other Dominionists, believes that the terrifying predictions of Revelation and Daniel were largely realized in the first century AD when the Jews were scattered from Israel. Dominionists are hoping for a Second Coming, but they don't expect the political and social upheavals of the Tribulation or a satanic world government under the direction of the Antichrist. They're also quite scathing about apocalyptic Christians.

This sounds like a moderate perspective, compared with the doomsaying of Tim LaHaye and John Hagee. But DeMar's complaint about Rapture enthusiasts—which he states repeatedly and vociferously during the debate that Tommy Ice has sent me—is that they deter other believers from pursuing a more ambitious form of Christianity. "Millions of Christians," DeMar insists, "will see no reason to get involved politically because the Rapture is just around the corner." Gary DeMar wants American Christians to stop looking to the skies for a heavenly evacuation. If evangelicals can rid themselves of the idea that the Rapture and the Tribulation are imminent, they can organize American society on strict Bible principles. Homosexuality and abortion are out; the laws of Moses are back in.

Dominion Theology celebrities like Gary DeMar fight running battles with the likes of Tim LaHaye and Tommy Ice. (They also maintain Web sites dedicated to persuading hapless Rapture believers that, for example, Prince William can't possibly be the Antichrist.) From the recordings of Tommy's debate with DeMar, I was surprised at just how cutting the Dominion people could be. DeMar and his allies couldn't resist making weak puns about Tommy's name—"He's on thin Ice again!"—and there wasn't a lot of Christian love on display.

Tommy didn't show up for our meeting in London. I suggested a little café at the top of a bookstore near Piccadilly Circus and absentmindedly told Tommy to take the elevator rather than brave all six flights of stairs. But as I waited and waited for his arrival, I started to worry that he'd virtuously chosen to walk up and had been put off by the photos of book signings that lined the walls. Nearly all the pictures featured a cheerful liberal titan who'd recently visited the bookstore on an author tour. Things started out bad, with Bill Clinton a few steps up from the entrance, but then got worse as you puffed your way toward the café at the top. By the time you reached the sixth flight, you were assailed by Jane Fonda, Michael Moore, and—the final insult—a demonically smiling Hillary Clinton. Did Tommy get this far, then simply turn around? I'm not sure, because he didn't reply to my messages. I shouldn't have made things sound suspicious by urging him to take the elevator.

INSTEAD OF TALKING to Tommy, I'm waiting in a diner just off the main road from San Antonio to Dallas, hoping to chat with another DTS graduate and prophecy scholar named Randall Price. Randall is a good friend of Tommy's and another associate of Tim LaHaye's prophecy research center. He's also a trained archaeologist, and his interest in pursuing physical evidence of the Bible has earned him a reputation as the Indiana Jones of the prophecy movement. His publisher has even equipped him with a fedora in an author photo, though he doesn't look entirely comfortable wearing it.

Randall has written books on just about every exciting topic in Bible archaeology: the Temple Mount in Jerusalem, the Dead Sea Scrolls, the location of the Ark of the Covenant. He has a Ph.D. in Middle Eastern Studies from the University of Texas, and he's conducted fieldwork in Jerusalem and in Qumran (where the Scrolls were discovered after the Second World War). He's built a reputation among Christian evangelicals as a respectable figure in a landscape of charlatans and confidence men, and he combines a passion for archaeology and Christianity with an academic's reticence. Randall would love to find the Ark and to prove that it is "a radio for talking to God." (Not Randall's line—I got that from Belloq, Indy's nemesis in *Raiders*.) But he's not going to distort the evidence or to claim that he's on the verge of uncovering it.

The Temple treasures and the quest for the Ark seem a long way removed from the Lone Star Cafe, squeezed between the freeway and an enormous outlet mall outside of San Marcos, Texas. The mall builders have run riot with the St. Mark's theme: the upscale stores are punctuated by clock towers and terracotta facades, a Venetian pastiche that seems unusually pretentious for this part of the world. The Lone Star Cafe isn't having any of this: it's a low building set apart from the rest of the mall, and it's managed to resist the temptation to ape a palazzo.

When Randall arrives, he doesn't look like Indiana Jones. He's a bit portly, with graying hair and a stubby mustache. As we sit down, he instantly asks me whether I'm coming from an "adversarial" perspective. (I've already admitted to being a vegetarian, when confronted with the Lone Star Cafe's unforgiving menu.) I tell him that I'm not a Dominion Theology person, and that I'm simply trying to explain Bible prophecy to an audience that doesn't know much about it.

"All right," he says. "Christian fundamentalists are worse than terrorists, because they're putting God into the political arena? Jerry Falwell and other types, they're affecting the Bush administration Bush is making policy decisions based on some kind of evangelical perspective, the end of the world?"

I ask him if any of that is true.

"I certainly wish we had that kind of influence!" Randall laughs. "I've never seen it. I don't know any of those people personally. Well, I know Falwell personally, but he doesn't know— the influence just isn't there. The fact is, no one is trying to affect anything, except what the Gospel of Jesus Christ says."

The waitress arrives at our table. Randall suggests that we share some food, but I can't see enough on the menu for one vegetarian, let alone two. He sensibly orders some fried mushrooms. Without really thinking about it, I ask for broccoli and green beans. It occurs to me, too late, that this is the kind of snack that only a crazy person would order.

I ask Randall about evangelicals and politics. Are Bible prophecy believers trying to make an impact on Washington? "Do we get involved in the social or the political? Yes, but what's the reason? The purpose is not some strange, nefarious manipulation of politics, to serve some apocalyptic end; it's to see men come to Christ and the world redeemed." I'm not totally sure I understand the distinction, but Randall insists that he's not trying to preempt the End: "That's going to happen on God's timetable and not mine."

Although Randall knows at this stage that I'm not in the Dominion Theology gang, he carefully explains why they're wrong about prophecy and politics. On the face of it, Bible prophecy people and Dominion Theology types are both fundamentalists:

they believe in treating the scriptures in a "serious and literal manner." But Randall can't see the point of searching the Old Testament for guidance on how to dress, how to eat, or how to fashion every law. "If we're talking about the sociological development, where distinctions are made over the version of the Bible you use, or dress codes, or more narrow aspects, I would not find myself there."

Our food arrives. Randall tucks into his mushrooms, while I find myself looking down at two bowls. One contains a few bulky florets of broccoli, which will be impossible to eat without a knife and fork. The other contains a sad pile of beans. This looks like the sort of meal you'd give a preschooler. I console myself with the fact that a Dominionist would have an even harder time at the Lone Star Cafe, since much of the menu wouldn't make it past the Book of Leviticus. (The house specialty is Chicken Fried Shrimp.)

At first glance, the Dominionists seem to take the Bible more literally than prophecy people like John Hagee, Tim LaHaye, and Hal Lindsey, since they're hoping to transfer the legal and political models of the Old Testament to the twenty-first century. (The English Parliament tried something similiar in the early 1650s, after dispensing with Charles I.) But Randall, with a quiet logic, tells me that Dominion Theology is actually a kind of ersatz fundamentalism—as phony and unsatisfying as the Venetian touches of the San Marcos mall. Here's the crux of his argument: although the Dominionists are happy to get hyperliteral with their biblical laws and cultural restrictions, they simultaneously ignore the specific promises of a Second Coming in scripture, or they turn prophetic promises into metaphors that effectively "spiritualize" (Randall's word) their material force.

Randall is convinced that, when Ezekiel talks about an End Times battle, or John talks about Gog and Magog in the Book of Revelation, those predictions are literally true. If you think they're metaphors, or you believe they already happened in some relatively minor political blowup in the first century AD, you've opened up every part of the Bible to metaphorical interpretation. At that point, with metaphors spreading out in all directions, and Bible truth dependent on the imagination of competing interpreters, there'd be no revealed word of God around which to build your faith. In talking to Randall, one can easily see the truth of prophecy as a burden rather than a fatalistic obsession. Perhaps it would be easier if this stuff wasn't in the Bible, but it's there and so it can't be dismissed or dodged.

When Randall has polished off the Dominionists, he offers a much broader critique. Our secular, liberal society is wrong to believe that the world can get better over time, that one generation can improve upon the previous one. "As we see things unfold," he explains, "we understand the scripture *not* to say that mankind is getting better, that there's an evolutionary process." Randall thinks that this comfy worldview has "dismally failed," and suggests that the culture has begun to agree with him. "The general understanding in our culture wherever you are, not just this culture but around the world, is that we're headed toward some kind of ultimate climax in history, and that it doesn't seem to be good." I wish I could refute this conclusively, but, of course, he has a point. "The nuclear threat, the environmental threat. The Avian bird flu." Randall has just seen an ABC News special predicting 300 million deaths if bird flu crosses over into humans: How can people retain any faith in the progress of history when they have this to look forward to?

We're also in a moral spiral, Randall tells me. "You can look at the generations previous to us, and see a much higher concern for how people spoke, how people thought, how they dressed, how they ordered themselves." People feared God, Randall suggests, even if they weren't Bible readers or churchgoers. But all this has gone, along the lines predicted by the prophecies for the End Times. "Look at *The Da Vinci Code* today. A fictional work is claimed to be fact." Dan Brown's book is full of "ludicrous statements," and Randall can't believe that it's been so widely devoured. "John tells us that many Antichrists have already gone out to the world," he observes sadly.

Randall briefly mentions the other religious *bête noire* of the season—*National Geographic*'s television special on the so-called Gospel of Judas, which suggests that the treacherous disciple wasn't such a bad guy after all. "I was sitting in a coffee shop recently," Randall says, "and that special on the Gospel of Judas came on TV, and the people in the coffee shop said, well, that'll put a final nail in the coffin of Christianity." He's getting indignant as he relives the experience, and I take the opportunity to cut up my broccoli. "I'm not a full-time prophecy person, my area is archaeology, this is my fourth year directing excavations at Qumran, and so I stepped in and simply explained what the Dead Sea Scrolls were . . .

"You actually approached the folks in the coffee shop?"

"Yeah. Because people have no frame of reference for these things."

I wonder how the unwitting skeptics dealt with Randall's intrusion, assailed by his stories of the Gnostic roots of the "Judas" manuscript and its marginal status within early Christianity. But Randall will strike up a conversation with strangers to ensure that the slow drift downward in these final days—marked by the splashy irreverence of *Da Vinci* or the rehabilitation of Judas Iscariot—doesn't blot out the Christian message. Randall thinks that the Bible paints a pessimistic view of human history, but he won't let me call him a pessimist. "We have the greatest message of hope to hold out. The Bible predicts that things will get worse. But look what the results are going to be. The one who made the world is coming back into the world. The one who came as a savior is coming not only to redeem people spiritually but to rule and to reign over this earth, and to bring ultimate justice and to transform it into the kind of paradise that people have prayed for."

———

TO THE EXTENT that prophecy scholars are focused on spiritual decline in America, their commitment to the End Times view seems austere and, in an abstract kind of way, honest. But Randall, like John Hagee and virtually every other prophecy writer, is also an active participant in debates over the Middle East conflict. In 1992, he co-wrote a book with Tommy Ice called *Ready to Rebuild: The Imminent Plan to Rebuild the Last Days Temple*. In the foreword, John Walvoord declares the book to be a "masterpiece" which "presents all the various views" about the Temple. In fact, Randall and Tommy struggle to contain their enthusiasm for a very inflammatory outcome: the replacement of the Islamic Dome of the Rock in Jerusalem by a new Jewish Temple, which would fulfill another theological precondition for the Second Coming. They acknowledge the political difficulties of destroying the Islamic sites—the Temple Mount, after all, contains the third holiest shine in Islam, and it was Ariel Sharon's visit here in September 2000 that sparked the second Palestinian *intifada* and helped to destroy the peace process. Randall and Tommy remain convinced that the Temple will be rebuilt, because prophecy tells them so.

Like John Hagee's red heifer, it's easy to dismiss the Temple restoration movement as kooky and basically harmless. *Ready to Rebuild* has the obligatory section on the search for a red heifer. (Randall spices this up by suggesting, Indylike, that the ancient ashes of the red cattle that were burned nearly two thousand years ago might be used to purify priests of the rebuilt Temple, if these ashes could be located by intrepid archaeologists.) Randall and Tommy also get excited about the reappearance in the Mediterranean of a rare snail that supposedly provided the special blue dye required for the Temple robes. ("The unusual appearance of the snails has been hailed by some Orthodox Israelis as a sign of the imminent coming of the messianic age since it heralds the possibility of the revival of the Temple priesthood.") But beyond some of its more extravagantly literal speculations, *Ready to Rebuild* has a lethal message. It encourages American Christians (and extremists in Israel) to look forward to a political and religious controversy that would plunge Israel and the Muslim world into an all-out war.

Randall has written more broadly about the Middle East. Soon after 9/11, he published *Unholy War: America, Israel and Radical Islam*. This book must have seemed very edgy in 2001. Back then, there was more wariness in the United States about painting Islam with a broad brush; even President Bush made strenuous efforts to distinguish between radical Islamists and the essential purity and decency of the Islamic faith. Randall's book was ahead of the curve. Drawing on what the publisher describes as "his intimate knowledge of Islam," Randall links the motivations of suicide bombers to the hostile nature of Islam itself. He also contrasts this aggressive faith with the essentially peaceful fundamentals of Christianity.

If you get hold of a copy of *Unholy War*, you'll be familiar with many of its sweeping arguments about Muslims and the imperialist dictates of their faith. This stuff has now leaped over into the mainstream, and you can find it on the editorial pages of major newspapers as well as throughout the blogosphere. In a chapter entitled "Does Prophecy Affect Politics?" Randall offers a jarring assessment of the emerging religious war waged by jihadis against the West. Having noted that prophecy belief has emboldened Christian evangelicals in their support for Israel, and that Islamic radicals have developed their own apocalyptic view about a Middle East war, Randall suggests that you simply have to choose the right apocalypse before the End Times arrive:

> As the unholy war stretches on, those who are religious on both sides will be staking their lives on their beliefs that their interpretation is the correct one. However, the problem is not

one of fundamentalism per se, [. . .] but which fundamentalism has the correct scenario of the future. Someone will be
right, and someone will be wrong.

Unholy War darts between prophecy, theology, and politics,
but it builds inexorably toward a simple conclusion: there's no
prospect of any Middle East peace, or "the permanent peace for
which our planet longs," until the return of Jesus Christ.

IN THE LONE STAR CAFE, Randall talks wistfully about the Israel
he remembers from his graduate school days in Jerusalem, when
there was even the odd marriage between Palestinians and Jews.
He heaps the blame for the religious revolution in the Palestinian
territories on the PLO: "It was an Islamic agenda from the beginning," he insists. "To think of this being a national movement,
their own statements say otherwise." This doesn't make much
sense historically: the Palestinian struggle was waged by secular
nationalists in the 1960s and 1970s, and the big turn to Islam and
parties like Hamas is a much more recent phenomenon. Randall
chooses to believe otherwise, because he sees Islam as relentlessly
expansionist, always seeking to take back land and to impose its
rule over non-Muslims.

I ask him about the Palestinian Christian community, which
used to comprise 10 percent of the population and is still strongly
represented in towns like Bethlehem. Have these hundreds of
thousands of people—Christians living under Israeli occupa-
tion—simply found themselves on the wrong side of Bible prophecy? "Palestinian Christians are growing in their knowledge,"
he says cryptically. "There's been dialogue with the messianic
community." But surely the residents of Bethlehem would reject
the Christian Zionist perspective? "No, not necessarily. More
educated ones do not." Randall thinks that Palestinian Christians
would have a much better time under Israeli rule, since "Islam

is not a friend to Christianity." He wishes he could introduce me to some of his Palestinian Christian friends, who have apparently come round to this point of view.

Before we finish talking, I ask Randall how he feels about televangelists and popular writers, the John Hagees and Hal Lindseys who have made a lot of money out of the prophetic message. He's quite gracious about them, and he tells me that "popularizers" are important to every religious or political effort even if they don't always get the point across with the right degree of circumspection. "Luther was a scholar, but he was a popularizer," Randall says. "A lot of people haven't had a background at all; they lack some of the background that helps you to rightly discern certain things. And, at the same time, what they're doing is very helpful to us. We sometimes tend to sit in our ivory towers and not get involved on the popular level, and we need that enthusiasm and encouragement to get our message out."

After saying good-bye to Randall, I thought about his claims that apocalyptic Christianity wasn't political. He's certainly not a date-setter, and his books are much more sober than *Jerusalem Countdown* or the *Left Behind* series. But it's hard not to see him as a kind of backstop for the popularizers, a figure who gives intellectual respectability to this project of viewing the Middle East in apocalyptic terms. While a firebrand like John Hagee takes an extreme line on Iran or the West Bank, Randall reassures an evangelical audience that, sooner or later, the clash between Islam and Judeo-Christianity—and between one vision of the apocalypse and another—is inevitable.

MY NEXT STOP is one of those popularizers that Randall mentioned. Nearly an hour's drive north of Dallas, past the little towns of McKinney and Princeton, you'll find a small compound that's the home of Lamb & Lion Ministries, one of the many Christian groups dedicated to spreading the news about the End

Times. It's a very isolated spot, and quite pretty in its own way. The surrounding countryside looks desolate by comparison, while the Lamb and Lion compound is full of shady groves and simple clapboard buildings.

I've come out here to see David Reagan, who founded Lamb & Lion Ministries back in the 1980s, and who now hosts a weekly show on the Daystar TV network called *Christ in Prophecy*. Dave is an archetypal Texan: he's friendly but determined, warm but fiercely committed to his point of view. His route into the world of Bible prophecy was unorthodox. He was born near Waco in humble circumstances, but after excelling as an undergraduate at the University of Texas he was accepted into a prestigious graduate program at Tufts in Massachusetts to study international relations. Religion wasn't a part of his life back then. Dave was surrounded by students who were looking to make it into the CIA, the State Department, or academia. After graduating, he spent twenty years teaching international law and politics at a series of colleges. It was only after he'd built an academic career that he decided that his calling lay elsewhere.

When I arrive at the compound—which is called Maranatha Acres, after a Greek word that loosely translates as "Until His Return"—Dave has popped out on an errand. His assistant directs me to another Lamb & Lion employee, who's named Gary. He's a youngish chap, and I'm instantly overwhelmed by his energy. He finds me a bottle of water, ushers me into his office, sits me down, and all the while speaks at extreme speed and without interruption. He's very friendly. He asks me about my last name, and then he offers to put it into a cool genealogical Web site that he knows about. He launches into a description of an hours-long conversation he's recently had, on matters related to salvation and prophecy, with a sixteen-year-old girl named Claire. He's still processing the experience. "I found out more in that conversation than you would from four years of theology!"

Gary seems dangerously interested in external stimuli; I imagine that the fridge is filled with bottled water since it's not safe to put him within range of fizzy drinks. He is *relentlessly* friendly. Within five minutes, he asks me if I have a place to stay. (I have, back in Dallas.) He insists that I consider staying with him, out here on the compound, where there's a spare room and a warm welcome. I say thanks, but I need a place with wireless Internet because it's my wife's birthday and I want to talk to her later via video messaging. He understands completely, but the offer's still open.

Dave Reagan eventually arrives, and steals me away from Gary. Dave is tall, sixty-seven years old, with receding gray hair. He's wearing a shirt that's printed with Christian fishes. On his belt is a very large Star of David buckle. Dave suggests that we go on a tour of Maranatha Acres before we sit down to chat.

When I'd parked my car, I hadn't realized how big the compound was. Beyond the office buildings, there's a mail room filled with Dave's books and brochures. Hanging on the walls is a series of tourism posters promoting Israel to vacationers—the earliest one, jarringly, reads PALESTINE. Past the mail room is a cavernous television studio that allows Dave to produce all the segments for *Christ in Prophecy* from Maranatha Acres. I recognize some of the sets from the broadcasts I've seen. On one side is the cozy front room in which Dave interviews his guests; across the studio is the newsroom set, which has a map of the Middle East and a pair of desks for Dave and his co-anchor, Dennis Pollock. Instead of a newsreader's script, each desk has a large Bible, opened somewhere in the middle. Dave shows this off proudly, and I'm impressed.

Christ in Prophecy is a mixed bag. Most weeks, Dave introduces a particular prophecy topic before discussing it with a special guest. Halfway through the show, there's a musical interlude from Jack Hollingsworth, who represents something called Acts 29 Ministries but who appears to be on the Lamb & Lion payroll. In one of his songs, Jack roams across the studio in a brown suit, pointing impishly to heaven and singing:

I'm getting ready to leave this world,
I'm getting ready for the gates of pearls,
I'm keeping my record bright,
And watching both day and night,
I'm getting ready to leave this world.

At various points, usually during key changes and other musically critical moments, Jack runs up and down on the spot excitedly. When he's finished ("Hallelujah!"), Dave looks at the camera and thanks him for his "lively song." He then adds, in a scripted aside that's wearily delivered, that Jack will be a pretty good singer one day "if he ever develops a little enthusiasm." Jack used to be homeless before he came to Christ and found his way to Lamb & Lion Ministries. You can buy an inspirational video about his life from the Lamb & Lion Web site, which also features more of his musical numbers.

Dave Reagan's big insight is that Bible prophecy isn't rocket science. There's a rigor to his Bible interpretation, and it's obvious that he's harnessing pedagogical skills he picked up in his many years as an academic. But there's also a folksiness about the show that takes the preachy edge off some of the theological discussions. Here's how Dave and his co-anchor, Dennis, try to persuade the viewers of *Christ in Prophecy* that the Rapture is definitely going to take place before the Tribulation, and that all true Christians will get to dodge the apocalyptic bullet:

DAVE: We don't need to suffer during the Tribulation in order to be purified! And those who argue to the contrary are, in effect, converting the Tribulation into a Protestant purgatory!

DENNIS: The idea becomes even more absurd when you consider that the Church is the bride of Christ. Do you really think that Jesus is going to beat up his bride for seven years and then marry her?

(Dave chuckles in the background, which makes me think he wrote that line.)

> DENNIS: What bride would want a bridegroom who behaved like that? Jesus is the church's blessed hope, not its abusive husband!

Despite—or perhaps because of—his years in academia, Dave isn't a snob. His own books on prophecy are clearly arranged, and he notes on the back cover of one that you can read the whole thing or "skip around," taking in whatever appeals to you. He makes a virtue of plain speaking and he's quite up front about what he can and can't answer.

"SOMETIMES, I have to say to you, I'm embarrassed to be a Bible prophecy teacher because of all the nonsense that goes on in the field; there's just incredible nonsense." Dave is sitting with me in the Maranatha Acres conference room, and he's impressing upon me that he's not some kind of prophecy nut. "You've got a lot of guys who are sensationalists—they're trying to sell books, they're trying to sell tapes, Y2K is going to be the end of the world." The supposed Y2K meltdown was a particular bugbear of Dave's. He was asked to give a paper on the topic at a prophecy conference in Tyler, but he was disinvited when the organizers realized that he was planning to debunk the survivalist scenarios about bunker building and "getting a machine gun."

But this isn't the most bizarre End Times scenario he's been forced to endure: "The idea that the planets are lining up, the building blocks of the Temple are gonna be assembled, and there's one in every Kmart in the U.S.!" (I've Googled this one, but I can't find it.) "Buzzards are gathering in Israel and, you know, it just makes me sick to my stomach to see this kind of sensationalism. And there are even people who have big names in the field of Bible prophecy who are very much involved in sensationalism." I try to draw him out on this, but he isn't talking about Hal Lindsey. Or John Hagee, whose only failing in Dave's assessment is that he's too optimistic about the effect of Christian opinion on U.S. foreign policy.

Dave, although he's not a sensationalist when it comes to hovering buzzards or the concealing of the Third Temple in Kmart, is remarkably negative about the United States. One of his recent books is called *America the Beautiful? The United States in Bible Prophecy.* The cover is an illustration of the Statue of Liberty, drawn from behind—the statue is looking away into the sunset, and the effect is rather disconcerting. Perhaps it's an oblique reference to Dave Reagan's famous namesake, Ronald: "It's morning in America," the president used to tell cheering crowds as he took on the Soviets abroad and the labor unions at home. Not anymore, Dave's book suggests.

According to *America the Beautiful?*, there are no explicit references to the United States in Bible prophecy. The vague phrases which other interpreters have connected to America—the "tall and smooth people" of Isaiah 18, or the "young lions of Tarshish" in Ezekiel 38—are actually references to places in Africa or Europe. Instead, the United States has been treated by God much as he treated the nation of Judah, one of the offshoots of the original nation of Israel in Old Testament times. Judah was once a mighty nation that glorified God and the world, but its people fell away from the true faith, and they were eventually destroyed for their sins.

Since Dave has training in international law and politics, when he transfers this idea to the present, he sounds unnervingly like Tom Clancy or Donald Rumsfeld. "In military thinking," he tells me, "you have to think about all the possible scenarios. I was taught that in my study of international politics, and I apply it to the Bible." So what's in store for the United States? "I looked at the entire Bible prophecy, and I had to conclude we're not going to be a major player. I think we're going to be removed from the scene very quickly." He's already seen this happen to one super-power: Dave spent some time in Russia soon after the Soviet Union had collapsed, and he was amazed to see the poverty that had swept across America's once mighty adversary. But a sudden economic collapse is only one scenario in his prophetic war gam-ing. "We're so vulnerable. You know, all you have to do is float a merchant ship into New York Harbor with an atomic bomb and a suicide crew. And that can happen any day. They set off the thing, New York's gone, the stock market's gone. We lost seven trillion dollars on the stock market from the last attack. If all of New York were destroyed, think what would happen?"

But why would God punish America, given that it's a nation of more than 150 million Christians and it's led by a man who says that Christ changed his heart?

"I often make the point that I consider us far more danger-ous to the world than the Soviets ever were." Dave pauses to let this sink in. "I travel all over the world, and the moment I turn on that TV set, I know I'm going to see the most immoral and most violent American television programs and movies. We are the moral polluter of planet Earth." Worse, Americans are smug about their standing with God. "I think that for many people in America, they believe that God is sitting on a throne wrapped in an American flag." Dave tells me that God has already visited "remedial judgments" upon the United States—the attack on the World Trade Center and Hurricane Katrina—and he's got more in the pipeline. "I think 9/11 was a wake-up call, and I think, like a sleeping man, we rolled over and hit the snooze alarm and went back to sleep and God is calling and calling." Is the alarm going to sound again? Will there be another 9/11? "It's gonna take something worse than that," he says.

I ask Dave to define the moral and cultural malaise in Amer-ica, and it's an interesting and quite complex reflection. At the most basic level, Dave is cranky about modern America because

he can remember a more innocent age. Listening to him holding forth on this, he sounds like any other nostalgic senior. He
looks back fondly to his childhood in the 1940s and 1950s, when
"people trusted each other, nobody locked their homes, nobody
locked their automobiles," and so on. I can only imagine the horrors that the 1960s held for Dave, who presumably had to endure
some of the excesses of the student movement from up close. (He
turned thirty in 1968.)

But beyond this nostalgia, he has a strongly Christian vision
of decline. Once upon a time, "you had Christmas plays, you
had Easter plays in schools, and you had presidents talking all
the time about God and about God's role in our history." Today,
the culture has been "paganized and secularized to the point
where, you know, it's politically incorrect to mention anything
spiritual."

What has been fatal to America's moral health, and its providential standing with God, is that this drift away from Christianity has coincided with a big influx of immigrants. For Dave,
the United States was founded on "Judeo-Christian principles."
Unlike America's leaders, he thinks that the ideas of liberty and
democracy aren't portable: "I think President Bush is absolutely
nuts to think he's going to change the Muslim world with democracy because democracy will never exist there." Similarly, the nation as a whole is making a big mistake by encouraging "a flood of
immigrants from non-Christian areas." In recent years, millions
of immigrants have come to America "without a Christian background" and have demanded that the nation's values should be
changed to accommodate them. By doing this, they're "under-
mining the very basis of the nation."

The problem isn't just the non-Christian immigrants, but the
sleepy Judeo-Christians in the United States who have let down
the drawbridge. Dave tells me a story to illustrate the point. The
villain of the piece is Goldie Hawn. I was surprised enough to
see John Hagee drag Goldie into the Bible prophecy arena, with

his claim that she was one of the entertainment-industry Jews "in whom all the nations of the earth shall be blessed." Dave has also taken note of Goldie, but he doesn't share John Hagee's confidence in her redemptive qualities.

Dave made a trip to India a few years back, and he wasn't impressed by what he saw. "I have never seen such poverty in all my life, such suffering, just pathetic. And it's rooted in their values, rooted in their religion. When you believe that you can't eat a cow, you can't eat any animals, there's animals everywhere and people are starving to death because you can't eat them, when you have a chapel that worships rats . . ." He trails off, but I get the impression that he could keep going if he needed to. "This has an effect upon the society, and on the standard of living."

When Dave got back on the airplane to return to Texas, "they showed a film with Goldie Hawn. Now, you talk about an airhead! Here's Goldie saying [he adopts a strained falsetto for this part], 'Oh, I came to India because I wanted to see a white elephant, so I went to the elephant temple and I offered a sacrifice to the elephant, and I said please let me see a white elephant and then I saw this white elephant and I am a fulfilled person.'" Dave pauses for effect, and then resumes as Goldie but drops the falsetto. "'And I just don't understand why we can't have the wonderful values of the Indian people; it's just such a wonderful society.'" Coming out of his guise completely, Dave shakes his head. "And I'm thinking, what an idiot. Two-thirds of the people are starving to death and you're talking about what a wonderful place this is."

Dave keeps reminding me, in a good-humored way, that England already provides American Christians with a model of a country that's tumbled from God's favor. He's visited Britain on a few occasions. "I was astonished at how pagan England is. The biggest joke over there is that the Church of England's not a church, it's a real-estate agent." He laughs incredulously. "And most of all they're giving them away to *Muslims*, who turn them into *mosques!*" In the nineteenth century, Dave reminds me, Britain sent missionaries around the world, and most of the great hymns were written by British Christians. This proud religious heritage has vanished in a few generations.

Dave's trips to Britain have been underwhelming for a variety of reasons. He's managed to turn out decent audiences for his sermons, but he's been alarmed to discover that they're mostly Plymouth Brethren and other fringe groups. His problem with these sects is that, like the Dominion Theology crowd, they have countless rules on how to dress and behave. These are an unpleasant reminder of the strict Protestantism practiced in Dave's childhood church in Texas. Ruefully, he recalls his conversations with the Brethren organizers on his tour. "I even asked, 'What if a woman just wanders in off the street, wants to hear the Gospel?' And the guy said, 'She won't hear it unless she puts something on her head.' Ain't that sad?"

I agree that it is, especially when Dave tells me that one of his Scottish appearances was canceled when the organizers found out that he owned a television and that his wife had short hair. Although Britain is a lot further down the road to perdition than the United States, he can glimpse the outlines of this in America's future: the liberals and the secularizers will drag most of the country into atheism, while the Dominionists bind the Christian remnant to the rigid cultural practices and religious laws that Randall Price warned me about. (And which got Christ into no end of trouble when he occasionally fenced with the Pharisees.) For Dave, America's spiritual, moral, and cultural decline leads downward, past a series of hair-raising catastrophes, toward national annihilation.

Dave is especially irritated by Europeans who declare that Bush is steering the nation toward the End Times. Not unreasonably, he suggests that we Europeans believe this only because we're so remorselessly pagan that we've lost the ability to distinguish between a churchgoing Christian and a prophecy believer.

"It's very true that many Americans in high positions of authority are in churches like the Methodist Church, the Presbyterian Church, and the Episcopal Church—President Bush is a classic example—and they go to church regularly, they're committed Christians, I have no doubt about their salvation. But they don't know anything about Bible prophecy."

But surely George Bush . . . ?

"I don't think President Bush knows *beans* about Bible prophecy! He's not into Bible prophecy, he doesn't know anything about Bible prophecy, he's not trying to fulfill Bible prophecy. He's gone to two churches, the Methodist and the Episcopal church, and both of those believe in replacement theology, and the only sermons he's ever heard on Bible prophecy are, God washed his hands of the Jews in AD 70, he's replaced them with the Church, there's no purpose left for Israel . . ."

SINCE DAVE SPENT twenty years teaching international relations, I expect him to have a different take on the Middle East than John Hagee or Randall Price. He mentions his "unique viewpoint" and his knowledge of international law and politics, but in our conversation, whenever the dictates of international law clash with some of the more perplexing projections of prophecy, Dave knows which side he's on. "I got more inside the world of politics by reading the Book of Daniel than I ever got at university," he says proudly. He doesn't make much effort to reconcile the divine grant to Israel with the Geneva Convention.

"How can a person really appreciate what's going on in the Middle East unless they understand that God is in the process of performing one of the greatest miracles he's ever performed in human history, the regathering of the Jewish people from all four corners of the earth?" None of this is very surprising, given what I've already heard from Randall and from Hagee. But when I ask Dave about John Hagee's new lobbying group, Christians United for Israel, he says something that stops me in my tracks. "I'm not sure it's going to turn around American policy, because American policy right now is very pro-Palestinian, and I just don't see it's going to be turned around, I really don't."

How can anyone imagine that the Bush administration is pro-Palestinian?

Dave tells me that the Israelis are "more subject to pressure than any other nation on planet Earth," and that American policymakers are only interested in appeasing the Arabs and securing access to oil. Dave shares John Hagee's belief that the land of Israel has been given to the Jewish people in perpetuity by God, and he tells me that there's a double standard in the way that Americans treat Israel. "The world doesn't realize how restrained Israel is," he continues. "They could wipe the Palestinians off the face of the earth in two or three days. If someone started shooting Katyusha rockets across the Rio Grande river into Texas, how long do you think it would take for us to go down there and wipe 'em out? And yet we say to Israel, 'Oh no! You can't do that! Don't take any action!'"

Dave also differs from John Hagee in his assessment of the Israeli government. "My greatest frustration in the world today," he declares, "is with Israeli leaders. They've deceived themselves into believing that they can gain peace through appeasement. If you know anything about history, you cannot gain peace through appeasement." Now we're back on familiar ground—Hagee likes to quote from Winston Churchill, and he spent a good deal of his speech at the CUFI Washington banquet retooling Churchill's speeches against Nazism for the fight against "Islamic fascism." But Dave has a couple of theories to explain the reluctance of Israel to use its might and to squash the Palestinians once and for all.

First, he tells me, the Israeli leaders are secular humanists. "They believe in the essential goodness of man," he says, somewhat implausibly, "which is directly contrary to what the Bible teaches." (As an example, he mentions that the Israeli soldiers who seized East Jerusalem in the Six-Day War didn't destroy the Dome of the Rock.) Because Israeli politicians haven't accepted the dark view of human nature outlined in scripture, they're still clinging to ideas of universal brotherhood that their Islamic enemy can only see as a form of weakness.

Dave is building up a head of steam here. "Number two, is because they want the respect and approval of the world." He reaches back to the Old Testament, and mentions that the Jews under Samuel refused to accept the benign rule of judges and demanded a king just so they could be like all the neighboring countries. Samuel told them it was a bad idea; it would cost them more money, and they'd have to give up their power completely to a sovereign. But they went ahead regardless because all the other nations had kings, and they wanted to fit in.

Then, abruptly, he offers another example. "*Fiddler on the Roof*. What does he say all through that thing?"

I've never seen *Fiddler on the Roof*. I don't know what to say. "'If I Were a Rich Man'?"

"He says, 'God, why couldn't you have chosen someone else? Why us? Why do we have to wear this funny clothing? Why do we have to be different?' The Jews desperately want to be accepted, and they believe with all their heart that if they do what the world tells them to do, they'll be accepted."

But, of course, they're wrong. "It doesn't matter what they do, the world will still hate them." Dave has crossed the globe and has found people in the unlikeliest places who hate Jews. People in Japan, even. "You see, I believe anti-Semitism is supernatural. Satan hates the Jews, and Satan doesn't want to see a single one saved." He lists a number of reasons why Satan is particularly vexed by the Jews, and tells me that this was what the Holocaust was all about. (He pronounces it "holy-caust.") Then, ominously: "That's what it's going to be like during the Great Tribulation."

Does he get frustrated when Israel's leaders keep trying to

conciliate their Arab and Muslim neighbors? I suggest that when he talks about his frustration with Israeli governments, he sounds like a parent trying to get through to an unruly kid. "I know! You want to take 'em and shake 'em till their teeth rattle!" But Dave knows that, according to the prophetic sequence, there's not much he can do to save the Jews from the delusion of an eventual peace deal, brokered by the Antichrist. He's happy to make calls to Congress insisting on Israel's right to the land, but he isn't "trying to manipulate some particular End Times scenario." Although Dave is empowered by the knowledge of what's going to happen, his faith in its political usefulness seems modest.

AT THE END of our chat, I ask Dave to tell me what's wrong with organizations like the United Nations or with high-minded concepts like international law. He pauses for a few seconds before letting out a big laugh and saying, "I don't think we have enough time for that!" Then he elaborates just a little: "I think the Bible makes it very clear that it is not God's will for nations to give up their nationhood, their sovereignty. The one time they tried to do that, and came together into one great empire, God poured out his wrath upon them." (He's talking here about the Tower of Babel.) Dave tells me that although he doesn't have a problem with international dialogue over issues that affect us all, he's suspicious of the "arrogance" that underwrites any effort at global government. "God sets the boundaries of nations, and when we start crossing those boundaries and unifying into organizations like the UN or whatever, we're going to start challenging God."

Dave is genuinely perplexed at why British people have been willing to get involved with the European Union: "I would think the British would be having their eyes opened today to the nonsense of getting into cross-national organizations like the European Union, which says, get rid of your weights system that you've had for hundreds of years and we're gonna put a little grocer in jail here because he wants to sell in weights that people understand." Dave remembers being in Britain in 2000 and watching bemused motorists at petrol stations trying to convert liters into gallons. "They have a chart on each pump to try to convert, and people are trying to figure out how much they're buying. Next thing you know they're telling you how high your hedges can be. Have the British woken up to the fact that they've surrendered their sovereignty?"

Lurking below this is a more hard-edged politics which, as we say our good-byes, begins to unnerve me just a little. Dave's complained about the European Union, and he talks about the coming Euro Super State in which 500 million people will submit their sovereignty to one man. (That would be the Antichrist.) Well, I suggest cheerfully, a super-state worked out just fine for the United States, didn't it? His face darkens.

"The United States right now . . . it's a bureaucratic mess. Our government is so overblown, that . . . Probably if we were to last another twenty-five years, we'd probably have a major revolution on our hands. On the part of people who are just fed up with this nonsense."

I'm taken aback, but Dave is getting angrier still. "You've got to understand that there's a lot of very independent people in the United States." At this point I'm nodding in a wimpish, you're-so-right way, because Dave is readying himself for battle. "You're in an independent country right now. Texas. Texans are a very independent people. And you think we Texans are independent? Go up to Idaho, you'll find survivalists, and those kind of people."

Dave, like a lot of conservatives in the southern and western states, is heir to a long tradition of skepticism about the federal government and what it does with its power. This may come as a relief to liberals who are nervous about the supposed evangelical takeover of Washington, D.C. Although things might change if the Religious Right consolidates its power at the ballot box, many evangelicals are profoundly suspicious of national power and are wedded to the idea of defending their patch. There's a reason why George W. Bush likes to take a month's holiday in rural Texas every year, and why he's commissioned those insignias for the "Western White House," which adorn the walls of his press room in Crawford. Dave's revolutionary rumblings about America's bloated bureaucracy are cut from the same cloth.

Randall Price and Dave Reagan assured me that their principal commitment is to saving souls, rather than manipulating the Middle East to conform with their End Times vision. Both men were frustrated that many of their fellow Christian conservatives had missed the evangelical potential of an apocalyptic message. Dave had heard plenty of Christian pastors say that prophecy seemed pie in the sky, irrelevant to their congregations who were struggling with profane problems like adultery, drugs, or alcohol. Dave insisted that these were precisely the people who needed to know about the End Times: "It will motivate people to live holy lives because they will realize that we're living on borrowed time and Jesus could come at any moment. We're living in the season of the Lord's return, and you'd better get right with God."

But Randall and Dave are also engaging with national and international affairs, presenting their readers and viewers with ideas about Israel, Islam, Europe, and the future that can't help but cast a shadow across the political process. Although they may not have identified a particular policy objective as they craft their books and broadcasts, their emphasis on historical decline—the world spiraling downward into the clutches of Satan—is a brittle foundation for any American who wants to understand and perhaps even to resolve some of the global challenges facing the United States.

BEFORE I LEAVE Maranatha Acres, Gary calls me back into his office. He produces a laptop, which isn't plugged in, to demonstrate that the compound has wireless Internet and that the offer of a room for the night is still good. Gary's hospitality is sincere and appreciated, but I turn down the offer and thank him again for his kindness. Then he hands me a sealed envelope, and says he'll be in touch. The envelope remains unopened on the seat of my rental car as I drive back to Dallas, and I forget about it until much later that evening.

Inside is a page from a genealogical Web site explaining the origins of my surname. There are also two printouts crammed with weird extracts and symbols: the Agriculture Department's Food Guide Pyramid; the great seal of the United States; a short history of brewing in Munich; and a library card for a book called *Bees Don't Get Arthritis*. There's also a newsletter about an apocalyptic sect called Koreshan Unity, which briefly gathered in Florida at the beginning of the twentieth century. The Koreshans were led by a man named Cyrus Teed who believed that he was the messiah. Teed was the first American with this belief to change his name to Koresh; the second was Vernon Howell of Texas, who became David Koresh in 1990 and died in the burning Branch Davidian compound at Waco in 1993.

I'm not sure why Gary has given me this packet. I think that Tom Hanks's character in *The Da Vinci Code* would spend a long time trying to decipher it. Here's what Gary wrote on the envelope: "This is my two cents' worth. One for what it is *not* worth!! :)" When I inspect the contents again, I see that Gary has taped a golden penny to the back of the newsletter.

5

American Apocalypse

Ronald Reagan loved talking about America's special destiny. "You can call it mysticism if you want to," he told an audience in 1974, when he was governor of California, "but I have always believed that there was some divine plan that placed this great continent between two oceans to be sought out by those who were possessed of an abiding love of freedom." The idea that God has a special mission for the United States has been a mainstay of presidential rhetoric since George Washington's speeches, but today's apocalyptic Christians don't seem persuaded by it. For them, there's no role for America in the End Times. Many believe that their country is already tumbling into a moral abyss.

There's some precedent for this pessimistic view in the debates about America during the earliest period of English settlement. Back in the 1620s, when the Puritans settled at Plymouth and Massachusetts Bay in the hopes of riding out the religious persecution of Charles I, they wondered if there was some cosmic purpose to the events that had led them into exile. One of their supporters in England wrote to Joseph Mede, the Cambridge prophecy expert, to ask for an informed opinion about American colonization. Mede's reply was polite but not encouraging: the role of America in Bible prophecy was to provide a home for Satan. The devil himself had set up shop in the New World, and was scouring the continent for recruits before the final battle between good and evil at Armageddon.

But what about the godly believers who had built new towns on the rocky Atlantic coast since the arrival of the *Mayflower* in 1620? Mede stood his ground: the continent had been seized by Satan long ago. The devil had persuaded the Indians to leave Asia and to follow him into the New World. Eventually, when the time arrived for the battle of Armageddon, they would be his foot soldiers against Christ. (Mede suggested that the Indians were "Gog and Magog," the evil duo named in the Book of Revelation.) Mede didn't doubt the sincerity of the Puritan settlers, and he wished them well in their efforts to roll back the Indians and Spaniards who vastly outnumbered them. But the best they could hope for was to annoy Satan—"to taunt the Devil in his own home"—rather than to found a New Jerusalem in America.

This more pessimistic view of America wasn't terribly popular with subsequent generations, and Ronald Reagan is only one of many American orators to argue that the people on the *Mayflower* traversed the Atlantic with a special mission to save the world.

In fact, most Puritans made the trip for a much more mundane reason: they didn't like Charles I and the way in which their religion was suffering under his Catholic-friendly regime. The first New England colonists saw their new home as a good place to ride out the storm until Charles I regained his senses or was replaced by a more reliably Protestant king. Among the first generations of settlers, very few believed that America was at the center of the apocalyptic scheme.

This isn't to say that the Puritans dismissed Bible prophecy. In

New England, there was a great deal of interest in mapping current affairs onto the vision of Daniel or the Book of Revelation, and some American theologians—like John Cotton, who advised Oliver Cromwell on the Hispaniola invasion—became famous for their prophecy interpretations. But this interest was overwhelmingly directed back at Europe, and toward the English Civil War in particular. New England settlers were fascinated by the conflict between Parliament and the king after 1640. Many of them preached sermons urging on the parliamentary cause. Others wrote poems against monarchical oppression. New Englanders speculated on the prophetic meaning of the war, and its tumultuous course persuaded some colonists that the End Times were approaching. After 1640, hundreds of colonists returned to England to get closer to the action.

One of them was Thomas Venner, who was born in the southwest of England and spent nearly fifteen years as a barrel maker in Massachusetts. Venner returned to the fervor of republican London in 1651, and quickly became a Fifth Monarchist. By 1655, he'd been arrested for plotting to kill Cromwell and blow up the Tower of London. A beneficiary of Cromwell's lax policy on religious zealots, Venner was released a few months later, and continued to agitate for the Fifth Monarchy even as Charles II was restored to the throne. In 1661, it was Venner who led the bloody attack on London that resulted in nearly fifty deaths. He received nineteen wounds, but somehow survived to stand trial for his actions. After delivering another speech to the unsympathetic courtroom on the imminent return of Christ he pleaded guilty to involvement in the London attack but denied that he had been its leader. (That role belonged to Jesus.) Within two weeks of the attack, he was hanged, drawn, and quartered outside the meetinghouse in which he'd planned his apocalyptic revolution.

Venner was an extreme example, but there were plenty of people in New England during the 1640s and 1650s who cheered on the English Revolution from an apocalyptic perspective. There were also those who fretted about the purpose of the American settlements, now that the Puritan cause appeared to have triumphed back at home. Perhaps, as many English revolutionaries were claiming, the defeat of Charles I could actually lead to the millennium promised in those brief verses of Revelation. If this was true, surely every Puritan should head back across the ocean to join the struggle against the Antichrist?

As the first colonists grappled with the anxiety that they were prophetically obsolete just two decades after the founding of New England, they reached for an apocalyptic pretext that might justify continued settlement in America. The Indians, who had been the villains in Joseph Mede's scheme, unwittingly provided this. Even before the first contact between New England settlers and Indians in the 1620s, Europeans had begun to speculate on what God had in store for America's native population. At first, these ideas verged on the genocidal. The Indians of New England had fallen victim to European diseases even before the *Mayflower* colonists had dropped anchor, attacked by alien microbes that had already landed in Spanish America and Virginia, or in the English and French fishing vessels that had tracked the northern shores for decades. The Plymouth settlers were amazed to discover villages that had been mysteriously emptied of their residents, and corn that had already been planted in the ground, and they concluded that God himself had prepared for their arrival. The Indians had been struck down by a plague to allow for true Christianity to take root in America. They were modern-day Canaanites in the new American Israel.

By the 1630s, some colonists had suggested a completely different role for Indians in God's scheme. Roger Williams, a controversial preacher who was eventually banished to Rhode Island for his religious views, was a keen student of Indian customs and languages. In 1635 he wrote to a friend in England with an extraordinary suggestion: Could Native Americans be one of the missing tribes of Israel, who'd lost their way nearly two thousand years earlier and had now washed up on the other side of the world? Were the Indians Jewish?

This may seem crazy, but in listening to the Indians speaking to each other, Williams believed that he'd heard similarities between their languages and Hebrew. The idea was intoxicating, not only for its way-out weirdness but because it suggested a role for America in the End Times after all. Suppose that the fight between Charles I and his opponents in England was the battle that would usher in Christ's kingdom, perhaps even the personal return of Jesus. The scriptures might be vague on exactly when this would happen, but a number of the Bible's prophetic passages insisted that the Jews would be converted to Christianity during the End Times. Assuming that Roger Williams was correct in his speculations about American Indians, here was a role for the English settlers that could justify their presence in America and complement the work of the Puritans back home. Perhaps God had intended New England as a huge ground for Indian conversions, a "spiritual factory" (in the words of one settler), which would turn long-lost Jews into Christians and move the prophetic clock one step closer to midnight.

This wasn't a view that persuaded everyone in America. Even Roger Williams eventually succumbed to doubts, and many observers remained unconvinced since the Indians themselves seemed entirely oblivious of Abraham, David, and the other giants of Jewish history. (One contemporary skeptic pointed out that, if the Native Americans really were Jewish, they would never have forgotten about it.) The English Parliament, on the other hand, voted funds for the work of Indian conversion in 1649, and sponsored books and pamphlets that investigated the Indian-Jewish question. The American missionary John Eliot sent a constant stream of reports on Indian conversions to Parliament, which sent back a steady flow of cash to sustain his work. The spiritual factory hummed with life, nourishing apocalyptic dreams on both sides of the Atlantic.

All this prophetic anticipation was dashed by the failure of the English commonwealth and the Restoration of Charles II. Americans, like their counterparts in England, had to accept that their revolution had failed—and that they'd been wrong to believe that Christ was waiting in the wings, ready to take over the government of the world in person when the Stuart monarchy had been overthrown. Some people dealt with this disappointment better than others: but for every Thomas Venner, who pursued his apocalyptic hopes into the Restoration period, when the odds became impossibly long, there were many more Puritans who resolved to trim their sails and shelve their predictions. John Eliot, in a particularly optimistic moment during the early 1650s, had written a book called *The Christian Commonwealth,* outlining how society and politics should be organized during Christ's millennial reign. After the Restoration, the nervous authorities in New England demanded that all copies of the book be collected and destroyed, and that its author should publicly declare his loyalty to Charles II. Eliot meekly complied.

AFTER 1660, American colonists were left with a profound caution about the role of prophecy in politics and history. As in England, there was little appetite for apocalyptic enthusiasm as the costs of the recent revolution were tallied. Since another Stuart monarch was now on the throne, had anything been achieved? Was the millennium any closer than it had been in the days of Charles I? Those bold prophecies of Christ's return began to seem deluded, even irresponsible, with the benefit of hindsight.

For the next hundred years or so, between the 1660s and the American Revolution, interest in prophecy waxed and waned. In New England, a colony on the distant frontier of the English empire, ambitious preachers and bumptious politicians occasionally aired their hope that America might have some prophetic significance. Cotton Mather, one of the Puritan ministers behind the

Salem witch trial of 1692 (and the execution of eighteen people), liked to say that America might be the location of the New Jerusalem of the millennial reign. But it's hard to determine just how seriously this belief was taken in New England. Millennial boasts were a good way to counter some of the snobbery and disregard with which the English naturally approached their far-flung province. Although it's hard for us to believe, given America's relentless power and influence in the present, the English mainland colonies were viewed as a backwater before the middle of the eighteenth century. (The sugar plantations in the Caribbean were the jewels of Britain's overseas empire.) Men like Mather in the frigid northern colonies, with their scholarly pretensions and their millennial self-regard, were easily ignored.

During this period after 1660, there was also a subtle but important shift in the interpretation of Bible prophecy in America. The struggle between Charles I and Parliament had mostly confirmed the view of the End Times contained in Ezekiel, Daniel, and the Gospel of Matthew: events on earth would take a scary turn, with earthquakes and wars and the other fireworks of the Tribulation, before Christ's return. But, with the exception of a nervous moment in the 1680s when England exchanged one king for another, the period between 1660 and 1770 was much more stable than the hundred years that had preceded it. In America, the colonies grew steadily and the frontier of European settlement was pushed farther back. When so much seemed to be going right, the idea that Christ's return would be prefaced by doom and despair became less compelling. On both sides of the Atlantic, theologians debated whether Christ could usher in his millennial reign without the global meltdown promised in the more lurid chapters of Revelation. Perhaps Britain and America could spread knowledge and religion around the world, and the resulting peace and prosperity (rather than despair and woe) could trigger the millennium.

Preachers in the colonies didn't usually tell their flocks to

expect the end of the world—and a political and social collapse—
in their lifetimes. Even those who discussed Bible prophecy in
detail steered clear of the more spectacularly depressing passages
in Revelation or Ezekiel. In the 1740s, the celebrated theologian
Jonathan Edwards was filled with excitement as a surge of religious revivals swept through his native New England and the
other colonies along the eastern seaboard. He wrote up an account of the revival—which these days is known to every American history student as the "Great Awakening"—and he shared his
hope that recent events might have prophetic significance.

Edwards's millennium didn't look much like John Hagee's
version. He steered clear of the darker passages of prophecy, and
looked forward to a kind of spiritual renewal in the world that
would flourish across a thousand years. Edwards sprinkled his
predictions with some textual detail—perhaps America was the
"Isles of Tarshish" described in Isaiah 60:9—but he explored the
idea of the millennium with a cool logic that sometimes departed
entirely from the scriptures. It was unlikely, he thought, that the
millennium would begin in Europe, since the Old World already
had the privilege of being Christ's birthplace. It also seemed rational to assume a special role for America in bringing on the millennium, since the discovery of the continent neatly coincided with
the Protestant rebellion against the Catholic Church—the beginning of Antichrist's downfall. Plotting a course around the chaos
that had enveloped apocalyptic preachers during the English
Civil War, Edwards imagined the millennium as a happy state that
could be achieved without the upheavals of the End Times.

Some historians have suggested that Jonathan Edwards played
the millennial card to outmaneuver his critics. Between 1740 and
1742, as the Great Awakening was at its height in churches across
New England, stuffier clergymen and churchgoers were appalled
at the enthusiasm of new converts. During the revival services
of Edwards and other evangelists, ordinary people would shout
with joy when moved by the spirit, or writhe in agony as they

experienced the throes of conversion. Edwards, stung by the suggestion that these expressions were phony or unseemly, upped the apocalyptic ante. It would be bad enough to oppose God's work in ordinary times, he argued in 1743, but to range oneself against the millennium would be a terrible mistake. Even those preachers who'd kept their peace on the topic, and had declined either to praise or criticize the revivals, were in the firing line. Edwards insisted that fence sitting was no better than throwing brickbats, at least in God's eyes. He had a direct warning for those writers who were tempted to go public in their criticism: before they reached for the presses and produced their articles and pamphlets, they should consider seriously whether God might not "go forth as fire, to consume all that stands in his way." There was a vengeful side to this millennial vision, but it was directed not at the Antichrist but at those laggards and cynics who refused to admit that the golden era was imminent.

Edwards was more admired than loved in his own time. His Massachusetts congregation, who tired of his demands and his strict theology, eventually removed him from his post. His millennial claims stirred some interest, but the Awakening sputtered to a halt just a couple of years after it had begun. John Wesley, the English minister who founded the Methodist Church, seized on reports of the American Awakening to promote his own religious revivals. But when he decided in 1745 to republish Jonathan Edwards's account of the Great Awakening, he simply deleted the entire section on the millennium. By 1750, the same year that Edwards was forced out of his church, few people in Britain or America would have agreed with Edwards's claim that the End Times were at hand.

The Great Awakening didn't produce a lasting millennial enthusiasm, but it did suggest a way of bringing together Bible prophecy and current events without the doom and despair of traditional apocalyptic books and sermons. Jonathan Edwards wasn't the first person to suggest that the millennium could emerge gradually rather than suddenly, or that the thousand years of Christ's reign might be symbolic rather than literal, but he helped to popularize this idea in America, which had a history that was better suited to this upbeat view of God's plan.

WITH THE COLONIES PROSPERING, why should Americans want the world to end? Much better, many concluded, to imagine a spiritual millennium in which American institutions and ideas could help to improve the continent and the rest of the world. Or even to promote this redemptive role for America without any reference to the prophecies of the Bible, thereby avoiding the difficulty of figuring out which country was the little horn or the Isles of Tarshish, and the embarrassment of setting a date for Christ's return.

After the American Revolution, many theologians and even politicians came to view the United States as God's vehicle for improving the world. This optimistic outlook usually avoided any specific reference to Bible prophecy: no predictions of Christ's return, no date setting, no attempt to unravel the mysteries of Gog and Magog. The Christian nationalism that took hold in America after 1776 was sometimes millennial, in that patriotic orators talked vaguely about a gradual improvement of the world under American tutelage. But it would be a stretch to describe it as apocalyptic. When Americans spoke of their providential mission to the world, and eventually of their "manifest destiny," they weren't preparing themselves for the Tribulation and the devastating rise of the Antichrist. If the millennium was the promised land, then the United States could go one better than Moses—and actually lead the world into Canaan without sacrificing its sovereignty or its special status in God's eyes.

This watering down of the terrifying predictions of prophecy— which encouraged Americans to look forward to a gradual increase of happiness and prosperity without enduring the Tribulation—

didn't convince every Christian in the new United States. The most famous apocalyptic preacher of the nineteenth century, William Miller, rejected this theory completely, and built an enormous movement around the older ideas about Christ's literal and imminent return. Miller was born during the American Revolution in Massachusetts, though his family soon moved to a farm on the Vermont–New York border. He was brought up as a Baptist, but like many younger Americans of the time he picked up some of the radical ideas about religion that had been generated by the European Enlightenment: the skepticism of Voltaire, and Thomas Paine's radical attacks on Christianity. (Stuck in a Paris prison after the French Revolution had gone sour, Paine occupied himself by writing a pamphlet called *The Age of Reason*, in which he set out to prove that the scriptures were filled with "obscene stories" that "corrupt and brutalize mankind.") These clever treatises gripped the young Miller, and he smugly declared that the Bible and the ceremonies of Christianity were outdated superstitions.

Miller's cocky preference for reason over faith didn't survive the War of 1812. He captained a U.S. Army company against the British, and his battlefield experiences gave him a taste of the arbitrariness of life and the horrors of death. After the war, he plunged into Bible study, and devoured the prophetic books with particular relish. His research led him to a stark conclusion: Christ was coming back to earth very soon. Miller held on to this secret for nearly a decade, but he was encouraged by his friends in 1831 to go public. In a series of lectures, and then in an 1833 pamphlet entitled *Evidence from Scripture and History of the Second Coming of Christ about the Year AD 1843*, Miller generated a sensation. As the appointed time for Christ's return drew closer, Miller's ideas spread across the country, and hundreds of thousands of Americans—perhaps more—seriously entertained the idea that the self-taught prophecy guru was right.

Miller's sermons and books still make for enjoyable reading, not least since he could be quite candid about the pitfalls of being a prophecy student. "There never was a book written that has a better connection and harmony than the Bible," he enthused in 1833. "And yet it has the appearance of a great store-house full of all the precious commodities the heart could desire, thrown in promiscuously." It was Miller's job to make sense of this jumbled treasure trove, and in his public lectures and newspaper articles he staked his reputation on the belief that the answer to the Bible's most tantalizing question was 1843. "If I have erred in my exposition of the prophecies, the time, being so near at hand, will soon expose my folly." But if he was right, "How important the era in which we live! What vast and important events must soon be realized!"

Miller and his followers were clear in their line of attack: the mainstream churches had, over the previous hundred years or so, retreated from a serious engagement with Bible prophecy in favor of a syrupy, feel-good vision of Christ's return. This "flattering millennium theory" sidestepped the literal, earth-shattering dramas of Ezekiel and Revelation, and encouraged Christians to approach the future with a false confidence. If the world was gradually getting better, Miller argued, where was the incentive for believers to reform their lives and turn away from sin? If, on the other hand, Christ was coming back within a decade, all Americans would be forced to accept Jesus Christ or risk his substantial wrath. Miller was, at heart, a moralist. The Second Coming of Christ, in his able hands, was the ultimate wake-up call for a sinful nation.

But he wasn't a politician. In fact, the Millerites came under attack from some of their old friends in the pressure groups of their day. Americans who were deeply engaged in the battle against slavery, or the temperance movement, came to resent Miller not only for distracting from their political campaigns but for encouraging passivity among potential campaigners. If Christ was coming back in 1843, they complained, what was the point of agitating against slavery? This is the same argument that Dominion Theology believers make against today's prophecy enthusiasts, though the Dominionist political agenda is a good deal scarier than the platform of antislavery Christians in the 1830s and 1840s.

Miller's popularity soared as the appointed hour approached. Although he encouraged believers to remain in their own churches, thousands of loyal followers traveled to Vermont and hoped that Miller would lead them into the millennium himself. Miller and his lieutenants organized huge camp meetings, in which thousands of believers came together to share their excitement about the impending apocalypse. In January 1843, with the day of reckoning at hand, these followers asked Miller to be more specific about timing. Would Christ come in the first half of the year? Should they plan for one last summer before the millennial reign? Miller was reluctantly forced into predicting that, if his calculations were correct, they could expect to see the Second Coming within one year of March 21, 1843. When Christ failed to appear by the spring of 1844, Miller and his followers were subjected to a wave of mockery—mixed with relief, presumably, on the part of those skeptics who'd dismissed the predictions.

The movement lasted for another seven months, as Miller's adherents circulated the suggestion that the actual date for Christ's return was October 22, 1844. Miller had always argued that he might be a little off with his calculations, and in the summer of 1844 he urged his followers to keep the faith and rally behind the new October date. Thousands obliged, many selling their property or neglecting to harvest their crops before gathering in public places to greet Christ when the day finally arrived. In Philadelphia, a large crowd gathered before daybreak on the twenty-second in the belief that the Second Coming would occur around 3:00 A.M. It was cold and wet in the city, and newspaper reports painted a scene of "wild confusion and misery" as "deluded parents" forced their children into tents to await Christ's arrival. Mothers told their children that Jesus would soon dry up their tears; some families had changed into "ascension robes" ahead of their imminent salvation.

The sun came up, the entire day passed, and the crowds began to thin. Some predicted that Christ was running late, and that the sun would set at noon on the twenty-third before Christ himself appeared at 3:00 P.M. But, as the newspapers gloated, "the sun shone through the day with unusual brilliancy. Scarcely a cloud was to be seen." In Philadelphia and the other big cities that had succumbed to Millerite excitement, these days became known as the "Great Disappointment." Miller himself admitted that there had been an error in his calculations, and he managed to convince some of his followers that he had been right in principle to forecast the imminent return of Jesus. One lasting institution emerged from all this—the Seventh-Day Adventist Church, which has its origins in one of the splinter groups that expected the imminent return of Christ even after the Great Disappointment of 1844. Miller himself was a figure of ridicule for the rest of his life, though he never gave up on the hopes he had raised in so many other Americans.

William Miller was a religious high roller. He'd built a hugely popular movement by offering a precise prediction about the Second Coming. The downside to this was that he'd exposed himself to utter humiliation if Christ didn't actually appear. After Miller's downfall in 1844, there was a lesson here for the mainstream churches that had watched his rise with disdain: the prophetic books of the Bible were dangerous stuff, with their mixture of momentous promises and bewildering images. Traditional preachers had warned their congregations to hold out against the wares that Miller was offering, and now they had been vindicated. The Church should hammer home the lesson that prophecy could mislead as easily as it could enlighten. This confirmed many American Christians in the more soothing idea that the United States could gradually ring in the millennium by spreading liberty and religion around the world. But many Christians reached a simpler conclusion: perhaps any attempt to decipher prophecy was a waste of effort.

APOCALYPTIC IDEAS didn't disappear from the United States after 1844, but the idea of the End Times retreated to the margins of American culture. A decade after the Great Disappointment, Tennessee minister Samuel Baldwin produced an enormous book called *Armageddon,* which argued that the references to Israel in prophecy were in fact references to the modern United States. Baldwin also argued, conveniently enough for a southerner, that whites would be the "guardians" of blacks during the coming millennium. When the Civil War broke out in 1861, and seemed to dash all this optimism about America's role, several Confederate interpreters tried to rescue Baldwin's framework. One Nashville author argued that, if the United States was the fifth kingdom imagined by Daniel in his dreams, then perhaps the Confederacy was the sixth kingdom (which Daniel had neglected to mention) and would lead the world into the millennial reign of Christ. Evidently there was life after William Miller for prophecy interpreters, though neither Baldwin nor his Confederate admirers won a significant following.

More important for our story is John Nelson Darby, a British preacher who founded the sect that would eventually be known as the Plymouth Brethren. Born in London in 1800 to a well-off Irish Protestant family, the young Darby became disillusioned with mainstream religion. The Church was much too involved in politics and society, he thought. True believers should immerse themselves in the Bible and remain aloof from the fallen world. This was quite a rebellion: Darby's father was a prominent merchant who had helped to supply the Royal Navy during the wars against Napoleonic France; his uncle served under Admiral Horatio Nelson at the Battle of the Nile in 1798. (Hence Darby's middle name.) Darby shunned this heritage. He wandered away to continental Europe, and then kept wandering for the rest of his life. Darby lectured on a variety of religious topics, and he came to America on seven occasions. In the United States, his ideas about the end of the world found a small but enthusiastic audience. Although he died in 1882, his influence on American Bible prophecy continues to this day.

Darby, like Joseph Mede and Joachim of Fiore, believed that he could gather together all of the prophecies of the Bible into a single system. To do this, he developed one of Joachim's ideas: that God had divided up the history of the world into distinct periods, and that he'd dealt with the world differently during each. Joachim had sketched three of these, but Darby suggested there were actually seven. One of the clever things about this idea was that Darby was able to explain why, for example, God seemed like a much tougher character in the Old Testament than in the New. If these were completely different periods in his wider scheme, there was no contradiction between all that smiting and woe in the first half of the Bible, and the emphasis on love and forgiveness in the Gospels. Darby's idea became known as "dispensationalism," and most American prophecy enthusiasts today consider themselves to be "dispensationalists."

Darby was the godfather of modern prophecy belief. Nearly all of today's prophecy celebrities—Tim LaHaye, John Hagee, Hal Lindsey, Dave Reagan—are indebted to his very specific discussion of the End Times. It was Darby who rescued the idea of the Rapture from a letter of St. Paul, and who gave true believers their escape route from the Antichrist. Darby cut through the confusing system of dates and intervals in Daniel and the other prophetic books, promising that the Tribulation that followed the Antichrist's rise would last for seven years. Most significantly of all, Darby rejected the idea that the Jews had somehow missed out on Christ and the prophetic promises. For Darby, the passages in the Bible about the restoration of Israel were literally true. Sooner or later, there would be a Jewish state once more.

All the talk about the Christian Church replacing Israel in God's scheme, or the speculative claim that "Israel" in prophecy actually referred to the United States, was totally erroneous. It might be hard for nineteenth-century observers to imagine Israel's return, Darby conceded, but it would happen nonetheless, just as the Bible had predicted.

Darby had mixed feelings about the United States. He thought that Americans spent too much of their energy on their jobs and their immediate surroundings rather than on their spiritual state. But he enjoyed speaking to the diverse crowds that turned out for his lectures, and he became so used to the humble lifestyle of the traveling lecturer that he was happy to visit some of the most depressed slums in America. On one trip to an especially deprived household, he had just tucked in to the modest meal that his hosts had prepared for him when he realized with horror that he was eating their son's pet rabbit. He refused to finish his dinner, and played with the bereaved child for an hour, though it's not clear whether this was much consolation in the circumstances.

In return, Darby's American audiences didn't rush to become Plymouth Brethren, and he was much more successful in spreading his ideas about the end of the world than in actually convincing American Christians to join his sect. He had a big influence on the Chicago minister Dwight Moody, though Moody simply grafted Darby's ideas about the Rapture onto his own evangelical scheme. Moody, who preached to enormous crowds in America and England from the early 1870s, was one of the architects of Christian fundamentalism in twentieth-century America. Beyond his revival sermons, he built an empire that included a Bible school, a conference bureau, and a publishing house. Before his death in 1899, Moody preached directly to tens of millions of people, an incredibly large number in the days before radio and television. Darby didn't like his more popular rival. In a dig at Moody's worldliness, Darby dismissed him as "that active man in

Chicago." But Moody helped to sustain dispensationalist ideas about Israel, the Rapture, and the Tribulation even after Darby himself had faded from memory.

Moody reached his enormous audience during the turbulent final years of the nineteenth century, when the gap between rich and poor widened considerably, and many working people turned to socialism, communism, and even anarchy to escape from their desperate condition. Some evangelical Christians saw this moment as an opportunity to improve the lives of the poor, especially in the big cities. Moody's message was quite different. The End Times were approaching fast, and there was little hope of improving the filthy slums or of solving the problems of unemployment and poverty. Christians should try to redeem souls, not society; Christ would take care of the world when he appeared in person.

On some occasions, apocalyptic evangelicals like Dwight Moody presented the tensions in American society as evidence that the End Times were at hand. Preachers in the nineteenth and early twentieth centuries weren't as brazen about this as their twenty-first century successors—who persistently warn that gay marriage or abortion are the trumpets of the Tribulation—but the connection between moral decay and End Times anticipation was clearly established long before Hal Lindsey or John Hagee came on the scene. What was missing was a sense of immediacy. If John Nelson Darby had been right about God's seven dispensations to the world, and about the literal restoration of Israel in the Middle East, American Christians would have a clear warning before the last days about their standing in the prophetic scheme. Until Israel was restored, there could be no Tribulation, no Antichrist, and no Second Coming.

THE CREATION of the Jewish State in 1948 provided the missing piece in the puzzle, generating the upsurge in apocalyptic belief

that has propelled today's most famous Bible prophecy interpreters into the mainstream. Many of them were alive when Israel
was founded, and claim to have realized immediately that this
was a uniquely significant moment. (John Hagee's recollection
of hearing the news on the radio, with his father listening beside
him, is only one example.) You have to concede their point: the
Jews had been scattered thousands of years earlier, but had now
returned to their original land in spite of the genocidal program
of Adolf Hitler. Bible prophets had talked of a Jewish return,
albeit obliquely; and John Nelson Darby, among other evangelicals, had explicitly insisted on the restoration of Israel when that
prediction was especially outlandish. Surely this was the most direct evidence yet that the scriptures were correct, and that Christ
would return as he had promised?

Among the many conservative theologians who delighted in
Israel's birth, few were more vocal and influential than John Walvoord, the president of Dallas Theological Seminary. Under his
influence, the faculty and students of DTS kept alive the teachings of John Nelson Darby, and keenly watched current affairs
for signs that Darby's precise chronology of the End Times was
coming to fruition. In his 1962 book, *Israel in Prophecy*, Walvoord
crowed at those Christian critics who had previously dismissed
the End Times scenario as "untenable, self-contradictory, and
hopelessly confused." Everything had suddenly cohered around
Israel. History and current affairs were finally on the side of the
apocalypse.

Walvoord was originally quite cautious in his prophetic teaching. Yes, events in the Middle East strongly suggested that the
world was entering its last days. Yes, the Rapture was a literal
promise from Christ to his followers, and true Christians could
expect to be whisked away from earth before the reign of the
Antichrist. But in the 1960s, in books like *Israel in Prophecy*, Walvoord merely prodded at the political situation of the day. To anyone who has read one of John Hagee's books, Walvoord's early

prophetic predictions seem positively coy. Perhaps Russia would be the source of that false philosophy of atheism that would spread throughout the world during the Tribulation. But, then again, Walvoord didn't find any specific reference to communism in the prophecies, so he didn't push the point.

Walvoord and his Dallas faculty were eventually overtaken by a new generation of prophecy interpreters who were bolder in their efforts to explain current events through scriptural predictions. The most famous of these was Hal Lindsey. Born in Houston in 1929, Lindsey served in the Coast Guard during the Korean War, and enjoyed a colorful career as a tugboat captain in New Orleans before coming to Christ (and to Dallas) in the late 1950s. Like many new converts, Lindsey chose to work for Campus Crusade for Christ, an evangelical group that still tours universities and colleges and tries to make the Christian message cool. Unlike John Walvoord and his seminary professors, Lindsey understood the youth revolutions of the 1960s from the inside. While he held on to his notes from his prophecy classes at Dallas, Lindsey quietly acquired the jargon and even the sensibility of younger, hipper Americans who had no time for the fogeys who ran seminaries or the creaking religions that they promoted.

In 1970, Lindsey wrote the most popular prophecy book in American history. *The Late Great Planet Earth* sold an astonishing 30 million copies and was eventually hailed by the *New York Times* as the nonfiction "bestseller of the decade." Part of Lindsey's success came down to timing. He plundered the headlines not only for news of Israel but for any indication that the world was on its last legs. The political preoccupations of the early 1970s were invariably gloomy: the global population crisis, the beginnings of the environmental movement, the battle to stop the war in Indochina. All these suggested that the times were out of joint, and gave Lindsey abundant evidence that the End Times were approaching.

Lindsey also had a knack for writing like a stoner. Before you even consider its prophecy predictions, *Planet Earth* overwhelms you with offbeat and seemingly random observations. Most of these, I think, are deliberate. Lindsey had presumably talked to enough hippies during his years as a campus preacher to know the best way to reach the younger generation. The book doesn't set out to judge readers, but instead opens the door wide to anyone who's been searching for answers. If you've tried astrology, faith healing, "vibrations," and even science fiction, but you're still feeling unfulfilled, Lindsey will help you to see that the Bible is the place you ought to be looking. If you think that being a Christian is dour and boring, the chapter titles and headings of *The Late Great Planet Earth*—a succession of jokes and puns—make it clear that you can follow Jesus without seeming like a loser. The chapters are also very short, which must have been appreciated by any real stoners who stumbled across the book in the New Age aisle of the supermarket (where it was often displayed).

Lindsey seems to have nudged the older generation as well. John Walvoord, who had previously been quite restrained in his predictions, wrote a much sexier prophecy book in 1974. *Armageddon, Oil and the Middle East Crisis* was, as Walvoord himself admitted, an effort to tailor his longstanding views on the End Times to the general public. His jumping-off point was the oil crisis that followed the Yom Kippur War of October 1973, during which Israel's Arab neighbors had clawed back some of the territory (and the pride) that they'd lost in the 1967 war. The prophetic insights were woven closely around the current situation in the Middle East, and Walvoord persuaded Lindsey's own publisher—Zondervan Books of Michigan—to release the book as a mass-market paperback. I bought a secondhand copy of the first edition, and the cover image is still striking: a large drop of oil, surrounded by four ugly blots of blood. In case readers didn't appreciate that his message was urgent, Walvoord inserted a screaming subtitle below a massive ARMAGEDDON: "What the Bible Says About the Future of the Middle East and the End of Western Civilization."

Armageddon sold nearly 750,000 copies, vindicating John Walvoord's decision to follow Hal Lindsey's example, and prophecy books found a huge crossover audience. The early 1970s were also the moment when American prophecy enthusiasts forged the first links with Israeli officials, and laid the groundwork for what would come to be called Christian Zionism in the United States. In 1971, the evangelical magazine *Christianity Today* organized a prophecy conference in Jerusalem with the blessing of the Israeli government. The first ever Prime Minister of Israel, the legendary David Ben-Gurion, met with the participants, who included John Walvoord and a number of Dallas faculty members. Naturally, the American participants shared their excitement not only at Israel's reestablishment in 1948 but at its recent victory in 1967 and the recapture of the Old City and the Western Wall.

Many of the elements of today's prophecy culture were in place by the mid-1970s: the enthusiasm of academics and popular prophecy writers for John Nelson Darby's system; the widespread excitement about Israel; and a commitment to take prophecy belief into the mainstream, in books like *The Late Great Planet Earth* or via radio and television. Mainline denominations steered clear of all this; if you were an Episcopalian or a Unitarian, you were very unlikely to come across any of these ideas in a sermon. But among evangelical churches, especially in rural areas and in the Bible Belt, the idea of the Rapture, a seven-year Tribulation, and the literal return of Christ was firmly established by 1975.

WHILE THE PROPHETIC MESSAGE was honed by Walvoord and Lindsey in the mid-1970s, Christian fundamentalism was on the verge of a political transformation that would remake American society after 1980. Fundamentalists have always been sensitive to the sins and the depravity of the world, though they have only sporadically made forays into the political arena to assert their agenda. One famous exception was in 1925, after a young biology teacher in Tennessee, John Scopes, deliberately disobeyed a state law that banned the teaching of Darwinism in the classroom. The Scopes trial that followed turned into a battle between the impassioned biblical reasoning of William Jennings Bryan, the former presidential candidate and a committed evangelical, and the massed ranks of liberal America: journalists, academics, and lawyers from the big cities poured into the small town of Dayton and made fun of the locals. The lead lawyer for Scopes was Clarence Darrow, who had recently made his name defending two Chicago boys who had murdered their parents. The highlight of the trial came when Darrow managed to get Bryan to submit to a cross-examination, which ended in a farce as Bryan proved unable to explain the many odd things that had happened in the Bible. Scopes was convicted and fined $100, but the big-city newspapers and academics who'd been cheering on Darrow and Scopes mocked William Jennings Bryan and the rural, religious culture that had drafted the anti-Darwinism law. They passed over Scopes's conviction (which was later overturned), and they concluded from Bryan's embarrassing appearance in the witness box that a secular perspective had now triumphed in America.

Christian fundamentalism spent a long time in the political wilderness, and maybe it benefited from the experience. Isolated from the increasingly secular culture of "mainstream" America, religious conservatives saw the decline in Christian beliefs across the nation as a justification for their focus on personal salvation. Perhaps they'd withdrawn to such an extent that many liberal Americans took their own political influence for granted. But in the 1970s, the ground began to shift once more.

Historians have offered plenty of explanations for the rise of what is now known as the Religious Right. Some suggest that southern preachers and politicians, steeped in fundamentalist Christianity, could only emerge when the issue of civil rights had been addressed. Although many African Americans would dispute the suggestion that this problem had been solved by the 1970s, the landmark federal legislation of the 1960s allowed southern conservatives to emerge on the national stage without instantly being dismissed as racists.

Other historians think that religious conservatism was stirred into political action by the protest movements of the 1960s and early 1970s, with their unapologetic demands for social equality and their fierce attack on American foreign policy. In this scenario, the Religious Right was a sleeping giant that was finally awakened by the sheer audacity of the American left: in the face of protest marches, flag burning, free love, and student radicalism, conservative Christians simply had to enter the political arena.

As late as 1976, the association between evangelicalism and political conservatism wasn't totally clear. Jimmy Carter, the Georgia peanut farmer who styled himself as a political innocent, was a born-again Christian and a Democrat, a combination that seemed impossible by the 1990s. His presidency was the final straw for many conservatives, who watched in despair as Carter refused to roll back abortion or to condemn secularism, homosexuality, and the other moral plagues that had supposedly overwhelmed America. Carter was even woolly on foreign affairs, initially talking up the possibility of peace with the Soviet Union, and failing to take a sufficiently hard line during the revolutions against American client leaders in Iran and Nicaragua. (He also had questionable views about Israel.) The Religious Right mobilized in earnest during Carter's brief stay in the White House, and by 1980 they had helped to create the climate for his successor, Ronald Reagan.

Apart from Bill Clinton's tenure, Republican presidents have been in office since 1981. During this time, they've become increasingly dependent on religious conservatives, both for votes and for the political organizing that gets voters energized around a candidate. Those religious conservatives, in turn, have taken their social and theological concerns directly to Washington.

None of this was happening in the early 1970s, when Hal

Lindsey and John Walvoord were racing up the bestseller lists with their apocalyptic readings of the current crisis in the Middle East. But in the decades since, the same people who believe fervently that the End Times are upon us—that things are going to get much worse, and that global catastrophes will be averted only by Christ's literal return—have become an important part of the most successful political coalition in modern American history. As the historian George Marsden has observed, there's a paradox in this: while fundamentalist Christians have made "massive efforts to transform American politics and culture for the long run," their increasingly popular ideas about the End Times have "suggested that for the United States there would be no long run."

This is what makes the current enthusiasm for prophecy both intriguing and perplexing. Historically, prophecy believers have been politically marginal, content to withdraw from the public arena while awaiting Christ's return, and conditioned to believe that terrible times are a prerequisite for the Second Coming. The Americans who are reading John Hagee or Tim LaHaye have held on to the part about terrible times, but now have the conviction to seek out senators and representatives in the nation's capital. "We're not in Washington to sing 'Amazing Grace' on the Mall and to get sunburned again," John Hagee told the evangelical delegates during the Christians United for Israel banquet in July 2006. "We're going to invade Capitol Hill tomorrow!"

There's plenty of variety among prophecy enthusiasts, and some people are a lot more convinced than others by the need to take Ezekiel and Daniel to Washington, D.C. But for Americans who aren't sold on the idea that the Christian apocalypse is upon us, and who might be nervous about the application of the Bible's cryptic promises to politics, there's an obvious challenge: How do you start a dialogue with people who are convinced that the world is coming to an end?

6

The Dirty Old Fishpond

f Texas is the epicenter of the Bible prophecy movement, Palm Springs is its retirement home. Tim LaHaye moved out to the desert when he quit his ministry in San Diego, and he lives in the upscale community of Rancho Mirage to the southeast of downtown Palm Springs. Hal Lindsey has also settled here, in another of these "Desert Cities," which spread across the valley between two mountain ranges. But these titans of Bible prophecy haven't put their feet up. Although LaHaye is eighty years old, he still travels across the country promoting his books, and he collaborates closely with Jerry Jenkins in Colorado on the latest manuscripts in the *Left Behind* series.

Hal Lindsey is seventy-six and going strong. Until January 2006, he had a cable show on Trinity Broadcasting Network, the undisputed gorilla of Christian television. But then he fell out with the TBN owners over Islam (about which more later) and moved over to Daystar, an upstart Christian satellite broadcaster that competes with TBN for viewers and talent. Lindsey is even more active than LaHaye, producing a thirty-minute show from his local television studio in which he puts a prophetic spin on the week's headlines. On his Web site, Lindsey sells an extraordinary range of videos and books about the End Times. If you're interested in the role of the United Nations in the Tribulation, or the prospects for the U.S. during the reign of the Antichrist, Lindsey has a video that you will want to see.

Just before you reach Palm Springs on the freeway from Los Angeles, you find yourself in a vast field of wind turbines. They crowd the road on both sides, they peer out from distant hilltops, and they seem to stretch for miles into the valley. Thousands of white propellers spin briskly in the warm breeze and give you a false impression about what lies ahead. While this spectacular gateway suggests that the Desert Cities (like many other parts of California) might be kookily right-on when it comes to sustainability and energy use, the reality of the area quickly overwhelms. The sprawl of towns runs for nearly twenty miles, and an enormous amount of water and energy is dedicated to denying the obvious: this is the desert, and people aren't supposed to live here in large numbers.

The experience of visiting Palm Springs is like watching a cigarette commercial from the 1950s in which a doctor cheerfully describes how smoking is good for you. The underground water that originally drew people to this area is now being gulped by strip malls and resort hotels, and everyone seems to be living on borrowed time. There are, according to the local tourist office, more than a hundred golf courses in Palm Springs. I didn't believe this when I was booking my trip, but thanks to a mix-up I found myself upgraded to one of those resort hotels and I could watch carts zipping up and down the fairway below my window.

The golf courses are especially lush, but these towns expend their water reserves on much more besides—as you drive (no one walks) to the mall or the multiplex, you're reassured by bushes and grassy banks on both sides of the street. In an act of denial on the part of the developers, the new mall in Rancho Mirage is actually called "The River." It's built around a sweeping concrete canal that divides Barnes & Noble from Starbucks. This is the kind of place that could easily send you over the edge. There's a barbecue restaurant in the mall called *Babe*'s, which is bafflingly licensed from the movies about the cute talking pig. Here and there, beyond a broken pipe or a misdirected nozzle, the grass withers in the fierce sun. Palm Springs, like Las Vegas and many of the cities in the Southwest, is an unnatural place, and it's growing larger every year.

Tim LaHaye had already agreed to meet with me in Colorado, so I didn't go looking for him in Desert Island, the super-swanky resort where he makes his home. Apparently his air-conditioning had given out while I was in town, which would give you an unpleasant idea of what hell might be like. (There's a sign outside one downtown church with a cheerful take on the oppressive weather: "SMILE! YOU KNOW THERE ARE HOTTER PLACES THAN THIS!") Instead, I wanted to find Hal Lindsey, and I followed a lead to the local church where he occasionally lectures and sells his prophecy gear. The week before, I'd been in Cornerstone Church in San Antonio, and I wasn't sure what to expect from a Palm Springs service. It was a very different experience. For one thing, the church was much smaller, and was obviously tailored to the tourists and others who passed through the town each week. After Cornerstone, it was also reassuringly amateurish.

Pastor Mark, who led the service, didn't need a musical warm-up. When the congregation had arrived, he launched right into his thirty-minute sermon "Why Church?" I'd never seen anyone preach using Powerpoint before. Pastor Mark wandered around the stage with his remote control, and we followed along on two big projection screens. We'd also been handed a packet as we entered the church that contained a kind of worksheet for the sermon. (This came with punch holes to let you file the notes in a binder.)

WORSHIP _____ GOD
WORSHIP _____ GOD
WORSHIP _____ US

The outline matched up with the Powerpoint presentation, and the church regulars scribbled in the missing words as Mark moved through his slides. There was nothing here about gays or Muslims—just a series of simple messages about submitting to Christ.

The music was also a surprise after the slick performances at Cornerstone. A choir of a dozen was led by a bearded man in his sixties, and a round lady played the piano bombastically as the congregation belted out traditional hymns. Occasionally the words—projected onto the big screens—were out of synch with the music, which left the choir to soldier on without us. The only worshipper who seemed Cornerstone-zealous was a burly man at the front wearing a blue shirt and bright green trousers. He threw his hands into the air during the hymns, which was de rigueur in San Antonio but which marked you out in this crowd. During "Holy Holy Holy," I noticed that when he got to the part about the blessed Trinity, he screwed up his thumb and pinkie and left his three middle fingers in the air.

When the hymns were over, we were treated to an ambitious finale. The speakers began to play what sounded like the theme from *Magnum, P.I.*, and the choir attempted a complicated number called "Worship the Lord!" They didn't seem completely comfortable, partly because the music was on tape so this was effectively karaoke for them. The congregation listened politely but nervously, worried about the choir's chances of getting through the song but grateful that it wasn't being Powerpointed for the rest of us to butcher. Perhaps the guy who wrote the *Magnum* theme tune, or someone else who made their money in L.A. writing TV music, had come to Palm Springs and written devotionals in their golden years. I scanned the room for Hal Lindsey, but there was no sign of him. When "Worship the Lord!" concluded (to relieved applause), Pastor Mark gave the blessing and sent us on our way.

When I got back to my hotel room, I had an e-mail from an unexpected source. Before I'd come out to California, I'd written to David Chagall, the host of a cable show on Bible prophecy called *The Last Hour*, which is produced in Agoura, just north of Los Angeles. I wanted to meet David because he seemed like a good example of someone further down the prophecy food chain than John Hagee or Tim LaHaye.

The Last Hour has been running on cable stations from New York to Hawaii for nearly ten years, but I'd first seen it on the Manhattan Neighborhood Network, which helped me to place its reach and influence. MNN is a public access station—everyone in New York with a cable box can watch the network, and local communities are encouraged to produce their own television shows or suggest other community-produced programming from further afield. (Such as *The Last Hour*.) Although the audience is potentially huge, in reality the content is often quite amateurish and attracts a niche audience. When I lived in Manhattan, I'd occasionally catch an MNN show in which performance artists wandered around the city pretending to vomit in front of unwitting passersby. The footage was accompanied by Frank Sinatra singing "New York, New York" as the hapless locals tried either to console the faux-vomiter or to look the other way. (*The Last Hour* was preceded by a program on dowsing.) If David Chagall was keeping this kind of company, then he was probably more of an enthusiast than a player in the Bible prophecy universe.

Although he still produced the show in Agoura, David e-mailed to tell me that he'd moved to Palm Desert, a few miles down the road from Hal Lindsey. He's seventy-five years old, and he'd left the suburbs to enjoy the "desert living" that billboards all over town promote to visitors who might be thinking about retirement.

(The word "desert" is attached to everything in Palm Springs, as if deserts were universally held to be a good thing—there's even a "Desert IMAX.") I called David and told him that I was interested in hearing how he got into prophecy, and that I was trying to explain the prophecy perspective to people who hadn't read the *Left Behind* books or seen his TV show. Come on over, he said, and told me how to find him in a gated community on the edge of town.

THE ENTIRE PALM SPRINGS area is a monument to old people. The streets are named after local residents who linger in the memory as permatanned survivors: Bob Hope Drive, Frank Sinatra Drive, Kirk Douglas Way, Gerald Ford Drive. But the dedicated housing complexes for seniors are something else. You're allowed to buy a place only if you're over fifty-five, and these developments are dominated by cheery retirees with plenty of energy and money.

To get to David Chagall's house, I have to wait in a line of cars to have my credentials checked by a fit-looking guy in his late sixties, wearing the community's uniform of white polo shirt and white shorts. It seems that everyone, even the staff, has to have gray hair to get into this place—it's like *Logan's Run* in reverse.

When they've waved me through the guardhouse, I drive nearly two miles along a boulevard that's flanked by greens and bunkers. Like my hotel, the development has been built in the middle of a golf course. Residents can literally walk out of their houses onto the fairways, and a fair number of them seem to be doing just that, taking advantage of the fact that it's early and that it won't be unbearably hot for another hour or two. David lives on the outskirts of the complex, where the artificial green smudges and then disappears into the browns and yellows of the desert. Nearby is the freeway that rises away to the east, up into the mountains and the wilderness of Joshua Tree National Park. There's a black billboard beside the freeway that says, in simple white letters,

"ONE NATION UNDER ME—GOD."

The Last Hour doesn't have any of the slickness of other prophecy television. The production values are a world away from Hagee's broadcasts, or the show that Hal Lindsey puts together each week in Palm Desert. Sometimes David appears alone, but he often has a "co-host," a guy named Steve who interviews David (confusingly identified as the "host") and asks him scripted questions about the End Times. There doesn't seem to be an autocue, which forces Steve to look down at his notes and read quite sophisticated theological questions to David, while making them seem like off-the-cuff inquiries that any of us might come up with.

The first time I watched the show, this didn't go well at all. David looked more nervous than I've ever seen anyone look on television. He'd splutter at the end of his prophetic apostrophes while Steve looked on with a fraught helplessness, and the whole thing was hard to watch. David spent a long time pointing to a diagram of what appeared to be a woman in a miniskirt and leggings. (On closer inspection, this was a mock-up of the statue that appeared in the dreams of Nebuchadnezzar from the Book of Daniel.) But the creakiness of the show—along with the title sequence, in which THE LAST HOUR crawls up the screen against a blurry astronomical backdrop, accompanied by 1980s synthesizer music—somehow persuades you that these people are for real. David tells me that he's never taken a penny from his ministry, and given the money that some preachers are making from predicting the apocalypse, this seems genuinely admirable.

"SO ONE DAY I was trying to get rid of a drug problem I had." David is talking about his conversion to Christianity in 1984, which had been prefaced by a predictably Californian roster of self-help strategies: Buddhism, "Eastern meditation," and so on. "And in the middle of my meditation, I heard a voice say, 'Ask Jesus.' And to me, a Jew, that would be the equivalent of saying 'Ask Hitler,' you know, the God of the enemy." (I should have mentioned: David is Jewish.) "And I quickly denied that, and went out and rolled a big bomber, and did that three days running."

But the voice persisted, and so David struck a deal with God: "'If you are truly real, and you have the power, take away this addiction I have, and I'll know that you are who the Bible says you are.' And at that point, it's strange, a weight lifted off my chest. The idea of smoking grass or taking LSD was so abhorrent to me, that I realized he had done it. And I thought, well, okay, my end of the bargain was that I'd follow you."

David grew up Jewish in Philadelphia. His father was an officer in the local synagogue, and his grandparents were devout Jews. But after his bar mitzvah, David wandered away from the faith. Looking for fame and fortune as a writer, he moved to England in the 1960s and became a novelist. He published a couple of novels— including one tortured reflection on religion and existence, *A Century Without God*—but he wasn't making ends meet, and so he moved back to the United States and began working as a journalist. He wrote about politics, producing exposés for *Los Angeles Magazine*, *TV Guide* (which used to cover the political beat), and other publications. David didn't tell me this, but I found out that he'd even written for *Penthouse*. If you look up the June 1976 issue, the cover of which has a montage of topless soft-focus shots by the legendary adult impresario Bob Guccione, you'll find an article by David entitled "The Vote Business." As if to give some idea of how far away this is from the world of evangelical Christianity that David now inhabits, readers of that month's *Penthouse* were also treated to a piece on the Moonies, and an angry article about the Israeli attack on the USS *Liberty* during the 1967 Six-Day War.

David described some of his journalism to me, and it sounded like hard-hitting stuff. He'd snoop around political campaigns looking for evidence of vote buying and ballot stuffing, and he'd try to counter some of the spin that was increasingly applied to the political process. He even accepted a commission from a Canadian magazine to write what David would call a "hit piece" on the Christian entertainment business in the 1970s, and the money that some people were making from it. "Did you lie? Did you tell them you were born again?" I asked him. "No, but we weren't exactly advertising that the story was going to be called "'Big Bucks on the Jesus Circuit.'"

David hit the peak of his career as a journalist in 1980, when he did a book for Harcourt Brace—a very respectable publisher—on the political consultants who'd taken over American politics in the 1960s and 1970s. *The New Kingmakers* tracked some of these men and presented a depressing picture of their effect on democracy. Candidates were being shaped and packaged with ruthless cynicism, and even Jimmy Carter—a born-again Christian— was happy to go along with the dictates of his image advisers. (David recalled his disgust at seeing Carter walking from an airport carrying his own suit in a bag, a populist touch that one of the image consultants had devised.) There was money in this line of analysis, but David's newsletter for Washington insiders— giving the lowdown on political campaigning—wasn't lucrative enough to keep him above water. His drug problem got worse in the early 1980s, until the about-turn in 1984 and his new life as a committed Christian.

I asked David if his conversion had cost him, in terms of his contacts in journalism and politics. He admitted that he'd badgered some of them into deserting him. "The first thing a new believer does is want to tell other people about it, and of course they don't want to hear anything about it, because they know you from another campaign, so to speak, and they, a lot of my old friends, began drifting away. A lot of people in show business don't want anything to do with a believer." So David started to work for the Roper Organization, a polling firm, and enrolled in a course in television production at his local community college. He also became interested in Bible prophecy, and was convinced soon after his conversion that God wanted him to spread the message of the Second Coming. When he'd gotten his qualifications as a broadcaster, he scared his local preacher by trying to bring cameras into church to televise the Sunday service. Spurned, he decided instead to produce a cable TV show on Bible prophecy, and *The Last Hour* was the result.

DAVID'S WIFE, JUNEAU, joins us during the interview. They're a sweet couple. David tells me that, as a Jew, he'd always been told to avoid Jesus, the Republican Party, and the New York Yankees— he succumbed to the first and flirted with the second. I'm not sure where he stands on the third, but he adds mischievously that he "even married a *shiksa*" so he could easily be a Yankees fan. Juneau's a photographer and an artist; she took the photos for the back of the jacket of *The New Kingmakers*, and David tells me that the pair of them were invited to the Carter White House to see some of the image consultants up close. Juneau apparently found Christ at the same time as her husband—Holy Week, 1984—though she made the leap after being inspired by Hal Lindsey's book *The Late Great Planet Earth*. They know Hal a little, and he was flattered when Juneau told him that his book had opened her eyes to Jesus.

These days, Juneau's art has a strongly religious theme. On the wall behind the sofa where I'm sitting, there's a painting of a stick figure suspended above the flames of hell, reaching desperately for a rope that leads upward to heaven. David's really taken with the picture. "That's the sinful soul, clinging to the rope that's coming from heaven." He comes back to the painting at various points in the conversation, and it's a reference point for his feeling about what he can do as we approach the End Times.

David and Juneau are happy to admit that, for those of us who haven't become evangelical Christians, the idea of the Rapture seems farfetched. "Before we were Christians," admits Juneau, "I thought, these people are crazy! You're going to leave little piles of clothes?!" But now that they've come to Christ, they're convinced that this is going to happen soon, and that their mission is to win as many souls as possible before Jesus returns in person to gather up those lucky believers who'll get to sit out the Tribulation.

How could people who'd been so involved in politics have wandered so far from the left, where Juneau and David had spent their time before the 1980s? "We were very idealistic in terms of politics in the early days," David admits. They put a lot of faith in the Democratic Party in the 1960s, and they went on peace marches against the Vietnam War in the 1970s. But the experience of grassroots corruption discouraged them even before Jesus helped David to overcome his drug addiction in 1984. He tells me about a magazine article he wrote in the mid-1970s, about a Democratic candidate for lieutenant governor in a southern state who was eventually defeated because he refused to tolerate his own party's shenanigans at the polls. David spins a lurid tale of Democratic insiders going to black churches with bags of money, and paying off ministers to promote particular candidates in their sermons. The publisher of the magazine stood behind his story, but David maintains that dark forces were conspiring against it. When the article was published, "the unions and the Teamsters" intercepted copies of the magazine and threw them from the loading docks before they even reached the newsstands. The magazine went out of business, and the Democrats were able to keep a lid on the scandal.

This wasn't the only time David had reason to doubt the openness of the media. Another magazine commissioned him to write a "hit piece" on an up-and-coming politician, but David met the guy and decided that he wasn't so bad after all. When he submitted his profile, the editor was furious: "Well, what's this?" David explained that he'd quizzed the politician, and that he was persuaded that his views were genuine and his motives were sincere. The editor spiked David's article, commissioned a new writer to be the "hatchet man," and made sure that David never worked for the paper again.

"And that's the way the system works," he tells me. "There are a few people, and only at the top, that consciously know what's going on." I ask him if he can name any of them.

"George Bush. President George Bush, he knows what's going on."

IT BECOMES APPARENT that David's political disillusionment hasn't just made him an evangelical Christian. He's also a paid-up believer in the New World Order, the shadowy global group that supposedly controls what you read, the laws under which you're governed, how you vote, and even what you think. When he first brings up the New World Order, he doesn't explain the acronym: I've asked him about where America will be in the End Times, and he says that he's "inclined more toward the NWO vision." I didn't follow up on this, partly because NWO stuff seems kind of crazy to me and peripheral to Bible prophecy, and partly because many NWO conspiracy theorists are anti-Semites so I imagine that this is just a side interest for David. But since he keeps coming back to the idea of a secret global government I realize that it's an important part of his thinking.

"It came out of Rome. Rome was the embryo of this New World Order, and they were very wise in the way they administered their empire. They knew that you had to give people very specific power here and there, you had to syncretize the religions, you couldn't have just one religion, and so you had the Pantheon. And I believe that the world order of today is based upon the same thinking, that you have to rule, but do it in such a way as to make people think they have these freedoms." David still buys the local newspaper, just to see what the NWO is saying, but he's under no illusions about who controls the media. "They're all part of the game, and the game is to keep you and me and every other citizen under control, and under the illusion that they live in a free sort of way, when in reality they're being monitored, and if you get out of line then you'll be cut off."

I ask David to narrate how we got from ancient Rome to the present, and he suggests that the embryo of world government has always been nurtured by powerful secret societies: he mentions the Bilderberg Group, the Illuminati, the Masons, and the Trilateral Commission. Occasionally things go off the rails—he reckons that the American and French revolutions weren't part of the script—but the NWO's well-placed members have been able to reassert control and to put the world back on its proper course.

These suspicions about backroom elites have turned David against America's most recent political dynasty. I'd already seen him complain about George H. W. Bush in an episode of *The Last Hour*, reminding viewers of Bush's promise to the U.S. Congress that he'd create a "new world order" in the aftermath of the first Gulf War in 1991. (The elder Bush did actually use that phrase, though if he was a shill for a secret global society, he didn't choose his words very carefully.) Meanwhile, David alerts me to the fact that the young George W. Bush was inducted into Yale's most exclusive secret society, Skull and Bones, though he seems sketchy on what actually takes place there.

How does the NWO operate? What does it want? I tell David that this book will be published in the U.S. by HarperCollins, a big corporation, and I ask him how far the conspiracy goes. Does my editor in New York know about it? "She doesn't." What about Rupert Murdoch, who owns the publishing house? "Rupert Murdoch knows." I ask lots of practical questions along these lines, and David supplies as many answers as he can. The NWO is interested in global integration, so it's the force behind trade treaties like NAFTA and the effort to extend a free-trade zone throughout Central and South America. It's interested in consolidating the energy resources of the Middle East, so it's hostile toward Israel and keen to court Arab regimes.

I'm still having trouble understanding how these people actually communicate with each other when Juneau remembers an article that recently appeared in a local Palm Springs paper. (*Desert Magazine*, of course.) David gets up to rescue it from the trash. It's about a businessman named Tim Blixseth, a billionaire from Rancho Mirage who made his money in timber and land speculation, who has just set up a club for other super-rich folk who want to hang out in exotic places. It costs $3 million to join, the membership fees are $75,000 each year, and members get to travel around the world to exclusive purpose-built resorts (Mexico, Paris, the Turks and Caicos islands) and to schmooze with other billionaires. One of the resort destinations is "so different and unique," Blixseth boasts to *Desert Magazine*, "that you have to join the club to find out where it is."

While David's away looking for the magazine, I confess to Juneau that I'm skeptical: Why would these super-rich people be interested in the NWO when they've already made so much money? At this stage in the game, wouldn't they just like to play golf with each other, unmolested by the rest of us, in some island paradise? (One of the resorts is at St. Andrew's in Scotland.) "Maybe they invite the president," she suggests darkly.

When David returns, I ask whether the NWO is going to be the incubator of the Antichrist. Will the false man of peace emerge from the ranks of crypto-globalists who have looked to rule the world for two thousand years? Is he already pressing the flesh at Davos or the G8 summits? David isn't sure. I'm surprised to hear him say that the members of the New World Order sincerely believe that they're acting in the best interests of mankind. Although they love power, they're trying to benefit ordinary people who wouldn't otherwise endorse their assessment of what's best for us. But sincerity is no guarantee of decency, David warns: even Hitler thought he was helping others. "You really underestimate and diminish your opponent by believing that he understands he's doing evil. I don't for a moment think that Tony Blair or George Bush or any of the other leaders know that they're doing evil."

The New World Order is trying to erect a system of global, secular government that sounds quite appealing to me. "In essence, their theory is very optimistic," David concedes. "If you want to look at it from that perspective. Get rid of poverty, get rid of illness, they have these wonderful world health plans, and they distribute the wealth, one-world socialism, that's the God of the New World Order and of secular humanism. To have this wonderful ethical society based on human principles of equality and justice, but on human terms."

I wonder whether the billionaires in Tim Blixseth's new club are talking about one-world socialism as they're enjoying lomi lomi massages in the Maldives, but Warren Buffett has just given $30 billion to Bill Gates's charitable foundation so I'm willing to hear David out. "So it's a project to redeem the world without God?"

"Absolutely. The key is, without God. That man is the sum of all things, and the New World Order has a system that's going to rule the world with beneficence, and do what the godly systems have never been able to do."

David's revelations about the NWO are hard to keep straight. One minute, he seems to be talking about a group of well-intentioned philanthropists who've forgotten to put God at the center of their vision for the world. But there's also a sinister side to their operations. When I ask why there haven't been any NWO whistleblowers, who might spill the beans in the way that, for example, some former Scientologists have done, Juneau initially replies that "they don't want to leave. They keep it in the family, like the Bushes!" Then David takes us back to the territory of seventies paranoid thrillers like *The Parallax View*. "They kill them. That's what the assassinations are all about. Some lone assassin, some mad demented person, in the end it's always someone who's overstepped their bounds, and it's kind of a mafia of power."

One of the consequences of this paranoia is that David doesn't have much faith in the political system. Although nearly a quarter of the members of the U.S. House of Representatives identify themselves as born-again Christians, he has a jaded view of Washington. Politicians are motivated only by power, and they play up their supposed religious beliefs just to get elected. When they're in office, they quickly scan the demands of genuine Christians— on abortion, on Israel, on gay marriage—and they throw them in the trash.

Even when the legislature backs a measure, it's still at the mercy of the courts. In 1994, David and Juneau worked on Proposition 187, the notorious California bill to deny health care, education, and other essential services to illegal immigrants. (David, like other prophecy enthusiasts, is driven to distraction by immigration.) The anti-immigration bill was approved by the voters, but then declared unconstitutional by a federal judge. After all this effort, David was confirmed in his belief that political change is impossible. The forces ranked against ordinary people are simply too great.

THE ENDURING IMPRESSION I got from David and Juneau is one of embattlement. If you hang out with John Hagee, either in San Antonio or when he sweeps through Capitol Hill, it's easy to imagine that Bible prophecy believers are intensely engaged with the political process. But the more I talk to the Chagalls, the more they insist that politics is the wrong way to go. Their estrangement is partly informed by their experience in the media—even before David's conversion in 1984, he was struggling to stay on top as a journalist, and he was disillusioned by some of the compromises that were required. Then there's the NWO stuff, a miasma of doubt and anxiety that stands between David and any more political adventures.

Perhaps this is just as well. I ask him what he'd do about the NWO and America's corrupt political system if he wasn't coming at all this from a Christian perspective. Like Dave Reagan, he'd storm the barricades. "I think if I were to sound a secular humanist alarm, it would be for mass revolution all over the world. Overthrow the yoke of these governments, and turn to a theocracy based on the Bible." But he knows this isn't going to happen. "The news media that control thought are going to destroy that notion immediately, so rather than preach universal revolution . . ." He admits that even grassroots organizing is impossible. "Even in this city! I could go next door and try to get . . ." He shakes his head, and I wonder if he's actually confronted his neighbors with the Rapture or the need for universal revolution. "People are so far gone," he tells me.

David insists that many Christians have turned away from Bible prophecy, and he thinks the idea of a Religious Right with enormous sway over the government is a liberal fantasy. Politicians are only interested in getting elected. (When I talk about George W. Bush's bold assertion in the 2000 presidential campaign that "Christ changed my heart," David sourly notes that this didn't cost him any votes at the polls.) Meanwhile, many of the most prominent Christian conservatives don't have much interest in the End Times. They push for social action as they promote conservative issues like abortion and prayer in the public schools, but they don't appreciate that time is running out for the world.

Worse, Americans are assailed by celebrity preachers like Rick Warren and Joel Osteen who promote a kind of bootstraps Christianity: God wants you to be rich, God wants you to get a better job, God wants you to live in a bigger house. This seductive argument tries to persuade Americans that if they go to church and donate to the ministry, they're going to have a wonderful life in this world before further rewards in heaven. In fact, as David keeps saying, you need to embrace Jesus for the opposite reason: this world is about to get very nasty indeed. He's read Rick Warren's runaway bestseller *The Purpose-Driven Life*, and he's not impressed. "It's become such an industry, and he may be a good guy, but I've read portions of his book and it's contrary to the word of God."

David hasn't completely lost his old political instincts, and he's razor-sharp on the subject of Al Gore's campaign against global warming. Gore's movie, *An Inconvenient Truth*, has just come out, and I'm interested in whether David's given much thought to climate change. I expect him to say that climate change is a sign that the end is near, or that true believers won't worry too much about the state of the world in fifty years because they'll be Raptured long before the ocean swallows up Florida and Long Island.

"Oh, Gore's just stumping for 2008! It's emotion. They're trying to get some theme that's going to emotionalize people. And, so far, all the Democrats have is 'Hate Bush!' And that's not going to do it; people are not going to come out to vote just because they hate Bush. So they need issues of fear, of the whole place blowing up and overheating."

Not only does David firmly refuse my invitation to behave like some kind of prophecy nut, he actually critiques the Democrats for manufacturing votes by spinning apocalyptic scenarios about global warming. Undaunted, I suggest that the idea of climate change might fit in with some of the more extreme prophecies of the End Times. "Oh no, I'm pretty much a man of the times. I have other sources, and studies that I'm looking at, that say that this is not so. Including the Smithsonian report. The notion that the world is heating, to such a point that all these catastrophes will take place, has no substance."

I don't think that David and Juneau take any pleasure from their marginalized place in the culture, or that they're self-righteous about what America has become in recent decades. David lingers on Ronald Reagan, and on the brief moment of Christian possibility that he seemed to offer the nation, but acknowledges that this was swept away by the tenures of Bush, Clinton, and Bush. The hope died even while Reagan was still in the White House: David's sure that the assassination attempt in 1981 was engineered by the NWO, and he thinks that Reagan was never the same after he'd been shot.

When I ask David if he still loves his country, he instantly says that he does, and scurries off to find something. "I've paid a price for it," he says sadly, producing a green box that looks brand new. Inside is his brother's Purple Heart. "He was killed at the Battle of the Bulge in Belgium, in World War Two, so yeah—my only brother paid his blood as a sacrifice." In spite of the Masonic symbols on the money, and his suspicions about the Illuminati connections of the Founding Fathers, David believes that America was founded for Christian purposes. "It breaks my heart, because the principles that were originally expounded, one country indivisible under God, with liberty and justice for all, I believe that stuff. In a sense it was a religion of its own, to worship this country, standing for those wonderful things, that God has ordained, and that's why it breaks my heart to see what's going on in this country, and in the world as well."

Would it be fair to say that his faith in America has been shaken by what it's become? "Oh, totally. I really don't have that faith in America, that I had as a kid, certainly. Even as an adult." So David shuttles between the hope that America could still wake up to its spiritual crisis, and the fear that it's already too late for the nation. He told me about his terrible feelings on September 11, when God clearly told the United States that he was no longer willing to be ignored, but the people wouldn't listen. He speculates that the "great city" described by John in Revelation 18, which will be destroyed in an hour by God, is New York. And he agonizes over whether the Antichrist will come to power through the European

Union, the restored version of the Holy Roman Empire, or whether America's own heritage of European immigration means that an American leader could eventually assume the mantle of the Beast. Perhaps the Rapture will condemn the United States to political irrelevance in the Tribulation period, he concedes, but the End Times could hit Americans especially hard.

BEHIND DAVID'S ATTACKS on secular humanism and the New World Order is an old fundamentalist assumption about the prospects of improving this world. For centuries, conservative Christians have argued against social change on the grounds that this world is inevitably imperfect. Although God didn't ordain evil or injustice, they are the necessary consequences of sin and human ingratitude. We shouldn't look for perfection, or even for significant improvement in the human condition, until we are judged by God and admitted to heaven.

I've seen this argument before. In the late eighteenth century, English conservatives suggested that inequality was a necessary condition of this world, and that the poor would receive their just deserts in the life to come. (One treatise in 1774 put the point less delicately: "If all were alike opulent, who must be left to build and decorate our houses?") In the nineteenth century, defenders of slavery in the American South attacked abolitionists as godless usurpers who wanted to tamper with God's providential arrangements. Slavery, poverty, and disease were, in the words of one South Carolina clergyman, the "badges of a fallen world." Abolition was a kind of social engineering that looked to deny God's control over the world. Many pro-slavery southerners angrily identified northern reformers with the French Revolution, and presented political and social reform as an attack on God himself.

David wouldn't thank me for making this analogy, and he's a very affable fellow. But it's clear that he hasn't simply checked out of the political sphere, but that he's come to think about political change in a fundamentally different way than he did in the 1960s or 1970s. Many people make the journey from the left to the right as they grow older; for David, the ground has shifted in a more profound way over these past few decades. "I had to give up my old gods, the gods of politics, the gods of blind idealism, of liberal idealism. I've exchanged my priorities. This world, I understand what it is. And in no way do I want to be loved by this world, because the Lord himself says that to be loved by this world means you'll not be part of my world."

David admits that international cooperation and world health organizations and antipoverty campaigns sound like good things. But, like many conservative Christians, he sees a terrible vanity at the root of this apparently altruistic thinking. It's wrong to create a system that focuses more on human problems than on the relationship between humanity and God—and the greater our success in triumphing over disease or indigence, the more we're inclined to worship ourselves rather than our creator. Secular humanism isn't secular at all; it's a religion with humanity, rather than God, as the object of veneration.

DAVID TELLS ME that he hasn't completely severed ties with politics. He supports an Israeli group called Women in Green, which opposes any withdrawal from the Occupied Territories. (The group created a sensation in 2004 by comparing the proposed Israeli withdrawal from Gaza with the willingness of Jewish ghetto leaders in Berlin in 1942 to "evacuate" their own community to the death camps.) But this is very much a side interest. "Most of my energies are spent trying to win souls for the ark, the ark of Jesus, the modern Noah's ark." David has very few nice things to say about Islam, and predicts that Ezekiel's war will soon engulf the Middle East and culminate in the false peace promised in Revelation. Perhaps the British Prime Minister will preside over this false peace; perhaps it will be the occupant of 1600 Pennsylvania

Avenue. But *The Last Hour* doesn't dwell on the need to write your congressman or senator about Hamas, or to demand that the president launch a preemptive strike on Iran. Instead, David and his co-host, Steve, meander through the same prophetic texts and eventually offer free prophecy guides and free Bibles (including a Hebrew translation) to any curious viewers.

David expects the secular humanists to triumph, albeit briefly. When the Rapture happens, the resistance to Satan and evil will be entirely gone. "Those who are left will say good riddance, these folks have just been causing a load of trouble, with abortion, prayer in the schools, and all that, and the secular humanists will have their way, and they'll feel free to . . ." He catches himself, unwilling to sketch the murky depths of a world without Christianity. "But we know what's coming, in sequence, and we'll be glad to be out of here. I won't shed any tears over it, because I think this is exactly what will be needed."

David has ceded the ground to secular humanism in the political sphere. Like Noah in the Book of Genesis, he's largely given up on the hope of persuading society to change course, so instead he's building his ark in a prominent place—or, at least, on public access television—and he's looking to persuade people to join him before God takes them up into the heavens. David accepts Tim LaHaye's argument that there will be another chance for Christians to win salvation during the Tribulation period, but he emphasizes that this is a much harder road to heaven than embracing Christ before the Rapture. "There's an old ad for oil filters, and it says: 'Pay me now, or pay me later.' There's a three-dollar oil filter you can buy now, and everything's cool; or you wait until it's too late, and you have to pay for a thousand-dollar engine, and the guy says pay me now or pay me later. And that's what I feel about salvation now. The door of the ark is open, and people can choose."

David seems resigned to the fact that his TV show and his ministry won't change the world, and he returns to an old preachers' adage: "We Christians are placed here not to clean up the dirty old fishpond of the world but to fish people out of it." He's especially sad that some of his own family—including his relatives in Israel—won't heed the call to embrace Christ. He's already sent them *Left Behind* books and videos, along with his own articles. Now he's hoping that the holdouts will be won over when the Rapture happens. "I've said, look—if Juneau and I no longer answer the phone, and you don't find any bodies or tombs where we've been laid, you know what's happened to us. And you'll have one more shot at making the right choice." David worries that the NWO will spin the Rapture and prevent people from realizing what has taken place; the media will probably blame the disappearances on "space people," he tells me, but he hopes that the little store of prophecy books and videos that he's sent to Israel will make a difference. Perhaps his Jewish relatives will find redemption even as the world descends into chaos.

THE LAST QUESTION I had for David was about the impending anniversary of *The Last Hour*. At the end of each show, David or Steve turns to the camera and says, without too much irony, "Until next time—if we're all still here." They've been doing this for ten years now, and I wondered if it felt weird to host a show on the imminent return of Christ for a decade or more. Did David feel disappointed that the Rapture hadn't already happened?

He didn't speak for a while. "Well, I feel that each day we're one day closer to it." He stopped again, unsure about whether to share his true feelings. "In fact, I've even schemed out . . . we're not supposed to set a date, and I really haven't got a date, but I do believe that the generation that sees Israel reborn will not die off until we see all these things take place."

So that means that the Rapture will happen within a lifetime of those people who were alive in 1948?

"Well, Psalm 90 gives the lifespan of a human being—three

score ten, or if by reason of strength, four score. So between seventy and eighty years. So 1948 to 2018 would be seventy years, so I believe we're going to be in the Tribulation by the year 2011."

David will be eighty in 2011, the same age that the very fit Tim LaHaye has just reached. David and Juneau tell me that they don't have any health problems, and that they feel much younger than their years. They get up at five every morning, in case anyone who has seen their show in New York calls for a Bible or a prophecy chart, and they go to bed early to prepare for the next day. "We have a nice life here," David admits, "but we would prefer to give it up right now. If the Lord shouts our name, as we're talking, and says, 'Come on up here,' then we're gone."

ON MY WAY OUT, David points out of his back window toward the edge of the seniors' development. Just beyond the property, the desert takes over and sweeps toward the mountains in the distance. A little way off is a faint scar that runs from right to left as far as you can see. Like a proud parent, David tells me what I'm looking at. "That's the San Andreas Fault! We're just on the right side of it. When that goes, and the rest of California falls off into the ocean, we're going to be okay over here." Whichever way the apocalypse comes, David and Juneau will be ready for it.

I walk back to my car, which the afternoon sun is doing its best to melt, and David and Juneau wave at me from the doorway. Just before they turn around, David shouts his special good-bye, the one they use with fellow Rapture believers: "We'll see you here, we'll see you there, or we'll see you in the air!" He laughs and goes back into the house, resuming his patient wait for the last hour.

7

Nuking the Hill

H ere's how Hal Lindsey says that he parted company with the Trinity Broadcasting Network: in the autumn of 2005, while Hal was in Jerusalem leading one of his popular Bible tours of Israel, God warned him to expect an imminent attack by Satan. Hal told his wife about this, since he remembered earlier satanic assaults that had coincided with important moments in his ministry. But the truth of God's warning became clear only when they returned to the United States. For twelve years, Hal had been presenting a prophecy newscast, a TV show that searched the week's events for signs of the apocalypse. This show, the *International Intelligence Briefing*, had been carried faithfully by TBN, the leading Christian television network. But soon after Hal got back from Jerusalem, TBN bosses told Hal that his show would be taken off the air. They even pulled a special that Hal had put together in Israel, which featured an interview he'd secured (improbably) with the former Israeli prime minister, Benjamin Netanyahu.

The Trinity Broadcasting Network was founded in California in 1973 by two couples: Paul and Jan Crouch, who still run the network, and Jim and Tammy Bakker, who went on to found a television ministry that was caught up in the 1980s in an enormous financial scandal that discredited the entire medium of TV evangelism. The Bakkers left TBN just a few months after it was founded, but the Crouches built the station into a powerhouse of Christian broadcasting. John Hagee has a daily show. So does Creflo Dollar, the gloriously suave African-American preacher whose very surname attests to what God can do for you as a Christian. TBN has provided a happy landing place for born-again celebrities who've left behind the sinful world of secular entertainment. Fans of *Growing Pains* can catch up with the child star of that sitcom, Kirk Cameron, in his TBN show *The Way of the Master*. (Kirk is also the star of the *Left Behind* movies.) Anyone with a soft spot for *The Love Boat* will appreciate *Back on Course*, hosted by former shipmates Gavin and Patti MacLeod. Oddest of all, the indomitable MC Hammer has also found his way to TBN. This is a broad church indeed, though, as Hal Lindsey discovered, it does have walls.

Hal's no fool when it comes to playing the media. Days after TBN suspended his Netanyahu special, he took to his Web site and told the whole story—about the divine warning in Jerusalem, and his long history of tension with TBN schedulers and "censors" over the content of the *International Intelligence Briefing*. Paul and Jan Crouch initially responded with wounded innocence. Paul published an open letter to Hal on the TBN Web site, claiming that the *Briefing* had been suspended simply because it wasn't very seasonal. TBN, getting into the holiday mood, was looking for Christmas programming in December. Hal had apparently been offered the opportunity to tweak his show accordingly, but he declined. In fairness to Hal, it's hard to imagine what a prophecy Christmas special would look like. "Silent Night" doesn't sit well with the Tribulation, and some Bible prophecy enthusiasts are so busy trying to identify false Christs that they barely have time to celebrate the real one.

Paul Crouch was understandably miffed when Hal started to talk about Satan. (Perhaps this drove Paul's decision to publish their entire correspondence on his Web site.) He wanted to convey his "utter disappointment and personal dismay" that Hal had described TBN's preemption as "part and parcel of Satan's plan of attack against you." He also threw the door open for a speedy return, though I can't help finding this invitation a little disingenuous: "Hal, if you will produce a Christmas themed program, we will be happy to air it this month!"

Behind the seasonal excuses, Paul hinted at his real beef with Hal: "It is becoming clear to us that your program has moved more and more away from biblical prophecy as it applies to world events and has become more and more a bully pulpit for an expression of your personal political views." Paul noted that TBN wanted to reach out to nonbelievers, including Muslims, and he suggested that Hal's tough line on Islam was getting in the way of this:

Nowhere in the scriptures does Christ speak negatively of those who persecuted him or his people. Surely we can agree that the Romans in Christ's day were just as violent, savage, evil, and in need of the truth of the Gospel as many terrorists are in the world today. TBN is making a great effort to reach the Muslim world with the truth of the Gospel by demonstrating God's love to all people. I am not aware of a single instance where making inflammatory, derogatory, anti-Muslim statements has led a single follower of Islam to Christ.

This didn't bring the sides closer together. By January, Hal had effectively cut his links with TBN, claiming that an "important part of [my] calling is to sound a prophetic alarm to America and the world about the dangers of the false religion of Fundamental

Islam." Paul continued to hope that a deal could be brokered, and even told TBN viewers that the *Briefing* would soon be back on the network. But then Hal accepted an invitation to appear on the Fox News show *Hannity & Colmes*, and he let rip once more on "Fundamental Islam" and the cowardice of Christian censorship.

Hannity & Colmes is supposed to be a lively debate on the day's events and newsmakers, conducted (in deference to Fox's famous "Fair and Balanced" slogan) by a conservative and a liberal co-host. The conservative is Sean Hannity, a right-wing superstar, and the liberal is Alan Colmes, who looks like the person everyone beat up at school. Hannity dominates the show, and Colmes occasionally pops up with a question or a comment that's supposed to guarantee "balance," Hannity gave Hal Lindsey the chance to repeat his attacks on TBN and on Islam. "When someone becomes devout and they begin to really get into the Koran," said Hal, "they become what we call a fundamentalist or a radical because the Koran itself and the Hadith teaches violence." Alan Colmes offered his usual tepid challenge: "So, Islam is a radical religion in your view?" Hal kept his nerve. "It is. I believe most Muslims don't read the Koran very much. That's why most Muslims are not radical, but when someone begins to really study the Koran and they begin to read the 109 verses that call for violence and war, they become very, very different. They become radical; they feel that they need to convert people by force."

This was too much for Paul Crouch, who sent one last, pained letter to Hal complaining about the "360-degree turn" that Hal had made over returning to TBN. A few days later, Hal announced that he'd found two Christian networks who'd carry a brand-new prophecy show that he was planning for February. *The Hal Lindsey Report* would offer "politically incorrect, alternative news that is biblically correct." Paul declared that Hal had now burned his bridges with TBN, and America's most successful television prophecy broadcaster parted company with the nation's most watched Christian network.

FROM HAL'S PERSPECTIVE, he'd been doing a show on TBN for a dozen years and banging the same drum all that time. But Paul suggested that his views had changed, and that the *Intelligence Briefing* had become more political and confrontational. Hal's books have always been in touch with the zeitgeist; *The Late Great Planet Earth* was a huge hit in the 1970s because Hal brilliantly reconciled his prophetic message with popular culture. One chapter begins with an awed description of the moon landing of 1969, before promising an even more amazing journey for those Christians who'll soon be Raptured. (This chapter is called "The Ultimate Trip," a slogan Hal cribbed from the poster for *2001: A Space Odyssey*.)

But changing times haven't just shifted Hal's cultural frame of reference. He's also reworked his warnings about the signs of the End Times. Back in the early 1970s, he was especially worried about spiritualism and the New Age philosophies that were sweeping across the United States. When he tackled foreign affairs, he had nothing to say about Islamic fundamentalism, or any link between Islam and the End Times. Hal fretted in *Planet Earth* about Egypt, but he was concerned about Gamal Abdel Nasser and his secular nationalism rather than any religious challenge. (He was also worried that the "black African nations" would rush to Nasser's aid in his battles with Israel and the United States.) The bad guy back then was the Soviet Union.

A decade later, Hal's next major prophecy book—*The 1980s: Countdown to Armageddon*—continued in this vein. Hal still believed that the world was about to end. In the introduction, he suggested that "the 1980s could very well be the last decade of history as we know it." Hal claimed that his predictions in *Planet Earth* had largely been realized a decade later (except for the big one, of course); this wasn't entirely true. Egypt, the bogeyman of the earlier book, made peace with Israel at Camp David in 1979.

The wave of spiritualism and alternative religions in America had subsided. Hal did his best to adapt discreetly to new realities. He predicted that Anwar Sadat, the Egyptian leader who had signed the Camp David agreements, would be assassinated by Islamic radicals—he got this spot on, and Sadat was killed by Islamists just a few months after *Countdown* was published. But he also predicted that Sadat would be replaced by a more radical leader who would renounce the peace deal with Israel, whereas instead Sadat was succeeded by Hosni Mubarak. Twenty-five years later, this still more pro-Western leader was still serving as President of Egypt.

In *Countdown to Armageddon*, Hal did identify Iran as an international flashpoint; he was, after all, writing in the shadow of the Islamic Revolution, which toppled the U.S.-backed Shah and installed the Ayatollah Khomeini in his place. But his fears centered on the weakness of the new religious government, and the possibility that the Soviet Union would invade Iran (as it had just invaded Afghanistan) and try to dominate the energy supplies of the Middle East. In fairness to Hal, this was the moment in which the U.S. administration began to support the mujahideen in Afghanistan, a policy that provided American funding for the radical Sunni resistance fighters who would eventually form Al Qaeda in the 1990s. Still, he was far less worried about the threat of political Islam than about the ambitions of the Russian bear. Even the kidnapping of more than sixty Americans at the U.S. embassy in Tehran did little to shake his views. The kidnappers only appeared to be Islamic, he explained in *Countdown*. In reality, they were "Marxist trained and inspired." Hal was on the lookout for a "charismatic Moslem leader" who could exploit a "religious fervor" that would unite the peoples of the Middle East, but he was shaky on the terminology: he warned of "a full-fledged 'Jahid' [sic] or holy war."

Things changed for Hal in the 1990s, when he produced another big book—*Planet Earth: 2000 A.D. Will Mankind Survive?*—that updated the ideas he'd laid out nearly twenty-five years earlier. As he did in *Late Great Planet Earth*, Hal cast a wide net here: he had chapters on "berserk weather," on the supposed political instability of post-Soviet Russia, and on the moral decline of America. ("Is 'Aids' Just the Beginning?") Hal gloomily worked on the manuscript during the first year of Bill Clinton's presidency, and the book came out in 1994.

Again, he predicted that the Rapture would take place before the end of the decade, but he also identified plenty of things to worry about in the meantime—developments that would be especially troubling if the Rapture was delayed by a few years. He'd read in *Time* magazine that, after 2000, secular humanists would try to destroy the nuclear family. ("Many women will live with other women. The *Golden Girls* television show might well be a model of such living arrangements.") He warned that the European Union would expand its influence and launch the Antichrist's career. Or perhaps the United Nations would give the Beast his leg up to international domination. Hal didn't like the idea that the UN would play a greater role in a post–Cold War world, and he warned that the UN secretary-general, Boutros Boutros-Ghali, was already "arguably the most influential individual on the face of the planet." (Two years later, Boutros-Ghali was unceremoniously removed from his post by the Clinton administration, and replaced by Kofi Annan.)

But Hal was clear in 1994 that "Islamic fundamentalism is the greatest threat to freedom and world peace today." What seems to have upset Hal most was the willingness of the Clinton administration and of the Israeli government to make peace with the Palestinians in 1993, in spite of the fact that a majority of Palestinians were Muslims. In *2000 A.D.*, Hal promised to outline the "new Islamic threat" not only in relation to Israel-Palestine but also the rest of the world. But he kept returning obsessively to the Oslo peace process, and the folly (as he saw it) of returning occupied land to Palestinian Muslims.

Although the Oslo framework collapsed in 2000, Hal's views

about Islam were by now very well suited to a world in which "jahid" had been replaced by jihad and the United States had begun to confront radical Islam directly. In 2002, Hal published *The Everlasting Hatred: The Roots of Jihad*, which put the events of 9/11 into a much longer context. The headline on the back cover of the book promised to describe "A HATRED THAT HAS LASTED 4000 YEARS," even though Muhammad himself was born around AD 570. Hal argued that the real conflict between Arabs/Muslims and Jews/Christians began when Abraham had a son out of wedlock with his Egyptian servant Hagar; this son, Ishmael, was cast out from Abraham's family and God's promises, and his descendants proved to be the first, natural adherents of the Islamic faith. (John Hagee says the same thing about Muslims in *Jerusalem Countdown*.)

There aren't any nice words about Islam in *The Everlasting Hatred*. From the cover, which juxtaposes a photo of an earnest Israeli soldier with a fanatical-looking jihadi wielding a machete, to the back-cover copy which asks why "most Muslims hate Jews," there's something depressingly one-note about Hal's investigation. The style is unchanged from *Late Great Planet Earth*. Hal is still arranging his chapters into short sections with catchy titles— "Face It: We Are in Deep Pooh-Pooh!"—but the focus on Islam rather than, say, overpopulation or the Trilateral Commission is relentless. Hal's gaze has narrowed to such an extent that, as the TBN bosses suggested in 2005, he seems a much more political figure than he used to be.

When Hal was working on *The Everlasting Hatred* in early 2002, Paul Crouch sent a letter to him and the other TBN stars insisting that, in spite of the new "war on terror," this was a great moment for Christian evangelism. Paul had gotten lots of letters and e-mails from overseas viewers as well as from Americans, and he was especially excited by the prospect of winning souls in the Middle East. TBN and its hosts could seize this opportunity only by thinking carefully about how to engage an overseas audience.

"So here's my point: let's be careful how we treat the Arabs and Islam. Let's not slam Mohammed and Islam. Let's reach out to them in love."

For Hal, this missed the point completely. Since he first became interested in Islamic radicals in the early 1980s, he's nursed the belief that Islam itself inspires hatred of Israel and the West. Hal doesn't talk about Islamic fundamentalism anymore but about "fundamental Islam." Any Muslim who takes his or her faith seriously has to become a militant, perhaps even a terrorist. A committed reading of the Koran entails rejecting Israel, embracing anti-Semitism, and pledging yourself to the extension of Islamic power worldwide.

I asked around about the Hal Lindsey/TBN spat when I was researching this book. The general feeling among prophecy believers was that Hal had been very brave to stand up to Paul and Jan Crouch and, more obliquely, to Islam itself. Some people thought that Hal had become a martyr of sorts, and that he'd inspire other people to speak out against the "political correctness" that clouded the judgment even of evangelical Christians. Others suggested that Hal was ahead of the curve. TBN would soon catch up with his views on "fundamental Islam," they told me, and Hal would return to the network in triumph. In January 2007, this is exactly what happened. TBN executives issued a press release praising Hal's "balanced coverage" of the Middle East—and announcing that *The Hal Lindsey Report* could now be seen every Friday on TBN.

HAL DOESN'T LIKE TALKING about his career. Some of his friends told me that this was because he'd been burned plenty of times by journalists who interviewed him at length, and then dismissed him as a wacko or distorted his point of view. But I tracked down his assistant and collaborator, Jack Kinsella, and he was happy to talk to me. Jack first got to know Hal in the early

1990s, and then worked with him on a couple of projects before agreeing to help out with Hal's Web site and his TV show. Now Jack is the editor of HalLindseyOracle.com, and the cowriter of *The Hal Lindsey Report*. Each Sunday, Jack puts together a rough outline of the script for the weekly show. On Monday, he talks to Hal about it—usually they chat via video messaging, and they spend hours fine-tuning the program before Hal does the taping on Tuesday in California. The rest of the week, Jack tends to the Web site, and works on his own Bible prophecy digest, *The Omega Letter*.

Jack is fifty-three years old and lives in North Carolina. Or, rather, he used to live in North Carolina, but these days he doesn't really live anywhere. In 2006, he got the call from God to take his prophecy ministry on the road. He sold his house and bought an RV with the proceeds. When I e-mailed him, he'd just driven down from the Canadian border to settle up some affairs in North Carolina. He was about to embark on another monster drive, this time across the South, up toward Chicago, and on to Hal's house in Palm Desert, California. He invited me to meet him in Branson, about fifty miles south of Springfield, Missouri, where he hoped to hook up with some of his newsletter subscribers at an RV park. Perhaps I'd be able to meet some of the subscribers as well, he suggested.

I first came across Jack when I was watching a show called *This Week in Bible Prophecy*. *TWIBP* used to be on TBN, though Jack later told me that it had originally started on Canadian television in 1992. (The producers of the program went on to make the *Left Behind* movies.) In the segment I saw, Jack wandered toward the camera wearing a sport coat and talking about the Bible's prophetic message. He seemed to be in a call center, though it wasn't entirely clear why, and his report featured a number of interviews with "prophecy experts" who predicted that the End Times were at hand. Jack had a handlebar mustache and a sonorous voice. He was really good at what he was doing—so good, in fact, that he'd be precisely the person you'd want to hire if you were making a spoof version of a Bible prophecy television show. In the segment I watched, he was amazingly deadpan, rattling off some of the more elaborate signs of the approaching Tribulation as if he were reporting for a local news station on a holdup in a grocery store.

BRANSON, tucked away in the Ozark Mountains, is one of the most popular vacation destinations in the South. On the drive down from Springfield, you start seeing the signs for Branson's famed nightlife almost as soon as you leave the airport.

YAKOV! DYNAMITE RUSSIAN COMEDIAN!
45 MILES AHEAD!

Yakov is an exotic and hyperkinetic fellow, invariably pictured with a bear hat and a stick of lit TNT. (His Web site invites you to join him on his journey "from Red to Redneck.") Most of Branson's shows have a local flavor, though the town is such a tourist draw that it boasts some elaborate attractions, like the world's largest *Titanic* museum. A couple of retired TV executives, who made their fortune working on *Who Wants to Be a Millionaire*, have built a model of the *Titanic* which is more than three hundred feet long and one hundred feet high. In a morbid touch, they've also built the iceberg as well. The hull and the 'berg are made from the same material—cement—though they're cleverly painted to suggest otherwise. Although the ship is stuck forever at the very moment of disaster, the museum seems like a cheery place. On the day I arrive, a Beatles tribute band (tenuously billed as "also from Liverpool") is about to take to the decks to entertain the crowd.

Running through Branson is the Strip, a winding boulevard around which the major hotels and attractions are arranged.

The traffic crawls along in both directions, and families gawk at the neon and the video screens that entice them to stop at Dolly Parton's Dixie Stampede Dinner and Show or at Dick Clark's American Bandstand Theater. Bart Simpson once observed that Branson was like "Las Vegas run by Ned Flanders," and it's hard to dispute this assessment. The casinos have been kept at bay by down-home entertainment and, in a distant echo of Palm Springs, there are endless opportunities to play mini-golf. Mini-golf has to be the biggest thing in Branson, and if you're so minded, then you can wield your putter in a variety of geographical and historical settings. My hotel is next to a pirate ship, which is crowded with families attempting to navigate unlikely obstacles. A little farther down the road, a massive diplodocus looks on impassively as other mini-golfers aim intently at its tail. Branson seems like a great place for a Bible prophecy get-together. There's plenty to do, and the town is friendly and wholesome.

Jack Kinsella has parked his RV in a campground on the edge of town. He's already told me that the place has stiffed him on Internet access, but it looks nice enough otherwise. He's waiting for me just inside the gate, and my first impression is that he looks a lot better without the mustache. He has shed that slightly cheesy appearance that came across on the old *This Week in Bible Prophecy* tape, and he doesn't look like a man who's been away from home for months on end.

I suppose you're never away from home when you have an RV. Jack had gotten his secondhand, but when I climb inside I'm very impressed. There are a couple of comfy sofas, and it feels surprisingly roomy. Up front are two enormous swivel chairs from which Jack and his wife, Gayle, can pilot the RV across vast distances. Recessed in the panel above the chairs is a big TV, which is hooked up to a satellite. Jack and I later joke about how it's been tuned to CNN in honor of my visit.

Jack is the friendliest and most relaxed of all the Bible prophecy people I've met. Very occasionally, a curse word creeps into his language, which is salted with Texas sayings and plenty of wit. He smokes a cigar, and he offers me a beer. There are only two in the fridge, and I get through both of them during the three hours we spend chatting. Jack drinks a soda.

Back in the 2000 election, pundits liked to say that although George W. Bush wasn't always an impressive politician, he appealed to voters because he was the kind of guy they'd like to have over for a barbecue. Jack seems a lot more intellectually robust than Bush, and he also passes the barbecue test easily. Whether you'd want to go to one of Jack's barbecues, on the other hand, depends on your willingness to talk to Bible prophecy enthusiasts. Jack's newsletter subscribers are coming over to do some grilling in a couple of hours, and I'm hoping that he was serious about letting me meet them.

SOME SURPRISING FACTS about Jack: first, he's Canadian. He grew up in Ontario on the border with New York State, and his dad crossed over every day to work near Buffalo. His mother died when he was ten, and his father remarried an American and moved the whole family over the border. Second, he was a U.S. Marine who served for nearly six years in Southeast Asia in the late 1960s and early 1970s. When he came home, he eventually decided to go into law enforcement. He spent most of the 1980s working in Texas. He was a patrolman for four years, then a detective, and finally a prison officer. At this point, "I'd had enough of the blood and guts and sin and misery. Mostly the blood and guts. It was pretty ugly."

Jack had his conversion experience soon after he got back from Vietnam. Yet again, it was Hal Lindsey and *The Late Great Planet Earth* that brought him to Christ. Jack's sister had bought a copy of Hal's book and seemed to be taking it quite seriously. The Kinsellas were good Catholics—"We went to church *every* Easter!"—and Jack didn't think it was smart for his sister to get mixed up in a "cult." So he read Hal's book carefully, looking to disprove it and to reprogram her. And he found that he couldn't dispute what Hal was saying.

"Worship, the worship of anything, it's a pretty serious thing. No one casually worships something. If someone worships money, they don't do it casually. And if they worship Muhammad, they don't do it casually. But we have a tendency to worship God as if, as if we kept him in a closet or something. We pull him out of a box." Although Hal's words tugged at Jack, he was reluctant to give up his rational perspective. "I don't want to spend my life dedicated to a myth," he remembers thinking, "and I don't want to follow a myth." So he subjected *The Late Great Planet Earth* to serious scrutiny, reading with a Bible in his other hand. He arrived at an informed decision to abandon Catholicism and to embrace prophecy.

Because Jack is such an easy person to talk to, I ask him to be specific about the conversion experience. Is it a sudden thing? Is it overwhelming? Was he totally transformed?

"A lot of guys that happens to. Not with me. It was like finally getting to meet someone that I'd always wanted to meet. Someone I'd admired and read about. For example, meeting Hal Lindsey. It was that kind of feeling like when I met Hal, it wasn't like, Oh my gosh, it changed my life. It's like, well, I finally met Hal Lindsey, he's a pretty nice guy! It was the same kind of process with God."

I spend such a long time quizzing Jack about the precise nature of his conversations with God that I start to feel bad about it, but he's not standoffish in any way and he seems genuinely interested in helping me to understand how all this works. For example, he appreciates that the second turning point of his life—after this conversion experience in 1975—sounds particularly crazy. He'd gone back to Canada in 1989 after ten years of blood and guts in Texas, and he'd applied to become a Canada customs officer. This is a very prestigious and exclusive job, not least because you get decent pay without enduring the human tragedies that Jack had been struggling through in his law enforcement career to date. There was a lot of competition, and the numerous national examinations and daunting waiting lists ensured that only a few applicants actually got the job.

Although Jack had done well on the tests, by 1992 he'd been waiting for nearly three years for a slot to open up. He was on unemployment in Canada, trying to support his wife and children, when he got a call from Peter and Paul Lalonde. These brothers eventually produced the *Left Behind* movies, but back then they were just starting out. They offered Jack an unpaid job in their ministry (Peter lived just up the road), and he wasn't sure whether he should take it. "I had quite an argument with God," he tells me. "The two of us . . . we went together in the bedroom with the door closed! We had a pretty long argument about it. And I said, okay—here's the deal. Where you lead, I'll follow. But it's up to you to take care of me."

The day after Jack said yes to Peter Lalonde, Canada customs called and told him to report to their training college immediately. "And I said, 'I'm sorry, I've taken another job.'" The woman on the other end of the line couldn't believe it. "She said, 'You don't understand, this is Canada customs!' And I said, 'Oh, I understand perfectly.'" Jack took this as a sign that God wanted him to pursue the ministry, and he's been following God ever since. "It sounds nuts, doesn't it?"

I guess it does. But how does it work? Do you hear God speaking to you? Is it an actual voice, something outside of yourself?

"It wasn't a voice; it was an understanding." Jack leans over, as if he's about to tell me a big secret. "You know, my voice and God's sound an awful lot alike. Sometimes I have an awful lot of trouble telling who's saying what. But, generally speaking, if you pay a little attention, you can tell. Because, generally speaking, when it's God, it's not really something you want to do."

––––––––

JACK'S NEW JOB with the Lalonde brothers quickly took off. Within a few weeks he was on the payroll, and soon he was writing and reporting for *This Week in Bible Prophecy*, which, Jack tells me, was an entirely Canadian production until it was eventually snapped up by TBN later in the 1990s. Jack's first piece for television was a report on the Clinton-Gore campaign in 1992; over the next few years, he found plenty of disturbing evidence of End Times decay during the Clinton presidency. The show went out on Canadian TV in a slot provided by the government for "religious programming." (In typically Canadian fashion, this was called "Mosaic.") "So we were sandwiched between a program about Wicca, and another one about Islam. We were just part of the Mosaic." I ask Jack how he felt about the Canadian government's commitment to religious diversity. "I was always in trouble with their censors, oh boy. I'm telling you. I was in trouble *all* the time."

It wasn't the censors who finally intervened but Jack's own discomfort with the direction in which the Lalondes wanted to take their ministry. Jack's circumspect about all this—he doesn't strike me as a man who bears grudges—but it's clear that he didn't feel comfortable when the Lalondes started bringing over actors and minor celebrities like Kirk Cameron, with a view to making Christian entertainment and End Times movies rather than prophecy newscasts. (We have a vigorous debate about whether Jeff Fahey counts as a movie star—Jack's more reluctant to concede this than I am.) "I'm not starstruck," Jack declares. This seems to have been a problem in a ministry which was morphing into a business, and which looked to dust a little Hollywood glamour onto Bible prophecy. Jack parted company with his employers.

Jack first met Hal Lindsey in Niagara Falls, when Hal agreed to do an interview for *This Week in Bible Prophecy*. They worked together a couple of times after that and Jack enjoyed their collaborations. By 2000, Jack had agreed to come out to L.A., and he spent a few unlikely months living in Venice Beach before Hal moved out to Palm Desert. Just before 9/11, Jack started up the new Hal Lindsey Web site. The timing was propitious. "When September 11 happened, it was the longest hundred hours of my life." Jack had four TV sets running, and he was bombarded with messages from Hal's fans complaining that the Internet was jammed and that they couldn't get good information on what was going on. So Jack stayed up the whole time, using the new Hal Lindsey Web site as a clearinghouse for the news he could gather from other sources.

Jack has spent a lot of time thinking about the news media in America, and he doesn't like what it's become. But his skepticism, like his approach to religion, is rooted in a faith in reason and truth. "In the United States, we have CNN, the liberal news network. And we have Fox, the conservative news network. The choice facing Americans is who lies to them. Not where the truth is. The truth is in between Fox and CNN. And that's where I am. I listen to both of them, distill out all the crap, get rid of the agendas, and what's left is what actually happened."

On the basis of this, I'm happily imagining Jack to be somewhere near the *Chicago Tribune* or the *Cleveland Plain-Dealer*. "So you put yourself left of Fox and right of CNN?"

"*No!* No! I put myself in the middle, because there's no left or right. There's liars on this side; there's liars on that side. We have an agenda-driven media, and in the old days they called it propaganda. Now it's called spin and it's respectable, but it's still propaganda. The media is supposed to report facts devoid of an agenda. But from 2000 forward, there's an unconcealed, almost celebrated agenda-driven bias that everyone's aware of, but they don't seem to mind anymore. Propaganda's okay."

I reckon Jack has an easier time watching Fox, and he doesn't say anything in our long conversation that makes me believe that he thinks that CNN is right half of the time. But I'm interested in how all of this links to Bible prophecy. Without any preamble, he says: "The Antichrist only has three weapons. His entire power structure is built on his control of the economy, his ability to deceive, and the willingness of the people to buy it."

We've been talking for nearly forty-five minutes, and suddenly he's dropped the word "Antichrist" into the conversation. Where did that come from? Jack admits that the word can be jarring. But he's suggesting that the Antichrist's rise to power will be dependent on spin and propaganda, that the "strong delusion" spoken of in 2 Thessalonians may be linked to the smooth editorializing of an Anderson Cooper or the pugilism of a Bill O'Reilly.

He's especially irritated by Christians who claim that they won't be deluded by the Antichrist. "I've listened to people who say, 'Boy, I tell you what, if the Antichrist ever shows up and wants to put a mark on me, I'll know it's the Antichrist and I'll run. . . .' No, you won't. 'If I ever see 666, good heavens, then I'll know, I'll know it's true.' Now, look at that barcode."

He's pointing at his soda can.

"It's been there twenty-five years, those long digits. That's computer for six."

You're saying there's 666 on this barcode?

"It's not a big deal; it's only a big deal because it proves that, you know, 'If ever I see 666 I'll run like a rabbit' is just so much crap."

If there are three sixes on every barcode, who put them there? "Actually, Europe." I laugh nervously at this, and Jack explains that the Europeans insisted on using sixes as separators in barcode language. (The Australians apparently used threes; the Americans used nines.) Jack then dredges up an old memory of a *Time* magazine article from 1991 discussing the European Union, which featured images from the proposed European currency that looked a lot like the symbolism of the Book of Revelation. Europa riding on a horse seemed to be the most striking one, and this reminded Jack of the Whore of Babylon riding the Beast in Revelation 17. (Hal Lindsey likes to call this figure "Scarlet O'Harlot.") Jack suggests that this can mean only one of two things: that European leaders are actively fostering the rise of the Antichrist, or that the Book of Revelation has perfectly anticipated the backdrop to the End Times.

So where are we in the narrative of Bible prophecy? Jack, like a lot of other American evangelicals, thinks that the terrorist attacks of 2001 were a pivotal moment. "September 11, I believe, began the war of Armageddon." He thinks, even without the prophetic insights, that there's plenty of evidence that the world is "flying apart at the seams." I ask him to be specific. "Go through the new movies, and see what they are. I mean, it's *End of Days*, and *The Omen*, and even *Mad Max*. Everything is an apocalyptic or post-apocalyptic future view. And that's because everyone is aware of the times, of what's going on." He tells me to sit down with anyone and ask them "objectively" where they think the world will be in twenty years. I admit that this is probably a gloomy topic for a lot of people, and he lays it out for me. "You know, what about Iran, what about Israel, what about the nukes, what about Russia, what about China?" He's not done. "And what about, you know, Islam? 1.2 billion Muslims." I ask him what he means. "Well, only 10 percent of them are mad at us right now, which is 120 million, but they're mad at us for the same reason that the rest of them would be mad at us if we do something to piss them off enough."

There's a harshness to all this that doesn't sit easily with Jack's convivial manner. But like Hal Lindsey, he's convinced that Islam is playing an important role in the coming of the End Times. He tells me that, despite the anguish he felt on September 11, the attacks had "vindicated what I believed in" and had borne out the truth of Bible prophecy. "We are in the midst of a global war in which there are only three major combatants. We have Israel, which is representative of the Old Testament and God's chosen people, and the whole Jewish religion. We have the United States, which is the crusader country; it's for good or ill the representative Christian country left in the world."

I read this back carefully, postponing the conclusion. "So we have the Jewish, the Christian, and . . . ?"

"And then we have Islam, the Islamic world. It's a civilizational war. Western civilization was founded on Judaism and Christianity. The Islamic world was founded on Islam. You have a religious war. You have the same religious war that ultimately ends on the fields of Megiddo."

(Megiddo is the site in Israel where the battle of Armageddon is supposed to take place.)

I ask Jack whether the combatants in this battle understand that they're fighting this kind of war. I tell him that I'm particularly interested in whether American policymakers see things in these terms.

"They're certainly denying it. You listen to George Bush, and he says, well you know, Islam is really one of the world's great peaceful religions; it was hijacked by terrorists. And you open the Koran, and you find out that there's not a word of that that's true. But at the same time, Bush can't say, yeah, we're in a civilization war, because there's still 1.1 billion Muslims who'd get pissed off with us."

Is it just tactics on Bush's part? "Yeah, exactly." And if Bush had his way, if he could say what he really thinks, you think we'd hear a different message from the White House about Islam? "Well, yeah. Don't you, again? Don't you?"

It's clear that Jack's views on Islam have, like Hal Lindsey's, hardened over the past few years. I ask Jack lots of questions about Muslims in America, and about the possibilities for a moderate Islam that might rein in a radical minority, but he's dismissive. He's willing to accept that many Muslims might be good Americans: "I'm not going to say that every Islamic guy is a terrorist. I'm saying that Islam itself is an ideology that spawns terrorism." Could Islam change? "No." What if moderates continued to denounce violence, to decry hate speech of all kinds, and so on? "Well, they could do all that, but that's not Islamic. They can change, but they change by changing their religion." The only way for Muslims to distance themselves effectively from the radical fringe, Jack suggests, is to "throw out the Koran and the Hadith and all the rest of it."

If you press him on the mechanics of all this, on the road that leads from Mahmoud Ahmadinejad to the valley of Megiddo, Jack will talk about high-tech weaponry and the language of the prophetic texts. At one point in our conversation, he describes the "pretty interesting weapons" that Israel has developed and which will be deployed defensively against the Iranian/Russian invasion. Then he gets up to find his glasses so he can compare Israel's nuclear arsenal with a passage in the book of Zechariah. He reads from a New King James Bible. He doesn't like the translation, but he sticks with it because the book was a present from Hal:

"'And this shall be the plague with which the Lord shall strike all the people who fought against Jerusalem. Their flesh shall dissolve while they stand upon their feet. Their eyes shall dissolve in their sockets and their tongues shall dissolve in their mouth.'"

And the plague is?

"A neutron bomb. You know, I'm not reading something into it that isn't there. There is no historical plague in which people melt. And they certainly don't melt in the midst of a battle. And there's no historical context in which you can place a battle where the combatants dissolve while they're standing upon their feet."

JACK, LIKE DAVID CHAGALL, loves the United States. "I've bled for this country," he reminds me, "I love this country." I'm surprised when he tells me that he's also fond of the separation of church and state, a concept which other evangelicals seem eager to discard. "It's absolutely indispensable," he says. While he'd love to see Bush govern according to his own version of Christianity, he doesn't want to live in a country in which a different president might bring a different religious agenda into the White House. (He mentions the Republican governor of Massachusetts, Mitt Romney, a Mormon who is about to enter the 2008 presidential race.) But when I push him on this, he suggests that the separation of church and state can go too far. He mentions the recent brouhaha in Alabama, where a Christian judge was instructed to remove a sculpture of the Ten Commandments from the lobby of his courthouse. Jack insists that the great British jurist William Blackstone based his legal system on Christianity; and that Magna Carta rests on the same foundations.

Jack's ambivalence about church and state is part of a wider difficulty in anchoring himself in America. He tells me about the "dual nature" of American Christians, how they strive to be citizens in heaven and also citizens of the United States. He says, offhandedly, that he's just "passing through" America on his way to heaven, by the grace of God. But it's clear that he loves his adopted country, and that he can't easily give up on it. The Book of Daniel insists that there won't be a fifth earthly empire, so Jack knows that America's days as a superpower are numbered. He can also see the writing on the wall: he reads a passage from 2 Timothy on the "perilous times" that accompany the last days, then he tells me that St. Paul was "basically laying out the liberal political platform of the Democratic Party in the United States right now." (The congruence between Paul's letter and the liberal worldview is "really kind of stunning," he assures me.)

But then he catches himself and qualifies this. "But we happen to be, despite the fact that we're the most powerful nation in the world, we also happen to be the most moral. And that's not really patriotic chauvinism—we just are."

How would you measure this? How would you convince a skeptic? "That's one of those things where, I could go down a list, and . . ." I throw out a sample list of objections, and Jack bats them all away. To an observer who would dismiss the United States as riven with gun crime, he'd reply that "guns don't kill people, people kill people." He relates an interesting experiment in which a New Mexico city insisted that everyone keep a gun at home, and the crime rate fell precipitously. ("Burglary dropped to *zero*.") But what about the moral pollution of Hollywood, and the Christians like Dave Reagan who feel alienated from the culture? "That, I suppose, proves my point. Because it doesn't seem to bother the French." He chuckles at the idea of the French protesting against smut and violence.

Jack isn't about to withdraw his faith in America's redemptive possibilities, or at least in the nation's ability to sustain its Christian status and to back Israel right up to the end. I keep asking him how the United States will come apart during the End Times, or when Christians will jump ship from a country that's slipping beneath the waves. As he's talking about Ahmadinejad and Iran, he puts it like this: "America's role in Bible prophecy is, to quote Ronald Reagan, to be that shining city on a hill. Until someone nukes the hill."

I'VE KEPT JACK TALKING for too long, and Gayle tells him that the newsletter subscribers have already started to grill. Jack invites me to come over and meet them. As I'm getting up, he stops for a second. He looks over at Gayle, then back at me. "I'd leave the beer behind." They laugh, and Jack repeats a line he's said earlier in the conversation. "You get ten Christians and you get eleven opinions."

There are actually more than a dozen subscribers at the cooking area. A few are in their forties, most in their fifties and sixties. They don't seem as friendly as Jack, but I guess they have reason to be suspicious of an outsider. I tell them what I'm doing with the book, and they seem interested but wary. Frank, a portly guy in a yellow polo shirt, tells me that these are exciting times to be a prophecy enthusiast. Reading the newspaper, he says, "is like watching the ticker tape of prophecy coming right at you."

Jack leaves me with one group, and he moves around the subscribers with ease. He's genuinely delighted to see them. Back in the RV, he told me the old story about the donkey that returns to the stable after being hired out for the day, and tells the other donkeys that he's had a fantastic time: "They were throwing palm leaves at me, they were cheering . . . You know, I think they're gonna crown me king!" Jack is wary of prophecy celebrities who confuse themselves with the message, and who forget that the important thing is the news that they carry. "Some guys are donkeys," he tells me. His subscribers seem to appreciate this about Jack.

But he also seems tougher, a little less ready to ruminate, as the barbecue conversation turns to hot potatoes like same-sex marriage or immigration. Jack's *Omega Letter*, which he mails out to these folks every morning, contains some acrid observations about the political scene. I hadn't seen much of that during our conversation (except for Jack's thoughts on Islam), but now he's around an audience that appreciates a firmer line. I wonder whether Jack was being politely reflective during our conversation (like that television tuned to CNN) or whether a group of like-minded people would make anyone seem more entrenched and uncompromising in their views.

When Jack mingles at the other table, I'm not sure how to keep the conversation going with the half-dozen subscribers sitting around me. I bring up the *Left Behind* books, which everyone has read. Back in the RV, Jack compared *Left Behind* to those old Chuck Norris movies in which a fearless veteran journeys back to Vietnam in search of American POWs. It's a kind of fantasy, Jack insists, to imagine that brave Christians could stand a chance against the Antichrist: "It's very American. It's just not very biblical." Jack doesn't have high hopes for those people who miss out on the Rapture. If you haven't assumed the number of the

Beast, he tells me, "you're going to stick out like a turd in a punch bowl." Given that the Antichrist will be a global dictator with unprecedented power to monitor every form of human activity, Jack is brutally honest about the chances of the rebels: "Nobody's going to get out of that alive."

The subscribers are more sanguine. An elderly woman named Helen tells me that she knows two people who've come to Christ by reading *Left Behind*. Her husband, Bob, says that he's read all the books and likes them a lot. Jack picks up on our conversation and wanders back over from the other table, insisting that the books are unscriptural because they ignore or actually contradict parts of the Bible. He rummages around for an example: apparently, one of the new Christian converts during the Tribulation ends up being saved by Jesus, even though he's taken the mark of the Beast.

When Jack says this, a young man named Jim—slight and geeky-looking, with a thin mustache—immediately corrects him with the zeal of a sci-fi fan. "But Chang Wong had been given the mark against his will!" Jack then leads a vigorous debate on whether it's possible to receive the mark involuntarily, and although he listens to other points of view, he gently nudges the group toward his own conclusion. Even Jim eventually concedes that the Chang Wong story is misleading, and Jack's view wins out.

A COUPLE OF WEEKS after our meeting, Jack dedicated one issue of the *Omega Letter* to something we'd discussed at length: Should apocalyptic Christians try to influence politics? This was, Jack admitted, a "conundrumy" question. He's cheered by the work of conservatives to defeat abortion, or to reform the public school system, or to remake the Supreme Court along more conservative lines. But his own role is to be a watchman for the End Times, and to win new souls for Christ: "The mission of the *Omega Letter* is to point out how trends dovetail with Bible prophecy, not to work to reverse them." Jack, like most prophecy writers, struggles with the paradox that things must get worse in the apocalyptic scheme before they can get better. As he told me in Branson, "The things of the spirit are always backward. Christianity is a religion whereby you gain victory through surrender." And, more humbly: "Death is the beginning."

Jack is still willing to explain what he believes to an outsider. But not everyone in the world of Bible prophecy feels the same way. Before I finish talking to the subscribers, Helen asks me directly whether I've accepted Jesus Christ as my savior. I don't know why I'm so surprised by the question, but I'm flailing instantly and, as the other subscribers look on, I feel quite uncomfortable for the first time during my travels. I mumble something about being in Branson to listen, and admit that the book won't be written from an evangelical perspective. Helen—without any rancor—asks a rhetorical question: "How can you write truthfully about Bible prophecy if you haven't accepted Christ?"

As I leave the campground, Helen presses into my hand a small blue book—the New Testament—and asks me to read it carefully. One of the other subscribers hands me some CDs containing lectures on the Book of Revelation. Jack shakes my hand warmly, and wishes me luck with the book. I do the same with his road tour, though the next few weeks are riddled with misfortune. Gayle tumbles from the RV and puts out her shoulder. In Chicago, Jack is electrocuted as he tries to plug the RV into a campsite power box. He suffers minor burns, and he bangs up his ribs quite badly when he slams into the ground nearly ten feet from the cable he was holding. On the way to California, a hit-and-run driver collides with the RV and smashes up the front end. But Jack keeps going in spite of the "nonstop onslaught from the enemy." The *Omega Letter* Web site is getting 2 million hits a year, and Jack's determined to spread the message as long as God allows him to.

I KEEP AN EYE OUT for the white iceberg on the way back to my hotel, even though it's dark and I'm sure the museum has already closed. But I can't find it amid the theaters and the mini-golf places that have now switched on their floodlights. Instead, I come across a thirty-foot volcano, still surrounded by families clutching their putters and searching for the next hole in the patches of gloom between the lights. The volcano is spewing purple lava, which gathers at the base in a sad pool.

When I get back to my room, I remember something that Helen said to me as I was leaving—"You can't sit on the fence"—and I think about the direction in which Jack and Hal Lindsey are heading. I don't doubt Jack's sincerity on the subject of donkeys and watchmen: he doesn't have the commercializing instinct of Tim LaHaye or the political ambitions of John Hagee. But his ideas about Islam and the West seem frozen at a moment of collision, like the *Titanic* model just down the road. Jack and Hal are happy to signpost the coming disaster, but they're doing nothing to avert it.

8

Tom Clancy with Prayer

J ack Kinsella is hardly a marginal figure in the Bible prophecy world. As Hal Lindsey's right-hand man, he reaches an enormous Christian audience that depends upon Hal to place current affairs in a prophetic framework. I was impressed, though, by Jack's decision to leave his old employers, the Lalonde brothers of Ontario, when they went into the movie business. On principle, Jack sidestepped one of the most unusual developments in the prophecy universe over the past decade or so: the selling of the apocalypse. Since the publication of the first *Left Behind* novel in 1995, a host of evangelicals, entrepreneurs, and corporations have turned the End Times into big business. In the process, they've been trying to reconcile the Christian message with the demands of popular culture. It's not hard to imagine some of the difficulties facing these doomsday impresarios. Can you make a feel-good movie about the Rapture? If you design a video game about the Tribulation, is it okay to let people play for the Antichrist's team?

Jack aside, this trend toward apocalyptic entertainment has

enjoyed the blessing of a surprisingly large number of prophecy experts. Some of them, like Tim LaHaye, have benefited financially from novels and movies. Others just seem to be along for the ride. About twenty minutes into *Left Behind: The Movie*, there's a scene in which the passengers begin to board Rayford Steele's 747 for its fateful flight from Chicago to London. Sharp-eyed viewers may well sit up during this scene and ask: "Hey—isn't that John Hagee?" Sure enough, John and his wife, Diana, are settling into their seats with a look of quiet confidence, as if they know that the Rapture is about to happen. They're not the only familiar faces on the flight. There's another famous prophecy couple, Jack and Rexella Van Impe. And just ahead of them, a living legend of the modern prophecy movement, the ninety-year-old John Walvoord.

The producers of the *Left Behind* movie recruited these guest stars to add some prophetic heft to their movie. The reward for Hagee and the rest is to disappear with the other Christians on the plane when the Rapture takes place. The remaining passengers—those "left behind"—wander forlornly around the cabin searching for their loved ones, and gradually begin to freak out. All that's left of Hagee is the very large Hawaiian shirt that we saw him wearing when he boarded the plane; in a sight gag that could have come from *Airplane*, a Hasidic Jew who'd been sitting near Hagee holds up the empty shirt as if to say—"Oy vey! He was right!"

WITH NEARLY 65 million books sold, *Left Behind* has influenced the whole entertainment industry. For the past ten years, other authors have been trying—with varying degrees of success—to emulate Tim LaHaye and Jerry Jenkins. Christian publishers have ramped up their output and hired more staff to deal with the upsurge in sales. Even Hollywood has got in on the act. In 2004, Mel Gibson's *The Passion of the Christ* brought in $612 million in cinemas around the world. The following year, *The Chron-*

icles of Narnia (a collaboration between Disney and a Christian production company) made $745 million. By 2006, Fox had decided to create an entire division that would focus exclusively on religious movies—FoxFaith. Explaining this move into evangelical entertainment, a Fox executive told the *Los Angeles Times* that "a segment of the market is starving for this kind of content."

Evangelical Christians have been producing and distributing their own End Times movies for decades. One of the most iconic was *A Thief in the Night*, a low-budget movie about the Rapture made in 1972 and screened countless times since at church movie nights and even in schools. Another classic of the genre was the 1979 movie version of Hal Lindsey's *Late Great Planet Earth*, a documentary about Bible prophecy narrated by Orson Welles. (It's worth remembering that, at the end of his career, Welles was happy to lend his voice to projects like the animated *Transformers* movie, in which he played the robot planet Unicron.) These two classics were succeeded by a slew of low-budget prophecy movies in the 1980s and 1990s, though very few got a theatrical release.

Evangelical Christians, especially those who were involved in TV ministries and Christian cable networks, continued to believe that the story of the End Times would eventually cross over to a mainstream audience. The first movie to really succeed at this appeared a year before *Left Behind* made it to the big screen and came from Hal Lindsey and Paul Crouch, the founder of the Trinity Broadcasting Network. *The Omega Code* was funded by TBN, and reached cinemas in 1999. To everyone's surprise, it did very well indeed, creeping into the box office top ten and eventually returning more than $12 million. It was no blockbuster, but it handsomely repaid its production costs even before it went to DVD.

The Omega Code is a retread of the End Times events depicted in the *Left Behind* books, but the writers (along with "prophetic adviser" Hal Lindsey) freshened up the familiar story with a modish subplot. Does anyone remember the Bible Code craze?

Back in 1997, when Paul Crouch was planning his apocalyptic movie, New York journalist Michael Drosnin published a book claiming that the Bible contained secret messages predicting future events. Drosnin claimed that, in 1994, he'd found a coded message warning of Yitzhak Rabin's assassination, a year before Rabin was murdered by a religious extremist. The U.S. media went crazy for the book at first, drawn to its claims that the Bible predicted the JFK assassination and that the Code clearly indicated the apocalypse would take place in 2006. The mania surrounding the book quickly faded when an Australian computer scientist demonstrated that the Rabin assassination was also predicted in *Moby Dick*. In 2004, the same scientist found references to 9/11 in the lyrics of Vanilla Ice records.

The Bible Code was still hot in 1999, and it played a big role in *The Omega Code*. The movie opens with an evil henchman, Dominic, killing an Orthodox Jewish rabbi to seize the secret of the Code. Dominic takes the Code to his boss, Stone Alexander, who's played by Michael York. York has been in a lot of big movies—*Cabaret*, the *Austin Powers* films. He was John the Baptist in Franco Zeffirelli's *Jesus of Nazareth*, but in *The Omega Code* he's switched sides. Stone Alexander is the Antichrist, and he's keen to get his hands on the Bible Code so he can use its warnings and forecasts to smooth his rise to world domination. With this novelty in place, the story reverts to prophetic type: Alexander takes over the European Union, and later the planet. He creates a single government, currency, and religion. And he's eventually undone by the return of Christ.

There are lots of odd things about the plot, but the strangest is the handling of the "false prophet" who helps the Antichrist to deceive the world. In Revelation (and in *Left Behind*, for that matter), this fellow is a rascal who shares the fate of his boss: the Antichrist and the false prophet are cast into the depths on Christ's return. In *The Omega Code*, on the other hand, the "false prophet" is a motivational speaker with a "doctorate in world religion and mythology from Cambridge University" who eventually turns out to be the good guy.

Michael York dazzles the world with the usual Antichristian tricks—a "high-nutrient wafer" that will end hunger; humanitarian awards from the United Nations; a spectacular castle located right next to the Vatican—but, even though he's got the Bible Code, he can't convince the world's Christians to renounce Jesus or prevent the Messiah from returning in the final reel. As some unkind reviewers suggested, this may have something to do with the fact that the Bible Code predictions (which spew from a printer in the basement of Stone's castle) seem to arrive just *after* the events occur, rather than before.

The DVD of *The Omega Code* is stacked with extras. The best is a documentary ("Behind the Codes") on the casting, the prophetic backdrop, and the special effects. Hal Lindsey makes an appearance, wearing a Hawaiian shirt and talking animatedly about the millennium. (I don't know why prophecy experts like Hawaiian shirts so much.) The highlight of the documentary is a breathless account of how the effects team managed to blow up the Dome of the Rock, or, at least, the 1/12 model of the shrine that they'd made for the movie. "The scale and the detail was *awesome*, and the day we blew it up was UNBELIEVABLE," says one crew member, apparently oblivious to the fact that this is an inflammatory act in more ways than one. The production's resident pyrotechnician, an elderly fellow who sounds like Hank from *King of the Hill*, talks us through his role as he sits in front of the soon-to-be-destroyed Dome: "I blow stuff up. I blow up eighteen-, twenty-story buildings. I've blown up a lot of cars." The technicians buzz around him, planting explosives in the roof of the model, as the explosives' guy talks about today's challenge. "We're simulating this mosque exploding," he says matter-of-factly. "Just one portion of the roof is gonna come out. In a fireball. That's basically it."

———

WHILE "THE OMEGA CODE" was filling cinemas in the autumn of 1999, the first *Left Behind* movie was in production in Ontario. Tim LaHaye and Jerry Jenkins had shopped around the rights, but they eventually decided to go with a Christian production company. Cloud Ten Pictures was founded by Peter and Paul Lalonde, who quickly built up a slate of apocalyptic films after parting company with Jack Kinsella in the mid-1990s. They managed to persuade reasonably well-known actors—not just Jeff Fahey—to star in their films. They also recruited John Hagee, who had a writing credit for their first film, *Vanished*, and a major role.

The release of *Left Behind: The Movie* was controversial. Tim LaHaye had high hopes for a blockbuster opening, but the Lalonde brothers didn't have the budget, marketing power, or distribution network of a Hollywood studio. They made the fateful decision in 2000 to send their film straight to video, then to use word of mouth in the Christian community to build popular interest ahead of a cinema release. When the movie finally appeared on the big screen in February 2001, it made only $2.1 million. Paul had brashly promised a week earlier that the *Left Behind* team was gunning for the number-one spot at the box office; the movie didn't even make the top ten, and slouched to a modest $4 million over the next month.

One viewer was especially unimpressed. Tim LaHaye brought a lawsuit against Cloud Ten even before the film had been released, claiming that he'd been promised a big-budget production: more than $40 million, Tim's lawsuit stated, against the $17 million that Cloud Ten finally spent on the movie. Tim was reportedly angry that he'd sold the rights back in 1997, before the book series really took off, and was now stuck with a creaky adaptation. Cloud Ten held its ground, and the suit was eventually thrown out by a judge. The first *Left Behind* movie sold more than

3 million copies on DVD and videotape, and Cloud Ten continued to make apocalyptic movies.

Perhaps Tim LaHaye was disappointed by the casting of *Left Behind*. The main roles of Rayford Steele and Buck Williams went to TV actors Brad Johnson and Kirk Cameron. Brad was great in the Steven Spielberg romance *Always* as the young firefighter who falls for Holly Hunter, but he's not done much since. Kirk, on the other hand, was incredibly famous in the U.S. during the late eighties and early nineties as the star of the sitcom *Growing Pains*, a wholesome retread of *Family Ties* (which was itself pretty wholesome). Kirk found Jesus in the middle of the show's successful run, and by the final seasons was exasperating his fellow cast members and the production team by rejecting dialogue and story lines that seemed un-Christian to him. Rounding out the *Left Behind* cast was the Canadian actor Gordon Currie, who plays the Antichrist with a thick Romanian accent that seems to have been inspired by The Count from *Sesame Street*.

Tim and Jerry have managed to get fifteen novels from the *Left Behind* concept, and the Lalonde brothers are similarly prolific. Their "Apocalypse" series—which began in 1998, and sketched a different End Times vision from *Left Behind*—produced four movies in three years. One of these films, *Tribulation*, brought together the unlikely trio of Jack Van Impe (the prophecy televangelist), Margot Kidder (of *Superman*), and Howie Mandel, the comedian who enjoyed a comeback as the host of *Deal or No Deal* on NBC.

The most recent movie in the series, *Judgment*, may be the first apocalyptic courtroom drama. The Antichrist—another Canadian actor, this time Nick Mancuso—has taken over the world and banned Christianity. Corbin Bernsen of *L.A. Law* has to defend a Christian woman who refuses to renounce her religion and accept the mark of the Beast. Most of the film takes place in court, though Mr. T has been recruited to play an underground Christian activist who wants to use violence against the one-world government of the Antichrist. ("Black eye for black eye!" he tells his band of righteous vigilantes. "Broken tooth for broken tooth!") The tagline for the film is "Supreme Court versus Supreme Being." Viewers who imagined that the apocalypse would be a largely extrajudicial affair may be disappointed. As one disgruntled Internet reviewer put it: "Isn't the end of the world supposed to be all gory with wars and killer locusts and dragons and stuff? Where was all that while we were watching this *Matlock* crap?"

After winning its legal battle with Tim LaHaye, Cloud Ten has continued to make movies based on the *Left Behind* books. The most recent entry in the series—*Left Behind: World at War*—features Oscar-winner Lou Gossett, Jr., as the president of the United States. Sony Pictures put up some of the money for the film, and then backed Cloud Ten in a very unusual release strategy. The movie opened in October 2005 on more than 3,200 screens across America, but didn't appear in any cinemas. The screenings were hosted by churches, which bought copies of the DVD and used their hi-tech projectors and sound systems to replicate the movie experience. (In many megachurches, the movie was actually shown within the sanctuary, using the same big screens that flash up video or song lyrics during Sunday services.) Peter Lalonde told *Christianity Today* that he wouldn't measure the box office in terms of tickets sold; he'd made it impossible to keep track of that, since the churches bought DVDs and were then allowed to decide how much to charge for admission, and what to do with the money. Looking ahead to the all-important first weekend, which can make or break a movie in Hollywood, he took a different approach: "The number we report to the press on the following Monday are the number at the altars—those who actually come to Christ. We're calling it a box office counted in souls."

AS I TALKED to Bible prophecy scholars and preachers across America, I was surprised to see how jumpy everyone was about the latest addition to the *Left Behind* family. In November 2006, a California company released *Left Behind: Eternal Forces*, an apocalyptic video game. I'd heard about the game earlier in the year, and I'd tried to stop by the headquarters of the company—Left Behind Games (LBG)—on my way back from Palm Springs to Los Angeles. They weren't keen to talk to me, and on balance I'm not surprised. LBG had stepped up their publicity effort in the spring of 2006, ahead of the first demos of the game during the summer, but they'd started to attract attention from Christian groups who had heard *Eternal Forces* was just another violent video game.

Since the 1980s, evangelicals haven't known what to do with video games. Pastors and Christian campaigners have railed against shoot-'em-ups like *Castle Wolfenstein* and *Doom*, while intrepid Christian coders have tried to create games that promote faith-based values. One of the more offbeat examples of this was *Super 3D Noah's Ark*, a Nintendo game from 1994, which actually made use of the graphics engine from *Castle Wolfenstein*. According to legend, the *Wolfenstein* programmers had become so exasperated by Nintendo's insistence that they tone down the violence in their own game that they leaked their graphics engine to a Christian games company, which went on to produce the only unlicensed game ever developed for the Nintendo console.

Players familiar with *Wolfenstein* were baffled by the new game. Instead of sneaking around a dark Nazi redoubt with a chaingun searching for the evil Dr. Fettgesicht, they found themselves wandering belowdecks on Noah's Ark firing melons at stray animals. The game's premise: a few days before the Ark finds dry land at last, the animals become restless and start running around wildly. Taking the role of Noah, your job is to fire food at them to send them back to sleep. The Christian programmers even retained the structure of *Wolfenstein*: each level ended with a "boss" character that you had to kill/feed. In an inspired touch, all the "boss" animals (elephants, bears, monkeys) were ritually unclean, according to the Book of Leviticus.

Although a number of Christian video game companies have emerged in recent years, the gaming industry has been dominated by secular fare, and by increasingly violent shooter games like *Grand Theft Auto* and *Half-Life*. Meanwhile, Christian watchdog groups fire off angry press releases lamenting particular games and the companies that make them. One of the most vocal Christian opponents of video game violence, Florida attorney Jack Thompson, insisted in 2005 that the role of Japan in promoting the PlayStation and its violent games amounted to "Pearl Harbor 2." It was Thompson who sounded the alarm in early 2006 about *Left Behind: Eternal Forces*. From what he'd read, this was going to be a "mass killing game" that could not be justified even in a "Christian context."

Left Behind Games began a charm offensive with the media, but struggled to avert the impression that they were making a violent game. The company president, Jeffrey Frichner, agreed to give a demo of *Eternal Forces* to Joel Stein, a *Los Angeles Times* journalist. Stein, who's Jewish, asked to try the multiplayer version of the game—Frichner agreed, and then allowed Stein to play as the Antichrist. "The apocalypse," Stein observed after losing to Frichner's Christian forces, "was a good excuse for Christians to just go nuts and unload a lot of pent-up stuff. Armageddon is like their version of divorce." Stories like this seemed to get around among the evangelicals that I visited. When I brought up the game, people invariably repeated the same line I'd read on Christian discussion groups and blogs—"Bang bang, you're saved!"—and shook their heads in disgust.

The controversy over the game eventually forced Troy Lyndon, the CEO of Left Behind Games, to issue a statement on the company's Web site. He complained about "journalists spreading misinformation," and assured potential buyers of the game that "it does not gratuitously depict violence or death." Having played the demo of *Eternal Forces*, I think the operative word is "gratuitously." LBG mentions in its investor reports that the *Left Behind* stories are "very action oriented and supremely suitable for an engaging series of video games." This means that some people in your virtual universe are going to get hurt.

When you boot up the demo and select one of the trial missions, you find yourself in the middle of New York City at the start of the Tribulation with a courier bag and the ability to convert passersby. This is quite cool. If you walk up to "neutrals" and select the "convert" button, puffy white clouds gather above you as you bring the pedestrian to Christ. Rather implausibly, the pedestrians don't run away from you when they see you coming at them with your Bible. When you've converted a character, they shimmer for a few seconds as if they've been through the transporter in *Star Trek*, then you get to control them as well. Helpfully, they let you know who's in charge when you click on them: "I'm ready for your direction!" they shout. "Enlighten me!"

As the game progresses, you wander around New York trying to bolster the Christian cause against the evil United Nations/ Global Community forces. You do this by bringing people to Christ, and buying and developing buildings that can serve as clinics, food courts, and military training centers. You can create soldiers and tell them to kill people, though the game designers discourage this (in single player mode) by docking "spirit points" if you behave in an un-Christian fashion. I was far too incompetent to actually kill anyone when I played. But a more accomplished gamer could certainly do some damage, given the firepower available even to the Christian rebels. Of course, if you decide to use the multiplayer option and choose the Antichrist's side, the sky's the limit.

Occasionally, the action stops for a public service message promoting evangelical causes. For example, gamers are told that the human eye is such a tremendously intricate mechanism that it disproves the theory of evolution. The apparently unintentional messages in *Eternal Forces* seem more troubling. When you move through the tutorial, you learn how to convert passersby and then how to train them to be soldiers, builders, or disciples. When you convert men, they transform into identical preppy kids wearing V-necks. Women suddenly sport an orange jumper, like Velma from *Scooby Doo*. If you only convert men, you can do everything you need to do in the game. But if you bring women to Christ, the game starts giving you polite reminders that your options are limited. "For the next operation," says the cheerful voice in the tutorial, "you will need a man. Take a moment to recruit a man before continuing!"

Girls can't do very much in *Eternal Forces*. Men can become disciples, builders, or soldiers. Women can't. You can train them to become medics, but that's about it. Even then, they're not indispensable: men can do this, too, along with their many other talents. Helpfully, random men keep sidling up to you and your female converts if you ignore the injunctions to convert them, though this seems quite seedy if you haven't understood the game's regressive sexual politics.

The full version of the game was released in November 2006, appearing in big shops like Wal-Mart as well as in megachurches and Christian bookstores. As one journalist unkindly put it, *Eternal Forces* was "crucified" by reviewers. It's hard to know whether the arrival of a *Left Behind* video game proves the reach of apocalyptic thinking in contemporary America or confirms its limits. Prophecy believers are willing to take their message into every part of the culture, and the very fact that the video game has made it into the shops demonstrates the determination of apocalyptic Christians to make the End Times cool. But most kids wanted a Wii or a PS3 rather than *Eternal Forces* for Christmas, and even those people who bought a copy may not have been thinking about the need for repentance as they clashed with Global Community troops or steered the Antichrist's forces to victory in the multiplayer version. Apocalyptic movies and video games have proved that it's possible to get prophecy into the cultural mainstream, but it's hard to control the message when it's out there.

"LEFT BEHIND" GAMES may be in trouble if *Eternal Forces* misses its target, but the publisher of the *Left Behind* books—Tyndale House—has made so much money from the series that it can afford to experiment a little. Between 1998 and 2001, as the *Left Behind* series took off, Tyndale's annual sales quadrupled from $40 million to more than $160 million. Beyond the twelve books in the original series, Tyndale devised spin-offs that could take the End Times message to an even larger audience. There are forty *Left Behind: The Kids* books, which cover the Tribulation period from the perspective of previously godless teenagers. There's the *Left Behind* audio series. And five graphic novels. And more than half a dozen "nonfiction" books about the End Times, several of them by LaHaye and Jenkins themselves. There's even a book of reader testimonies in which fans of the series share their personal stories with the editors at Tyndale House. In a crowd-pleasing move, this book is called *These Will Not Be Left Behind*.

Tyndale's determination to milk their cash cow has occasionally upset even Tim LaHaye. In 2004, Tyndale announced a new apocalyptic series called *The Last Disciple* to be written by Hank Hanegraaff, a Christian radio host. Tim seems to have been less annoyed by the competition than by the version of the End Times that Hanegraaff was peddling. Unlike the *Left Behind* books, *The Last Disciple* series argued that the events of the Book of Revelation were realized in the struggles of the early Christian Church in the first century after Christ. This would mean that the LaHaye/Jenkins vision of the End Times was mistaken. Tim, who'd already signed his massive book deal with Random House for a new series of apocalyptic novels, complained about this "stunning and disappointing" move on Tyndale's part. "They are going to take the money we made for them and promote this nonsense," he told reporters. Hanegraaff shot back that he was "not relying on some wooden, literal interpretation that is unsupportable." Reporting the squabble, one newspaper noted that these Tyndale authors would be unlikely to exchange signed copies any time soon.

Perhaps the oddest apocalyptic spin-offs came directly from the *Left Behind* stable. In 2001, Tyndale executives sat down with Tekno Books, a packaging firm from Wisconsin that develops book ideas and pitches them to major publishers. Tekno wanted to expand the *Left Behind* series and devised more than twenty ideas for possible spin-offs. The Tyndale execs went through them carefully and decided on two. The first was a political franchise, focusing on the events in the White House after the Rapture. "This series combines the explosiveness of the *Left Behind* universe with the immediacy of *The West Wing*," enthused the Tyndale Web site.

The second, which seemed to push the format beyond breaking point, was a military series in which readers would follow the adventures of a U.S. army ranger in the Middle East as the Tribulation begins. "Military thrillers are not a big thing in the Christian bookselling market," admitted Tyndale's business director in an interview about the Tekno/Tyndale partnership. "While this looks like two companies just did a business deal, nothing would have happened if God hadn't put it in our hearts to propose this."

"WELL, THE STUFF I did with the apocalypse is Tom Clancy with prayer." I'm talking on the phone with Mel Odom, author of *Apocalypse Dawn* and the other two books in the *Left Behind* military series: *Apocalypse Crucible* and *Apocalypse Burning*. Mel lives outside of Oklahoma City, and he's carved out some time to chat about his work. Ever since I found out about the military books, I've wanted to speak to Mel and ask him the obvious questions. Isn't Christian military fiction a contradiction in terms? How easy is it to combine the Tom Clancy stuff—obsessing over the details of the latest gun, tank, or plane—with the message of the End Times? And what about the fact that, in the world of *Left Behind,* the United States is on the ropes from the Rapture onward?

The *Apocalypse* books are Mel's first foray into Christian fiction, but since the late 1980s he's written more than 140 books. Mel's output seems downright incongruous for a *Left Behind* author. He's written strategy guides for video games, including *Leisure Suit Larry,* the notoriously lewd adventure series, and *Duke Nukem,* a violent action game in which the hero uses some very large guns to blow up alien invaders in Los Angeles. Mel has also written tie-in novels for action movies, including Angelina Jolie's *Tomb Raider* and the Wesley Snipes vampire flick *Blade.* To round out his CV, he's ghosted for Tom Clancy and written young-adult novels based on *Sabrina the Teenage Witch* and *Buffy the Vampire Slayer.* Mel is presumably the only Tyndale House author to have written two books about vampires.

Mel has a huge laugh, which he fires up on a regular basis. He's telling me about a Tyndale party at the Florida meeting of the Christian Booksellers Association, and his amusement at all the boozing that went on. "I was raised in a nonalcoholic church environment," he says. "Alcohol was a sin. I don't think it is now, but I was raised that way, and it still jarred me to be around a bunch of church people that were *drinking*." He pauses for a second. "And that weren't Catholic. HA HA HA!" (Mel actually makes the HA sounds.)

Growing up in Bible Belt Oklahoma, Mel originally saw Christianity as a very intimidating force in people's lives. "Back in the small towns I grew up in, the pastors were very much a part of the community. If you did something wrong, the pastor would show up on your door and tell you not to be doing it anymore." He decided in school that he wanted to write for a living, but had to wait until 1989 before he got his big break: a commission for the *Executioner* series. The *Executioner* novels chronicle the adventures of Mack Bolan, a former Green Beret who returns from Vietnam to take on the Mafia. After dismantling America's organized crime network across a series of novels, often with rocket launchers and other blunt instruments, Mack moves on to tackle international terrorism: "Bolan stalks a Mideast hellzone to save American lives" reads the tagline on one of Mel's *Executioner* books. The cover has the following quote, which may or may not be a compliment: "'Very, very action oriented' (*New York Times*)."

Incredibly, there are around six hundred *Executioner* novels in total. Mel has written nineteen of them, but by the late 1990s he was looking for a change of scene. "I talked to my agent at the time, and I said, 'Man, I want to start doing some of the young adult stuff.'" Mel's agent, Ethan, didn't think he was that kind of writer and tried to put Mel off the idea. (Ethan is the straight man in many of Mel's best stories. Since Ethan's Jewish, these funny stories multiply now that he's dealing with Christian publishers.) After getting the cold shoulder from his agent, Mel worked his own contacts in New York and successfully pitched a story based on the Nickelodeon teen show *Alex Mack* to an editor at Pocket Books. "So I called my agent and I said, 'Ethan, I've got a book contract offer for a young adult novel. Do you want to be my agent or should I get a young adult agent?' HA HA! He goes, 'No, no, I can take care of this for you.' So from there the editor asked me if I would do the *Sabrina the Teenage Witch* books. I'd seen it on TV, it was great. I loved the cat. So after that she offered me a *Buffy*, and I just got to do a lot of stuff."

I wonder how all this played with the folks at Tyndale House. In 2002, Mel went to Illinois to audition for the job of writing the *Left Behind* military series, and the Tyndale editors grilled him on his ideas and on his unconventional background. "Tyndale actually flat out asked me—well, how do I reconcile *Sabrina the Teenage Witch* and the *Buffy* work that I did? And I said, well, it's nothing to reconcile for me. I'm a single father with four kids and I've never once questioned the work that God put before me to take care of them. If God puts work in front of you that's not harmful to your children, how can it be bad work? And that was my argument with them, and that closed the door on the whole argument."

Mel left the Tyndale offices feeling disappointed. "When I walked out of the interview I didn't think that I had gotten that job at all," he confesses. But when he got back to Oklahoma that evening, God sent him a sign. "It was raining, and I got out of the airport and walked to my car, and the car next to me had a license plate on it, a personalized license plate, and it had the letters F T S T P S." He spells this out really quickly, and I have no idea what he's talking about. "So I looked at that and I thought *NO WAY!* And I'm telling you right now, Nick, this sounds like a made up story to tell you over the phone."

I'm frantically trying to work out what this means when Ethan, Mel's hapless agent, shows up in the story to bail me out. "And Ethan called the next day and he goes, 'I just got word, you got the job.' And I told Ethan, 'I saw this license plate parked right next to my car, and out of thousands of cars parked in the airport the one parked next to me has F T S T P S.' And he goes, 'Fort Stamps?' And I said, 'No, man! FOOTSTEPS!'"

Mel tells me the story about a Christian who complained to God that he'd been deserted. God denied this. "But look back in this path through the sands," said the angry believer, "there's only a single set of footsteps." God looked at the man and told him: "Those were the days I carried you." Mel is clearly moved when he remembers this story: "And it gives me chills right now to talk about this, but I mean how can you not believe? I don't know what's out there, I'm not a religious fanatic or anything, but I know something is beyond this place."

"LEFT BEHIND: APOCALYPSE DAWN" has an orange jacket with a grainy photo of an aircraft carrier sailing to war. The hero of the novel is First Sergeant Samuel Adams "Goose" Gander, an army ranger on a UN peacekeeping mission on the Syria-Turkey

border. Three hours before the Rapture, the Syrians team up
with the Kurds to challenge the Turks, and Goose finds himself in
the middle of a running battle. Meanwhile, back at Fort Benning
in Georgia, his wife, Megan, is trying to help Gerry, a military
kid, to escape from his abusive father. Megan's a counselor at the
base, and she eventually persuades Gerry to open up about the
latest beating he's taken from his unstable dad. Mel follows Goose
and Megan as their situations deteriorate: in Turkey, the under-
manned Ranger force buckles beneath an all-out Syrian assault;
back home in Georgia, Gerry escapes from the base hospital and
scurries in despair to the roof of a nearby building.

Apocalypse Dawn, unlike the original *Left Behind* novel, cannily
postpones the Rapture for nearly 180 pages. "I slowed down the
clock and I amped up the action," Mel tells me proudly. Things
have become wildly intense when the Rapture finally occurs.
Goose calls in helicopter reinforcements, but the pilots disappear, leading to a grisly midair pileup. (This made me think of
those online forums encouraging committed Christians to resign
from life-and-death professions, in case the Rapture happened
while they were on duty.) At precisely the same moment, Megan
watches in despair as Gerry throws himself from the top of the
building. His clothes land far below with a soft thump, but his
body is nowhere to be found. Megan subsequently finds herself
on trial for her involvement in the boy's disappearance, and Mel
does a good job of making this seem tense even though the Rapture ought to be a solid alibi for Megan.

There are one or two moments at which God seems to have
joined Team America, including an uncomfortable scene in the
underground headquarters of NORAD, the American air defense network. "Do you think God planned for DEFCON?" asks
one sergeant as the NORAD staff monitor the American nuclear
bombers that are speeding toward Russian airspace. For most of
the novel, though, things don't go well for Uncle Sam. Nearly a
third of the American military personnel in the novel disappear

in the Rapture. Goose finds his faith afterward, like Buck and Ray in *Left Behind*, but he's badly outnumbered and outgunned by the Antichrist. (Nicolae Carpathia uses his connections in the CIA and his devilish charm to swing American commanders to his side.) The overriding impression from *Apocalypse Dawn* is that the United States, in spite of its military might, will be totally besieged during the End Times.

WHEN "APOCALYPSE DAWN" became a hit, selling more than one hundred thousand copies, two of the editors from Tyndale flew down to Oklahoma City to hang out with Mel. "Because even the Tyndale people when they first met me were looking at me going, 'Okay, what is this guy all about?' Because I had the earring, the long hair." Mel keeps telling me, with another huge laugh, that he looks like a biker or a thug. ("I've had people who are afraid to make eye contact with me!") When the Tyndale editors arrived, Mel took them to the Murrah memorial, on the site of the old federal building that Timothy McVeigh destroyed with a truck bomb back in 1995. This is a somber place, with 168 empty chairs sitting in a neat park and symbolizing the people who were killed that day.

When they'd finished seeing the sights downtown, Mel looked to lighten the mood. "I said, 'You guys want to go to a gun range?' And I begged and borrowed every gun I could find from people, and we took about two dozen guns up to the range." Mel is especially tickled that the two editors were women, and they'd never done anything like this before. "And they got to shoot everything from a .22 pistol all the way up to a .500 Magnum, and they got to shoot shotguns and AK-47s. Because I have friends who are hooked up with guns. And the women had a blast!" He tells me that one of the editors still has the target silhouette (or what's left of it) on her office door at Tyndale.

But this story, like Mel's earring or his biker looks, is misleading.

As he talks about his faith and his writing, it becomes clear that he's neither a gun nut nor some kind of apocalyptic survivalist. One of the things he's proudest of is his baseball coaching: he manages a kids' Little League team, and in our conversation he keeps linking this to his books and his beliefs. Coaching Little League helps him to believe that "we're here to do something with our lives." Dealing with demanding parents taught him how to stay honest and to speak his mind. When he talked baseball in his Tyndale House interview, one executive suggested that "God has given you these kids to be kind of your church." Mel likes that idea. "I've got kids that are nineteen, twenty, twenty-one years old right now, who are still coming up to hug me, talk to me. I mean, they're from single-parent homes, their fathers weren't around, their fathers were gone, and they've turned out to be good men."

Although Mel is a committed Christian, he's a lot more open about faith than most of the prophecy writers I've talked to. He tells me about the time he had lunch with his local preacher and told him that he was unhappy with the way that some Christians interpret the Bible. "The preacher said, 'What do you mean?' And I said, the fact that all the Indians that lived here before Christianity reached this world supposedly are condemned to hell." Mel had recently found out that he was part Cherokee Indian, and the idea that his ancestors were damned unsettled him. The preacher didn't offer much solace—"Well, Mel, that's just how it is"—but Mel refused to accept this. "And I was like, I don't believe that. I believe that if you've lived a good life, and you've believed in something beyond yourself, that there's still room for everyone to live in heaven. It's not like there's limited space." He keeps returning to this point, and I'm struck by his emphasis on good deeds and on the many paths to God. "I'm not a dyed-in-the-wool, gotta-get-out-and-convert-everybody guy. I think God converts people, or your faith, whatever your faith, will convert you to what you need to be and what you need to know."

I'm surprised to hear that Mel has never even met Tim La-Haye. He ran into Jerry Jenkins at a conference a few years ago, but he's hardly taking orders from the series creators. "The thing of it is, Tim has his own ideas of what's going to happen and how it's going to happen. Now, is he going to be right? I don't know. It could be that we continue on for another thousand years." Whenever I invite Mel to be specific about what's coming next, he hedges his bets. "I have no idea of how the End Times are going to work out," he tells me, before launching into a very vague discussion of China and its energy needs in the coming years. (This bleeds into an enthusiastic review of the labyrinthine and quite left-leaning George Clooney flick, *Syriana*.) "It is *so* open to interpretation," he says of the Tribulation period. Most important of all: "You're not supposed to know when it's going to happen."

Many apocalyptic Christians offer disclaimers like this on the question of timing, but they also insist on the need to scrutinize every detail of the prophecies and to map those onto current affairs. Mel is amused by that approach and offers a few examples to demonstrate the pitfalls of literalism. "'In my father's house there are streets paved with gold': Is that really what they meant or is it just, like, there's no potholes? HA HA! 'I knew that you'd have needs, and you wouldn't want to be alone, and you'd want to be comforted'—does that mean sex?" Mel even brings up one of the more awkward moral problems in the *Left Behind* universe: If your spouse is Raptured, are you allowed to remarry during the Tribulation period? And if you do, what happens when you're reunited with your former spouse at the end of the Tribulation period, when Christ brings the Raptured back to Earth?

I tell Mel that this scenario is actually played out, uncomfortably, in the last novel of the *Left Behind* series, *Glorious Appearing*. Rayford Steele's wife, Irene, is Raptured in the first book. By book two Ray has found a new wife, Amanda, who was in the same Bible study group as Irene. (Amanda, who was left behind, was presumably a less accomplished student.) Ray's romantic misfortune persists as Amanda also disappears by book four—she's killed in a plane crash. Nonetheless, there's an awkward reunion at the Second Coming when Jesus Christ resurrects Amanda and retrieves Irene from heaven, then personally delivers both wives to a bemused Ray. The scene is no less awkward for the avowals of Jenkins and LaHaye that "the two [wives] get along without difficulty." Mel listens to all this and bursts into another laugh. "HA HA! That could be kind of complicated!"

SO FAR IN our conversation, Mel has rejected literalism, overconfident predictions about Bible prophecy, and a Christianity that excludes people. He wants to open up heaven to all those who've led a decent life and who've believed in a God beyond themselves. But what about his views on politics? The idea of combining *Left Behind* with Tom Clancy seems like an ultra right-wing fantasy: the United States military wages God's war against the infidels.

My suspicions about this had been fueled by the Tyndale press releases announcing the series. In an interview with one of the leading book distributors in the Christian market, Tyndale's business director admitted in 2003 that "some would say this is a bad time to publish something about wars and military." But he insisted that "God has accomplished great things through the horrors of war." *Apocalypse Dawn* came out in July 2003, just a few months after the U.S. invasion of Iraq, and the Tyndale representative joined the dots in his interview: "If we truly believe that all things work together for good for those that love God and are called according to his purpose, then that means that God can use war for something good. If there was ever a time when we needed to see how God plans the future to play out, it is now."

When I ask Mel about the war on terror, and Iraq in particular, he breaks ranks with the Bush administration. "I try to remain evenhanded; everybody has a different feel for politics.

I'm not happy at all about the fact that we're embroiled in this Iraq situation. You know, I was even more unhappy about the fact that there were no weapons of mass destruction found over there after we invaded, and this thing has turned into a situation that is not going to be something that is easily let go. Am I happy about that? No, I am not."

Since Mel is warm and willing to answer pretty much any question, I decide to ask him directly about Bible prophecy Christians and their political agenda. I mention some of the press coverage surrounding *Left Behind*, and the tendency of liberals and secular Americans to think that End Times evangelicals are not only nuts but a threat to the nation's future. Then I ask him, rather sheepishly: Is the United States threatened by the growing political influence of apocalyptic Christians?

"Apocalyptic Christians." Mel sighs loudly. "I start hearing these people and they start wanting to carry around the sign saying the world's going to end tomorrow, so they don't have to die! The thing of it is, they want to be called up, and that way they don't have to go through the whole death thing, but, you know, to every life there is a death owed."

I'd been expecting Mel at least to identify with the Bible prophecy crowd. Instead, he's offering to dissect them for me.

"And so where is the apocalyptic Christian coming from? Is it coming out of religion? 'Well, God is here to get us if we go ahead and trigger all of this massive stuff, we're going to make God come to us'? Or is it, 'We're just doing what God ordained, we're following God's orders'? Or is it, 'This is a good excuse to line our pockets with money'?" Mel compares today's leaders with the War Hawks, a group of American politicians from the southern and western states, who argued strongly for the War of 1812 because they knew they'd benefit financially from a fight with Britain. Perhaps some of these people have used Bible prophecy for cynical ends, he suggests. "Nick, I don't know where these people are coming from. I could sit down with them in a room and probably in fifteen or twenty minutes give you a better idea of where they're coming from."

It seems that, even though Mel has written three Christian novels with the word "apocalypse" in the title, he doesn't consider himself an apocalyptic Christian. I decide to come right out and ask him.

Mel pauses and gives this some thought. "No, I don't. Because I don't think I'm trying to trigger any kind of feelings one way or the other. I'm writing a story of good and evil." He talks about this eternal struggle all the time, and it's one of the ways he reconciles his other books (including his *Buffy* novels) with his *Left Behind* work. "When you boil it down, it's not *religion*. You know, people can brand this religion and everything else, but the stories I'm telling—it's good and evil."

BEFORE WE FINISH chatting, Mel admits that he's worried about America. "One of the things that's happened since 9/11, the government has taken more power here in the United States. I object to that. The baseline reason for them to take more power is because people don't want to be troubled with as much, making decisions for themselves. That's where you get a party line. That's where you get your apocalyptic Christians." Mel war-games this End Times mentality for me: "Well, let me be on that team. They don't even stop to think about what the team is all about. They look at the color, they look at whatever, and they're attracted." Mel's books go in a different direction. "I make myself think, I make my kids think, I take readers and try to make them think for themselves too."

He lets slip that he's planning a new series of apocalyptic military novels about a tank crew who find themselves facing impossible odds after the Rapture. It won't be a *Left Behind* series, and it may not even be a Tyndale book. Mel's agent is, as usual, the butt of the joke. "Ethan cracked me up because I'd presented another series that I wanted to do, and it had the Rapture in there, and he said, 'Mel, you can't use the Rapture! LaHaye created that!' HA HA HA!"

Mel's last story is about a trip he recently made to Texas. He was giving away copies of a book in Borders, and a man who'd read his *Apocalypse* novels came up and confessed that he sometimes had trouble keeping his faith. This man's wife had died of cancer five years earlier, and he still couldn't accept that "things are where they're supposed to be." But Mel drew from the bereaved husband a touching story: one of his colleagues at work didn't have enough money to send her daughter to college, so the bereaved husband paid for all the girl's college expenses and watched her graduate debt-free. Mel heard the man out, then told him what a great thing he was doing. After recounting the story, he tells me the moral: "That's what life's about. That's what I try to write about. And the Christian ideology, of exclusionary stuff—no, man. It's to bring people close to the fire, warm them, feed them, and give them a safe place to sleep."

I'M NOT SURE whether the readers of the *Apocalypse* series would necessarily follow Mel down all these paths, but if a person who actually writes these books can be this open-minded, it's possible that some of the 60 million *Left Behind* readers might have ideas about faith and the world beyond America that depart from the apocalyptic perspective. Mel is attracted to the End Times for the same reasons that any writer would be—there's plenty of potential here for exciting stories, and for morality plays in which ordinary people are forced to make difficult choices in extraordinary circumstances. At the same time, his brush with prophecy doesn't seem to have dulled his enthusiasm for vampires and the kind of video games that send evangelical leaders into a moral panic.

From a liberal perspective, there's a danger of stereotyping the evangelical Christians who've devoured *Left Behind*, and of assuming that the ideas of Tim LaHaye and Jerry Jenkins are instantly adopted by the people who read their books. Mel takes his faith very seriously, but he also enjoys *Sabrina the Teenage Witch*. He loves guns, but he's got cold feet about Iraq. These apparent contradictions have survived Mel's involvement with the *Left Behind* series, and his own take on the apocalypse makes it sound a lot like a *Buffy* episode: it's yet another way to retell the eternal story of good versus evil. The growing industry in apocalyptic entertainment—which is now turning out novels, movies, and video games about the End Times—has had problems connecting with a secular audience that's wary of a Christian message. It may also struggle with evangelical readers and viewers who are still capable of thinking for themselves.

9

Armageddon Comes Later

At Mardel's bookstore in Denver, Tim LaHaye has spent the past ninety minutes greeting his fans. The line is much shorter now, and from where I'm standing Tim's still looking good. But Beverly, Tim's publicist, comes over to tell me that the interview may be off. She reminds me about the multiple 6/6/06 junkets that she has organized, and the strain of all this on her eighty-year-old star author. She can sense that in spite of the smiles and the kind words that he's stored up for the crowd, Tim is starting to flag.

Eventually, when the signing line dwindles to nothing, Beverly leads me to a round table at the back of the bookstore and tells me to wait. Jerry Jenkins mops up the last few readers while Tim gets wearily to his feet. He suddenly looks drained, and Beverly points him toward my table even as she checks her watch. "Fifteen minutes," she mouths in my direction, leaving me with no doubt that this will be rigidly enforced. As Tim walks over, Beverly starts to unscrew the publicity banners that have been placed to one side of the signing table. Tim's wife has left, and Jerry is sitting at the table on his own. Perhaps I should have asked Beverly if I could talk to Jerry as well; after all, he actually writes the *Left Behind* books. It's too late now. Tim's bearing down on me, working up one last smile for my benefit. He sits at the round table and looks at me with polite resignation.

How to break the ice with the most famous apocalyptic preacher alive? I remembered something that I'd heard from Tim's neighbor, David Chagall, back in Palm Springs. I'd mentioned to David that the area looked a bit like Israel and the West Bank, a place I'd visited on a few occasions, and his face lit up. "God bless you, you're exactly right!" He told me that the mountains reminded him of the hills of the Judean desert; and, more implausibly, that the Salton Sea was the American double of the Dead Sea in Israel.

The Salton Sea was accidentally created in 1905 when a dike holding back the Colorado River burst its banks; after a few decades in which tourists flocked to its shores, the sea became so salty and polluted that the visitors stopped coming and the new resorts withered away. These days, the sea attracts only diehards who remember the good times, or misfits who see a strange beauty in this vast, dying place. (A recent documentary about the Salton Sea was narrated by John Waters, the director of *Hairspray*.) But the view is very different from Palm Springs, which is fifty miles to the northwest. If you ride the tourist tramway that runs behind David Chagall's house, and you take in the view from six thousand feet up Mount San Jacinto, the distant sea looks spectacular. This was the image that stuck in David's mind: "When I came out here and I looked, I thought, My God, this looks just like Judea."

David wondered if the same thought had occurred to Tim LaHaye and Hal Lindsey, who'd both been living in Palm Springs for more than a decade. So I decided that this would be my opening gambit in Denver. "The one thing I thought when I went to Palm Springs," I casually tell Tim, "is that it looked just like Israel."

He stares at me as if I'm crazy. "Really?"

"Yeah, you know—the mountains, the Salton Sea . . ."

Tim gives this some thought, then grudgingly concedes that you might get this impression "if you look at the dry side." But he's really excited about the built-up parts of Palm Springs, and the miracle of those golf courses and condos. "Where we live," he says proudly, "it's like a park. Have you been to Desert Island?" I spare him the story of my visit to Rancho Mirage, since I don't want to remind him about his air-conditioning problem while he's singing the praises of his condo complex. "That's where we live. And you get in there through the gate, and it's a twenty-five acre island around twenty-five acres of water, and seventy-five acres of golf course. And it's just like paradise!"

So much for David Chagall's romance with the biblical landscape of southern California. Tim's enamored of his desert oasis for lots of reasons that don't have anything to do with Israel. He likes to stay active even in his advanced years. Apparently he's still waterskiing, which must be some kind of record given that he's just turned eighty. He admits, though, that he's given up skiing on the slopes around Palm Springs. He has friends who've broken a leg or a hip and were never the same. "I enjoy life so much," he says with real yearning. "And I've got so much to do."

This makes me think of another icebreaker. When I'd met Dave Reagan in Texas, he told me that he liked to kid Tim about the *Left Behind* books, and the fact that there seemed to be no end in sight to the series. Dave liked the first novel, but he told me that he'd lost interest when Tim and Jerry had decided (with their publisher's blessing) to "drag out" the story across more than a dozen volumes. This led him to a joke which, I was sure, would amuse Tim.

"I was talking to Dave Reagan, and he said you were planning to write one *Left Behind* book for every year of the millennium. Is that true?"

As soon as I say this, it occurs to me that Dave hadn't been the biggest fan of the *Left Behind* series, and his crack actually sounded kind of sour even when accompanied by his deep Texan laugh. (When I check my notes later that evening, I discover with horror that Dave had also observed of the prolific *Left Behind* authors that "they're just milking it for all they can get out of it.") Tim looks at me without the slightest trace of amusement, and I find it hard in that moment to picture Dave and Tim sharing a laugh about this. "I think that's a joke," he says frigidly.

Just as I'm starting to despair of the interview, I stumble on a topic that gets Tim excited. I mention some of the people I've already interviewed, and I suggest that Tim must enjoy his status as the grand old man of the modern Bible prophecy movement. But he snags on one name that I've dropped—John Hagee—and bids me to come closer. "Many of us have been drinking at the same trough," he says quietly. "But I've become a little concerned about John . . ."

TIM FIRST HEARD about the Rapture when he was nine years old. His father had suffered a massive heart attack, and Tim remembers listening to his uncle, a pastor, giving the eulogy at the funeral. "This is not the last of Frank LaHaye," the sermon began. "One day he will be resurrected by the shout of our Lord; we will be translated to meet him and our other loved ones in the clouds and be with them and our Lord forever." This promise— that Tim would meet his father in the air during the Rapture— was "the only hope for my broken heart that day." He remembers that the sun broke through the clouds just as his uncle finished speaking.

Tim was born in Detroit in 1926 to a religious family that was buffeted by Frank's sudden death and the Great Depression. He didn't leave Michigan until he was eighteen, when he joined the air force and shipped out to Europe. After serving as a tail gunner in a B-29, flying over Germany, he returned to the U.S. in

1946 to continue his education. He chose the ultraconservative Bob Jones University in South Carolina for his undergraduate degree.

Bob Jones still makes headlines. In the 2000 presidential campaign, George W. Bush was forced to apologize for giving a talk at the university because of its ban on interracial dating. In the 1940s, when racial segregation was the rule rather than the exception, Bob Jones stood out in other ways. Tim fell in love with another student from Michigan, Beverly Ratcliffe, but until they were married they had to observe a strict code of conduct: dating students were expected to observe a "no touching" rule, which insisted on at least six inches of distance between the couple at all times.

After marriage and graduation, Tim and Beverly spent a few years in a series of small churches in South Carolina and Minnesota. But it was their move to San Diego in 1958 that positioned them as key figures on the Religious Right. In the 1950s and 1960s, southern California was becoming a hotbed of the national conservative movement. Ronald Reagan became state governor in 1966, and California native Richard Nixon captured the White House two years later.

Before the 1950s, the Republican Party had been a sort of political country club: dominated by powerful families and old money, the party groomed America's homegrown aristocrats for a career in Washington. But a new crop of politicians from the Sunbelt—epitomized by Nixon and the Arizona firebrand Barry Goldwater—shook things up after 1960. Goldwater won the Republican nomination for the presidency in 1964 by accusing Lyndon B. Johnson of being soft on communism, even though LBJ had just chosen to escalate the war in Vietnam. He lost heavily to President Johnson in the general election, but four years later Richard Nixon was elected president. For fourteen of the twenty years after 1968, the United States was led by a Republican conservative from southern California.

But Tim's entry into politics wasn't as straightforward as you might expect. By the time he got to California he was already a paid-up Rapture believer, a staunch opponent of world government and the other signs of the Antichrist's emergence. Since Marx and Lenin had openly yearned for a global socialism, Tim identified easily with the militant anticommunism of the era. Soon, his blend of conspiracy theories, religion, and patriotism led him toward the unnerving right-wing fringe group known as the John Birch Society.

The society was founded in 1958 in Indianapolis by an eccentric confectioner named Robert Welch, Jr. During the 1940s and 1950s, Welch made a fortune from Sugar Daddies and Junior Mints. When he retired from his candy empire, Welch created the John Birch Society as an alternative to the Republicans, whom he considered to be soft on communism. Like Senator Joe McCarthy and the infamous Un-American Activities Committee, Welch believed that there were Communists and Red sympathizers all over America. President Harry Truman had been one during his tenure in the White House, Welch charged; even Republican President Dwight D. Eisenhower had probably taken orders from Moscow. The society took its name from an American spy who had been killed by Chinese Communists in 1945. Loyal Americans would honor his memory by halting the Communist advance overseas and at home.

These ideas caught on nationwide and were especially popular in southern California. By the early 1960s, as Tim LaHaye was giving speeches at training seminars for John Birch members, Robert Welch and the JBS leadership had moved a step further in their conspiracy thinking. Perhaps the Communists and Moscow were just the front men for an even deeper conspiracy, with roots that dated back hundreds of years to the secret societies of Europe. Welch began to speak of "The Insiders," a group of international businessmen, politicians, and bankers who were really directing world events. (In a neat trick, this clandestine elite had even coordinated the socialist and Communist challenge to international capitalism.) JBS members circulated a variety of names and theories to explain all this, but they kept returning to one shadowy group in particular: the Illuminati, a secret society founded in Bavaria in 1776, which had been dedicated to global domination ever since.

Back in the 1960s, when the John Birch Society openly blamed the Illuminati for the world's dangerous slide toward godlessness and global government, Tim LaHaye enthusiastically followed the party line. (Even in his recent books he's argued that the rise of global humanism isn't just an accident: instead, it's "the result of the devilishly clever scheming carried on by this secret order.") But in spite of their shared paranoia, Tim's work with the John Birch Society in San Diego soon began to backfire. To the horror of many committed JBS members, the participants in Tim's training seminars would start attending his church services on the other side of town and then abandon their posts at the society. Staunch anti-Communists were transformed into meek, apolitical evangelicals, and the JBS organizers got mad at Tim. The San Diego area coordinator marched over to Tim's church to complain about the "neutralizing" of these right-wing foot soldiers.

The problem of the "Rapture Cult," as many John Birchers referred to it, became so extreme that the society issued a pamphlet with a new warning to its members: perhaps apocalyptic Christianity was also part of the evil Illuminati plot. Tim was upset by this—not only because it turned Bible prophecy into a secular conspiracy theory but because he believed it was possible to combine End Times thinking with political engagement. The tendency of apocalyptic Christians before the 1970s, as we saw earlier, was to stay away from mainstream politics and to direct their energies and hopes toward the imminent return of Christ. Tim used to think this way himself. Back in the 1940s and 1950s, he'd faithfully heeded the advice of an old pastor who warned him about the "dirty business" of politics. He fell into the political arena by accident in the 1960s. After a long struggle with the San Diego city council, Tim's church was denied a permit for renovations, a very mundane defeat that nonetheless convinced Tim that there were powerful enemies of Christianity in the secular world of politics.

After this low-key political baptism, Tim became the visionary who believed that a different route was possible: you could embrace the idea of the Rapture and the Tribulation, but also remain politically engaged in the here and now. In spite of the bruising encounters with his colleagues in the John Birch Society, he set about crafting a new form of religious politics that would unite prophecy and activism, and would ensure that the churches were filled with people who would vote in elections with the same enthusiasm and energy as they used to embrace the apocalypse.

I HADN'T PLANNED to get Tim onto the subject of John Hagee and *Jerusalem Countdown*, but he's extremely keen to get his point across. "You've read his latest book," he says, "where he's talking about the Jews who don't have to believe in Jesus as the son of God?"

I don't think this is exactly what Hagee's saying in *Jerusalem Countdown*, but I can see how Tim might get this impression. "The dual covenant theory?" I ask.

"Yeah," he replies. "That's nuts!" He cuts at the air with his right hand, a heavy black ring flashing past my face. "I've never heard that before. And I think it's heresy. Without Jesus, I don't care whether you're a Jew or a Gentile or whatever you are, you're not going to get saved."

Tim reminds me that Christ isn't just a man but the "specially created, virgin-born son of God." Believing in Jesus isn't optional, or something you can dodge in special circumstances, but an absolute prerequisite for salvation. We talk a little about Joel Osteen's appearance on Larry King, and Joel's reluctance to tell

Larry that he's damned unless he accepts Christ as his savior. Tim doesn't want to bundle John Hagee with Joel, though. "I think in fairness to John, he *loves* the Jews. And he hates it when the Jews take offense at something we Christians may have done or said and think that we're against them.

"And the Jews are so touchy! I was raised in Detroit among Jews, and I went to school with them, so, you know, I love them. But I know that they're very touchy. And they interpret anything that isn't for them as being biased against them. And when you say you have to be born again, you have to receive Jesus Christ, they go berserk."

For most of our interview, Tim exudes charm and the kind of cozy warmth that suggests he's a gentle soul. But here, as he considers the idea that the Jews have been given a pass by God on Christianity, or that you can get to heaven without putting your faith in Jesus, his tone changes completely and his face fills with color. Trembling a little, he looks me in the eye and says coldly: "I take vicious exception to that heretical viewpoint."

TIM'S FIRST BOOK about Bible prophecy, *The Beginning of the End*, was published in 1972 by Tyndale House, which would eventually publish *Left Behind* nearly twenty-five years later. My dog-eared, secondhand copy has a faded jacket that still looks garish: there's a photograph of Earth taken from space that has been tinted red (like the trippy sequence at the end of *2001: A Space Odyssey*), set against a bright orange background. I guess Tim and Tyndale House were hoping to capitalize on the success of Hal Lindsey's book, *The Late Great Planet Earth*, which was cleaning up in bookstores and even in supermarkets by 1972. Tim has borrowed some of Hal's tricks: just like *Planet Earth*, the book is divided into short sections arranged beneath snappy subheads ("Israel—A Miracle Nation!"). Each chapter begins with a clock face, the hands getting closer to midnight as Tim leads you through the signs of Christ's imminent return. There are plenty of other pictures to help you navigate the End Times—Jesus looms large in these, though he's a bearded, long-haired Christ with an uncanny resemblance to the man in the *Joy of Sex*, another iconic book that appeared in the same year.

Tim doesn't have Hal Lindsey's gifts as a writer. There's a tacit confession of this when, about sixty pages into the book, he simply reprints an entire chunk of *Planet Earth* (with Hal's permission) to get readers through the knotty question of Russia's place in the Book of Ezekiel. The rest of the book lays out the familiar scheme of the Rapture and the Tribulation, though there are some interesting flourishes that root you in that early 1970s moment, and remind you of Tim's anti-Communist sentiments. Soviet communism, predictably, is merely a smokescreen for the Antichrist's evil schemes of world domination. But Tim has a novel spin on that other mysterious line in Ezekiel 39, the one about God sending fire "among those who dwell in the coastlands." In *Jerusalem Countdown*, John Hagee speculates that this may refer to Americans living on the coasts, who'll be punished for the general godlessness of those regions. Tim argues in his first prophecy book for a much more precise deployment of divine wrath:

> This could mean that the Communist spies who have infiltrated positions of influence in the isles (such as America, Canada, Britain, etc.) will be struck by a ball of fire. From a practical standpoint, the F.B.I. may someday get help from an unexpected source—Almighty God. Suddenly the Communists on the university campus, the security risks in government, and agents hiding elsewhere would die by fire. In one dramatic moment, God will solve the greatest internal threat to the security of the free countries of the world.

Perhaps you can imagine these fireballs streaking down the corridors of the State Department in search of Russian sympathizers, or pausing at the office doors of university professors before obliterating Noam Chomsky and Howard Zinn. With the Communist fifth column destroyed, and the Soviet Union humbled by its disastrous attack on Israel, Tim has an unobstructed view of the endgame: the world will fall victim to the United Nations, a "gigantic exercise in futility" that will hasten the Antichrist's rise to global domination.

Unlike other prophecy preachers of more recent vintage, Tim has been publishing End Times books for thirty-five years. Today's apocalyptic Christians are united in their rejection of date setting: no one wants to look a fool by insisting that the Rapture will happen in a particular year, and the mantra from prophecy preachers is that we are living in the season of Christ's return but we can't pinpoint an exact time. But *The Beginning of the End* is now so old that some of Tim's predictions are catching up with him. Throughout the book, he returns to the First World War as a crucial event in prophecy. This was the conflict that started the prophetic countdown, he argues. It was also the war that made possible the State of Israel and the United Nations, each of which would play a crucial role in the End Times. In the final pages, Tim predicts that the generation that grew up during the First World War—people born between 1900 and 1909—will also witness Christ's return. There's the usual fuzzy math here, as Tim concedes that a "generation" may be seventy or eighty years, perhaps even longer. But he insists that we shouldn't expect "the entire generation to pass away before Jesus returns." Since the youngest of that generation will be ninety-eight by now, and we're still waiting on the Rapture, this is a rare slipup in Tim's carefully managed prophetic calendar.

THERE WAS NOTHING very political in Tim's first prophecy book, and you can imagine the brass of the John Birch Society reading *The Beginning of the End* in despair. But Tim didn't rest on his prophetic beliefs in the early 1970s. Instead, he branched out into education, science, and eventually politics. With the help of his congregation, he set up a network of Christian schools that could shelter children from the "humanistic" curriculum of the public education system in California. He also worked with the architect of the modern creationism movement, Henry Morris, to found the Institute for Creation Research in San Diego. In the past thirty years, the ICR has waged a dogged and amazingly successful effort to rehabilitate creationism in Republican circles; Tim was present at the beginning, and he's maintained an interest in the subject ever since.

Tim's interest in creationism was bound up with another odd obsession, the hunt for Noah's Ark. In 1969, he met Eryl Cummings, an evangelical Christian and amateur explorer who had been searching on Mount Ararat in Turkey for the remains of the Ark. (Cummings and other enthusiasts are known to each other as Arkeologists.) Tim became fascinated by the idea that, in spite of the forty-five hundred years that had passed since the great flood in Genesis, the Ark might still be sitting in a glacier waiting to astonish a skeptical world. After volunteering his services as pastor on an upcoming expedition (which was eventually canceled due to a lack of funds), Tim paired with John Morris—son of Henry Morris, and now the president of the Institute for Creation Research—and wrote a book about this exciting topic.

The Ark on Ararat (1976) isn't as loopy as it might initially seem. Or rather, it is that loopy, but there's a logic to Tim's involvement. Mainstream science has discredited the old creation timeline from the Book of Genesis, which holds that the world was created in 4000 BC and that the flood took place about fifteen hundred years later. Christians who stick to this traditional timeline are known as "Young Earth" creationists, and not all advocates of creationism or "intelligent design" believe in this old-fashioned timetable of human development. What's at stake here isn't so much timing as method. If Tim and the creationist movement can uncover the Ark, then they'll have incontrovertible evidence that our secular, scientific explanations for how the world changes over time—evolution and geology—are wrong. God will again be recognized as paramount, the Supreme Being who created the world supernaturally and will soon return to judge it.

Unlike some of the later books of the Bible, which feature wars and power struggles for which we can find some archaeological evidence, the story of Noah belongs to that misty period which even many committed Christians see as more mythological than historical. Modern science makes things harder still for the biblical literalists. If Noah's Ark really settled on the slopes of Mount Ararat, perhaps twelve thousand feet or more above sea level, what happened to all the water when the flood receded? (Tim's answer—that the ocean floors were created abruptly by God at this moment—flies in the face of modern geology.) And how did Noah manage to build a four-hundred-foot boat? The Chinese had pulled off this trick by the fifteenth century, way ahead of Western engineers. It would have been truly miraculous for Noah to figure this out nearly four thousand years earlier.

God could have helped him, of course, though here the picture gets even fuzzier. The problem with a recourse to divine assistance, as Tim knows well, is that it tends to drain away some of the credibility of the story. Creationists and advocates of "intelligent design" like to say that their theories are compatible with scientific observation and reasoning—if you need God to keep bailing you out with miracles, then you're losing the battle. So Tim looks for down-to-earth explanations of how a wooden boat might still be perfectly preserved after spending so long in the ice; he uses a theory of migration to explain how the entire animal kingdom may have naturally sent representatives to Noah during the 120 years in which he was building his massive vessel; and, most impressively, he does a labor analysis to determine that, even with only a few family members to help him out, Noah could have completed all the work on the Ark in only eighty-one years. (This would leave thirty-nine years "for vacations" and other business.)

Is there any evidence to suggest that the Ark might actually be up on Mount Ararat? Tim and his co-author keep getting close to their quarry, but the clues disappear just when they seem to be within reach. An Armenian guide told a credulous creationist in 1920 that he'd seen the Ark twice during hikes on the mountain. (His uncle had actually fired his rifle at the wreck, but didn't even scratch its strange surface.) During World War II, the Tunisian edition of the U.S. military's *Stars and Stripes* newspaper ran a cover story that featured a picture of the Ark taken by a couple of American airmen; the airmen and the newspaper have since disappeared. Photos were handed around in a Bible study class in California around 1940, but now they're gone. A group of public school alums *swear* that a picture appeared in a New York State geography textbook in 1950 (one student remembered that "the planking on the sides seemed quite visible"), but no one can locate the book. And then there's the Turkish Airlines calendar which definitely featured a photo of the Ark on Ararat. Also vanished.

The Russians, who used to have a front-row seat on Mount Ararat when Armenia was a part of the USSR, are part of the problem for Arkeologists. Tim notes that Soviet communism and atheism would be discredited if the Ark shows up, and he thinks that the Reds have a secret file in which they've buried their "considerable" knowledge of the Ark's resting place. Perhaps they've gone even further. *The Ark on Ararat* reprints a dark accusation torn from an American newspaper headline in 1974:

CHRISTIAN-HATING COMMUNISTS
DIG UP NOAH'S ARK AND BURN IT

Tim thinks that this story is "very interesting," though he's got his doubts about its authenticity; for one thing, its accompanying suggestion that the Ark had thirty frozen animals in the hold seems too cute. (Tim is less suspicious of the fact that the story comes from the *National Inquirer*.) But the dogged conspiracist doesn't give up easily, and Tim wonders whether the tall story may have been planted in the American press by the Russians to "discourage further exploration." Unbowed by this, he and his co-author urge Christian readers to scour their attics and leaf through their family Bibles just in case one of those old photos of the Ark turns up.

You're left waiting for an apocalyptic connection in *The Ark on Ararat* until the very end of the book. Somewhere in between the various prescriptions for personal and political action to find the Ark—contact your congressional representative to insist on better relations with Turkey, and "never miss an opportunity to ask for information from a Turk"—Tim shares his belief that God may have intended to uncover the Ark just before the End Times. There are plenty of parallels between the flood and our own times. Noah lived in an age of unprecedented wickedness, and God resorted to planetary destruction in order to purge the earth of its prideful inhabitants. Jesus made the connection between the age of Noah and the End Times in his apocalyptic prophecy on the Mount of Olives, and Tim thinks that the rediscovery of the Ark may be our last warning before the Rapture and the rise of the Antichrist.

Although Tim didn't talk much about the Ark in the 1980s and 1990s, he has revisited the subject in his new fiction series. The *Babylon Rising* novels, which began appearing in 2003, feature a Bible scholar and archaeologist (a sexier version of Randall Price) who ventures to Mount Ararat just before the Rapture and discovers the Ark. Even if this fictional scenario doesn't come true, Tim is convinced that the Ark will make an appearance during the Tribulation. The "trumpet judgments" of the Book of Revelation will melt the glacier that has encased the secret for so many thousands of years. Whether any of us will be paying attention at that point, as we deal with devastating earthquakes and the tyranny of the Antichrist, is another question.

————

IN THE 1970S, Tim went from being a local pastor to being a national political figure. Along the way, he produced more than a dozen books that seemed to have little to do with Bible prophecy, or with each other. In 1971, he published *Transformed Temperaments*, an unusual effort to combine personality testing with Christian evangelism. In 1978, two years after *The Ark on Ararat*, he wrote a book called *The Unhappy Gays*, demonstrating how homosexuals are—in spite of their name—a morose bunch. And in 1980, he wrote *The Battle for the Mind*, a book about the "subtle warfare" between Christianity and its "invisible enemy," secular humanism. In the middle of all this, he and Beverly also collaborated on what must be one of the oddest books of the decade, an eye-wateringly explicit Christian sex manual called *The Act of Marriage*. When he wasn't at his desk working on these and other books, Tim was helping Jerry Falwell build the Moral Majority, the religious lobbying group founded in 1979, which helped to establish the influence of the Religious Right on American politics.

Not many people have written a sex manual and a book about Noah's Ark, but Tim covered an astonishing range of topics back then. He also did a fair bit of research to prepare his various studies, especially *The Unhappy Gays*. According to Tim's preface, Tyndale House decided that "the Christian community needs a penetrating book on homosexuality" and asked Tim if he'd write one. He agreed, basing his work on his own experience counseling gay church members and on some intrepid reporting in the San Diego area. Tim spent time at the local zoo, talking to the keepers about whether homosexuality was a natural phenomenon in the animal kingdom. ("At the San Diego Zoo, acts of sodomy are said to be unknown among primates.") Going undercover, he also ventured into the city's gay bars in the hope of witnessing "homosexual life as it really is."

Tim was pushing fifty in 1978, but from his author photos I

reckon he could have fit in during these walks on the wild side. (On the back of his 1971 book, *Transformed Temperaments*, Tim's wearing a loud, brown floral shirt and what appears to be a white PVC safari jacket, complete with silver pocket clasps and enormous triangular collars.) Cruising the haunts of San Diego's gay community, Tim claimed to have "seen them in action" and brought back this chastened report: "I can assure you—it's a different world!" His adventures enabled him to compile a vocabulary of gay life, which he offered to his readers as a way of deciphering what their friends, neighbors, or even family members were up to. A couple of examples:

Butch: A masculine or super-masculine homosexual. Many wear boots, leather clothing, or extremely tight-fitting clothing that show off their muscles and emphasize their genitalia.

Trouble: Butch that may cause trouble.

In recent years, Tim's been asked by journalists about *The Unhappy Gays* and he hasn't backed away from its findings or its approach. According to a recent *Time* magazine interview, he considers the book to be "a model of compassion." You could read it that way, in the sense that Tim's interested in "saving" gays from their sins and converting them to a straight lifestyle. But he sees homosexuality itself as "ungodly, vile, against nature, and shameful." Tim thinks that it "leads inevitably to a 'reprobate mind,' that is a mind with a conscious bent toward sinning."

One of the more disconcerting aspects of *The Unhappy Gays* is Tim's certainty about the psychological roots of homosexual behavior. After styling himself as a personality expert following the success of *Transformed Temperaments*, he confidently devises diagrams to explain how good people might be drawn to the dark side:

THE FORMULA FOR PRODUCING A HOMOSEXUAL

A Predisposition
Toward Homosexuality
+
That First
Homosexual Experience
×
Pleasurable and Positive
Homosexual Thoughts
+
More Homosexual
Experiences
×
More Pleasurable
Thoughts
=
A Homosexual

I don't know how he figured out the details—why are some of these influences multiplied, while others are simply added together?—but the book is littered with more specific pointers to understanding the unhappy gay in your immediate circle. Look out for people who've been brought up by "smother mothers" and "dominant mothers," Tim warns. Also beware of onanists: "Almost every homosexual I have counseled or studied has been an early and heavy masturbator," he confides.

Tim rails against gays and their "deviant sex life," and insists that they should be prevented from teaching in schools or from holding public office. But he urges Christians not to "persecute" gays or to give up on the hope that they can be saved. There's a straightforward logic to keeping gays out of public life. Tim thinks that if American society learns to accept homosexuality, a host of bad things will follow. Gay teachers will try to turn their students into homosexuals (hence Tim's perplexing insistence that it would be better to hire a straight rapist in a girls' school than a gay man); there'll be an increase in "crimes and sadistic murders" because gays have a "much higher crime potential and tendency toward sadistic violence" than straights; and, most worrisome of all, God may take revenge on the entire nation if America accepts homosexuality as a "normal way of life." America may meet the same fate as Sodom, razed utterly from the earth for its embrace of "human depravity."

What does any of this have to do with prophecy? Just when you think that Tim has overcome his apocalyptic fixation, there's a surprise in the last pages of *The Unhappy Gays* that takes us back to the End Times. Tim has already suggested, in a brief aside, that there may be an international cabal of prominent gays who are pushing the world toward acceptance of the gay lifestyle. "Interestingly enough," he writes, "homosexuality is to be part of the buildup of the 'perilously evil times' that are prophesied for the last days."

Tim thinks that he's found biblical evidence of a connection between a gay upsurge and the rise of the Antichrist. According to St. Paul's second letter to Timothy, people will be "without natural affection" in the End Times (they'll be homosexuals). The Book of Daniel may offer an even more revealing clue, suggests *The Unhappy Gays*:

> Daniel 11:37 contains an interesting prediction about the anti-Christ, who is destined to rule the world just prior to our Lord's return to set up his Kingdom. "Neither shall he regard the God of his fathers, *nor the desire of women* . . ." This suggests that the anti-Christ *may* be a homosexual. If he is, that would explain the significance of the influential group of international homosexuals who are rumored to be gaining worldwide political influence.

Does it sound as if Daniel is outing the Antichrist? I'm not so sure. "He shall magnify himself above all," Daniel goes on to say. The Beast might as easily be a masturbator as a homosexual, though heavy masturbation is the slippery slope that leads to a gay lifestyle. Tim seems content once again to anchor his social agenda with Bible prophecy. If you can't get worked up about gays corrupting your children, capsizing American morality, or incurring God's wrath on the entire nation, then you need to realize that the Antichrist himself could be a part of the global gay mafia.

THIS IS THE POINT at which I get confused about prophecy and politics. Wouldn't a committed End Times believer simply batten down the hatches on learning that the Antichrist—whether he's gay, or a Communist, or both—is on the rise? Those frustrated John Birch Society officials accused Rapture enthusiasts in the 1970s of leading Christians away from political action. Of course, Tim wouldn't want gays in his own Christian school system, and he might feel the need to speak out against homosexuality to give other Americans the chance to acknowledge it as sinful. But if a gay explosion is a sign that the end is approaching, why would a committed apocalyptic Christian want to avert this outcome?

And yet *The Unhappy Gays* concludes with a political pep talk and a rejection of Christian passivity. "Somehow the prophecies of the 'perilous times' for the last days have immobilized the Christian community at a crucial time," Tim laments. If Christians work together, and enter the political realm, they can slow down the prophetic clock and postpone the emergence of the Antichrist. "God can yet save America from this onslaught of perversion," Tim insists, and he directs born-again Christians to write to their "local, state, and national leaders opposing any further leniency toward homosexuality," and to "vigorously campaign to elect Christians to public office."

"What is the future of America? It is entirely up to you!" That's the last line of *The Unhappy Gays,* and it's a useful reminder that Tim LaHaye's political influence has been based more on his withdrawal from the apocalyptic cliff edge than on trying to speed up the End Times saga through political action. Tim likes to walk along that precipice and to point out what lies far below in the abyss of the Tribulation, but he eventually entered politics because he wanted to use that bleak view to promote moral revival in America. Instead of becoming transfixed by the Rapture, Tim effectively embraced the Tribulation as a cautionary tale. Of course, he's an apocalyptic Christian with a very powerful commitment to politics. But, paradoxically, politics has become a way for him and his followers to postpone the triumph of the Antichrist and to keep God on America's side for a few more years.

I'M NOT SURE Tim has worked all this out. Back in Denver, when I ask him about the relationship between politics and prophecy, he gives me a tangled answer. Should Christians simply watch what's going on around them, as the prophetic narrative draws closer to the Rapture and the Tribulation? Or should they spend their energies opposing the global religion, global government, and global economy that will give the Antichrist his opportunity to enslave the planet?

"I've written several books that encompass that. I don't think it can be your hobbyhorse. I'm not going to spend the rest of my life speaking out against the global religion ... I'd be more inclined to speak out against the global religion because it damns the souls of men. But the global government—and the economy—I'm not an economist, I know the Trilateral Commission has got the idea now ..."

Tim trails off. Where is this going? We agree that the Antichrist might already be among us, that he could already be pulling the strings of global government. "But as a Christian," I ask him, "it seems as if you can't do anything about the Antichrist because this is going to play out according to God's scheme. Right?"

"That's right. But it's not necessarily God's scheme; it's God's forecast of what's going to happen. That's what prophecy is. I hope you will use in your book the simplest definition of prophecy: it's history written in advance."

Doesn't that mean you should stay out of politics because God's already figured out how the world is going to end? Tim sits up in his seat and interrupts me before I can finish the question.

"Well, wait a minute. I'm not . . . that's one of the places where we would have a disagreement with the English, with the British. Particularly the Christians who are kind of pacifists. We're not pacifists. We believe that we have a God-given, citizenship responsibility to become informed at election time and register and vote." Tim's looking really tired now, but he plows ahead with this, determined to bury my suggestion that apocalyptic thinking leads away from political action. "I think it is a sin against God and our country if we don't use our free enterprise system—free franchise system—to go out and vote."

Tim has been wrestling with this paradox for more than three decades: although he's tremendously excited about the Rapture, he's asked people to vote against homosexuality, abortion, and secular education in the hope that they can postpone the triumph of global humanism—and, by extension, the coming of the Antichrist himself. Back in the 1960s and 1970s, Tim's critics in the John Birch Society complained that Bible prophecy was itself an Illuminati conspiracy. When he eventually reflected on this accusation in a 1992 book, Tim hit back by trumpeting his political achievements:

In fact, one reason the Illuminati conspirators are running far behind their schedule to usher in the new world order is that the Religious Right in the 1980s registered and got out the vote of a record number of evangelical Christians in the election of President Ronald Reagan. His election didn't solve all our national problems; it wasn't intended to. But it lit the way for other Christians who could turn the conspirators back another decade.

As I'm talking to Tim about all this, I remember what he said at the start of our conversation: "I enjoy life so much. And I've got so much to do." Even while he continues to assure Americans in the *Left Behind* books that their days are numbered, he has found a way to pull back from the brink and concentrate his political energies on the here and now. When John Hagee pushes for a military confrontation with Iran, and mentions Ezekiel's war as a possible consequence, this sounds scarily like an apocalyptic manifesto. For Tim LaHaye, you could easily argue the reverse: that the apocalypse works as a kind of aversion therapy, an outcome that can be held off if enough Christians leap into the political arena.

THERE'S A SCHOOL of thought that identifies Tim LaHaye as the mastermind of the Religious Right, a man who has done more than anyone to bring evangelical Christianity into the political mainstream. In the 1970s and 1980s, he proved himself to be a visionary by reconciling evangelical Christianity with political action. Even a partial list of the organizations that he created or helped to shape is impressive: Californians for Biblical Morality, the Moral Majority, the Council for National Policy, the American Coalition for Traditional Values. Tim's influence faded for a while in the late 1980s, when he came under fire for his links to the controversial Korean evangelist Sun Myung Moon, and for some scathing remarks about the Catholic Church. But the *Left Behind* phenomenon once again revived his fortunes in the late 1990s, just as the Republican Party perfected its strategy of building election victories on a secure foundation of Christian voters. Tim's Council for National Policy has routinely interviewed Republican presidential hopefuls in recent years, and grilled George W. Bush on his evangelical credentials at the start of the 2000 campaign.

With all this success, and given the rock star status he enjoys among younger Republicans who have brought their religious faith to Washington, you could easily imagine Tim as a kind of apocalyptic Karl Rove, the Bible prophecy Svengali with the ear of the White House and a hand on the levers of power. But when I finally catch up with him in Denver, he seems as alienated and embattled as any of the prophecy writers that I've met on my travels. I suppose this is the kind of thing you could fake, but I find it hard to convince Tim that he's actually in the driving seat when it comes to culture and politics, in spite of the successes of the Religious Right and more than a decade of Republican dominance in Washington after the 1994 elections. "In America," he tells me, "we have some of the most powerful newspaper engines that the mind ever invented, and they're controlled by five major corporations." This sounds like Chomsky or Bill Moyers, until Tim gets to the part about secular humanism. "And they're all super-liberal. I think they're liberal socialists. They don't believe in God, they believe man evolved, and that man is autonomous and independent of God, and that there's no one up there telling them what's right and wrong."

In spite of the enormous success of *Left Behind* and the election victories of George W. Bush, Tim clings to a stark paranoia about the liberal undercurrent of American society. Back in 2000, he published a book called *Mind Siege* about the dangers of secular education and "postmodernism." Although he'd explored these ideas before, the book begins with a striking prologue, "It Could Happen . . . ," which seems to be borrowed from a *Left Behind* novel. An ordinary Christian named Bruce Van Horn lives a quiet life in the near future. Bruce becomes concerned about his teenage son, and bribes him with baseball tickets to report on what's happening in his school. It's not a pretty picture. Science teachers relentlessly attack Christianity and assign anti-creationist textbooks by "some Harvard dude." (The biologist Stephen Jay Gould.) History teachers insist that the Founding Fathers were all slaveholders. The kids are subjected to endless visits from Captain Condom, the promiscuous sex educator. And, in a chilling twist, a small group of Christian students is actually abducted from the schoolyard by a SWAT team for the crime of distributing pamphlets promoting intelligent design.

The idea of Christians being disappeared by a godless police state may seem farfetched, but I'm convinced that Tim's fear of a creeping, crippling humanism is real. Perhaps Bible prophecy is partly to blame for this. Tim looks around at our shrinking world and he feels a shiver of recognition, as if Revelation is being realized in every newspaper story of technological progress and economic integration. He's been looking for the secret rulers of the world for more than five decades: the Communists, perhaps, or the Illuminati who lurk behind them. All the while, he has carefully collected clues suggesting that something sinister is afoot. Jimmy Carter selects a vice president in 1977, Walter Mondale, who turns out to be a humanist. Ted Turner, the founder of CNN, tells the American Humanist Association in 1990 that Christianity "is a religion for losers." Bill Clinton keeps his job after the Lewinsky scandal because Ted and his liberal media friends use their power to shape public opinion. (In a chance encounter in the early 1980s, Ted Turner allegedly told Tim that "television is more powerful than the government—it elects the government.")

Tim hasn't tried to persuade the federal government to hasten the apocalypse through its actions at home or abroad. But he sees his political rivals in apocalyptic terms, and talks about the culture wars in America as skirmishes with the Antichrist, or at least with his advance guard. The irony in all this is that the tens of millions of liberal Americans who defend gay rights, abortion access, or the United Nations appear in Tim's schemes as unwitting pawns of Satan. As long as liberals try to remove God from the political debate, and insist that American history mandates the separation of church and state, Tim and his political followers will see the footprints of the Antichrist everywhere.

DURING MY CHAT with Tim, I console myself with the fact that he hasn't followed John Hagee and Hal Lindsey down the path of confrontation with Islam. Or so it seems, since he's entrenched in the old school idea that humanism (rather than jihad) will be the Antichrist's weapon in his global takeover. I ask Tim if there's even a chance that Islam will become the one-world religion prophesied in Daniel and Revelation, and he rules this out. "My understanding would be, Ezekiel 38 and 39, Islam is going to continue getting bigger and bigger, and they'll go down to Israel to snuff them out."

"Islam will go down to Israel"? But before I can ask him to clarify this, Tim's tone changes and he sounds like John Wayne. "And God will *wipe* the Arab world out, in one demonstration of his power. There are eight times in that passage of scripture where it says that 'all the world will know that I am the Lord.' Can you imagine, if everyone in the world, on CNN or whatever, saw all those armies coming down to Israel, and then all of a sudden they see the phenomenon of all phenomena, and all of the armies are wiped out?" Tim tells me that this will finally embarrass sacrilegious thinkers like the eighteenth-century philosopher David Hume, whom he pointedly identifies as "an Englishman," in case I'm not paying attention. (I'm relieved to report that Hume was from Scotland.) While generations of secular thinkers have embraced the argument that "Jesus Christ was not supernatural," Tim assures me that this impious presumption will meet its end in the same fires that consume the "Arab world" and Islam.

In our conversation, the Middle East seems like an afterthought in Tim's apocalyptic career. He's drawn his political energy from the End Times narrative, but he's tried to reshape American society rather than force the nations of the Middle East to initiate the prophetic sequence. This isn't to say that he's had no influence on American foreign policy. His steadfast opposition to the United Nations plays into the general aversion of the Republican Party toward international cooperation and alliances, a trend that has helped to isolate America from the rest of the world since the end of the Cold War. But given Tim's focus on social issues—and his implicit suggestion that the apocalypse can be held back, if America is remade as a Christian society—he seems like a more subdued presence in the post–9/11 debate about Israel, Islam, and America's role in the Middle East. Perhaps that's why he was so ready in our conversation to go after John Hagee, who'd been forced into theological gymnastics ("That's nuts!") by his ardor for Israel and his determination to initiate the Jerusalem countdown.

Tim's PR rep wanders back to our table and tells me to wrap up. I shake Tim's hand, and in spite of his tiredness, he gives me one more bit of advice. "Keep up the good work, and remember this. The best way to reach the minds of people is the printed page. God chose the printed page to communicate with mankind. So how can you improve on that?"

LATER THAT SUMMER, as Israel waged its nasty war with Hezbollah in Lebanon, I saw Tim and Jerry again, but this time they were on television. *Good Morning America* invited the *Left Behind* authors to New York to discuss whether the End Times were actually being realized in the Middle East. ABC's Robin Roberts cheerily introduced Tim and Jerry as "America's favorite authors of the Apocalypse," as if the End Times were a breakfast cereal. Then the producers flashed up the caption for the segment: "APOCALYPSE NOW: IS THE END NEAR?"

Tim and Jerry seemed surprised to be in the studio in the first place, and there was something surreal about the segment. Tim was wearing a shiny silver jacket and looking a little nervous.

Jerry seemed more laid-back; but behind his shoulder, looming menacingly in the background, was a yellow peanut wearing a top hat. Mr. Peanut, the corporate mascot of Planters, must have been positioned strategically on the opposite side of Times Square to catch the cameras in the *Good Morning America* studio. But with his spats, his white gloves, and his fixed grin, he could very easily have been one of the Illuminati.

Robin Roberts, meanwhile, seemed giddily excited at the prospect that the world was coming to an end. "When we see what's going on in the Middle East," she asked, "there are many people that believe it's just not by coincidence. How do you feel?" Tim and Jerry were happy to follow this line of questioning, and eventually they had to rein in their host:

> TIM: There's no alternative. You either accept Jesus, or you're going to go through terrible times.
>
> ROBIN: As my mom often says, you better get right—better get right in these times that we're living in.
>
> TIM: Amen.
>
> ROBIN: You see what's going on, the bombing in Haifa and Israel. And it's so close to the valley of Armageddon. And when you think about that and people see these and think about . . . is it indeed Armageddon?

For a brief moment, I was glad that Tim and Jerry were the experts here, rather than Robin. She seemed quite ready to pour the vials and sound the trumpets right there in the studio. Jerry eventually stepped in.

> JERRY: Well, we feel Armageddon comes later. But the big thing is, this is keeping the discussion on the table.

Throughout the five-minute conversation, the producers cut away from Tim and Jerry to run footage of the war in Lebanon, the devastation that followed Hurricane Katrina in New Orleans, people being swept up in the Indian Ocean tsunami of December 2004, and even an ice shelf falling into the ocean. (Robin missed her chance to ask Tim and Jerry how they felt about global warming.) These pictures of real events, along with Robin's sympathetic questions, only confirmed the connection between the world's problems and the devastating predictions of Bible prophecy. By the end of the segment, as Robin thanked Tim and Jerry for their "insight" into these questions, the viewers of *Good Morning America* could be forgiven for thinking that even if Armageddon was coming a little later than Robin had suggested, it was certainly on the way.

Epilogue

An Intercept from God

Most of the prophecy enthusiasts I've spoken with have one big limitation: they haven't successfully managed to predict *anything*, in spite of their claims that the Bible foretells the future. The world is coming to an end, yes; but whenever they get more specific—John Hagee's warning about a nuclear showdown with Iran before September 2006, for example, or Tim LaHaye's claim that the World War I generation would live to see the return of Christ—their predictions become embarrassing and are silently discarded.

What if an apocalyptic Christian guessed right for a change? What if he persuaded some people in Washington that he could actually predict the future on the basis of Bible prophecy?

The unlikely seer in question is a thirty-nine-year-old Washington insider named Joel Rosenberg. Joel, who was raised Jewish but is now an evangelical Christian, seemed almost completely lacking in prophetic insight during his early career as a political consultant. A case in point: he used to work for Steve Forbes, one of the more underwhelming presidential candidates in recent

memory. Forbes, whose grandfather founded the business magazine that still bears the family name, ran for the White House in
1996 and 2000 and was comprehensively defeated on each occasion. Michael Moore once made fun of him for his unsettling ability to speak for minutes in public without blinking. (Interestingly,
the actor Robert Powell once observed that he'd mastered this
trick before taking the title role in *Jesus of Nazareth*.)

If you could see the future in the late 1990s, you'd have backed
George W. Bush. Joel picked Forbes instead, and then moved on
to work for another big name: Benjamin Netanyahu, the former
prime minister of Israel, who decided to mount a campaign for
his old job at almost the exact moment that Steve Forbes dropped
out of the U.S. presidential race in 2000. Joel was looking for another campaign position. Netanyahu liked Joel. The two men decided to work together. Netanyahu was promptly muscled out of
the race by Ariel Sharon, and Joel had to add another campaign
defeat to his CV.

Then something odd happened. Joel decided in late 2000
that he would quit working on campaigns and take up a new
line of work: writing Bible prophecy thrillers. Within two years,
he'd signed a major book deal and published his first apocalyptic
bestseller, *The Last Jihad*. By 2006, he'd sold more than a million
copies of his four novels, and he'd become a fixture on Fox and
other news networks as a "Middle East expert" with particularly
strong views about Iran.

Along the way, he'd picked up a lot of press attention for a simple reason. His first novel, which he wrote in early 2001, opened
with a hijacked plane crashing into an American city in a kamikaze terrorist attack. Since the book wasn't actually published
until 2002, the media didn't immediately register Joel's uncanny
prediction. But newspapers and TV shows eventually woke up
to Joel when they found out about his accompanying plotline. In
The Last Jihad, the United States responds to the kamikaze attack
by invading Iraq and removing Saddam Hussein.

———

WHEN I CALL JOEL at his house in Washington, D.C., I ask him how he had the nerve to abandon his political career and turn to prophetic thrillers. I tell him that my wife would kick me out of the house if I pulled the same trick.

"Well, that was a concern," Joel admits. "I was helping candidates lose campaigns, but I was still making money. I wasn't sure that helping more candidates lose would be a long-term career for me, and I was ghost writing, but once you've ghost written for Rush Limbaugh and Sean Hannity and Steve Forbes, I was running out of major players to help.

"So, honestly, I began to pray about it. I sat down with my wife and my children, right before bed, this is now January of 2001, and I explained what I wanted to do. But I said, Daddy has never written a novel before, and Daddy doesn't know how, and Daddy isn't exactly sure what the story is. But apart from having no experience and no story, this is the plan for the family." (Joel delivers this part in an affecting deadpan.) "So I said here's what we're going to do. We're going to pray every night. Jeremiah 33:3—'Call to me and I will answer you, and I will show you great and mighty things that you do not know.' And I said, that's the verse for Daddy."

He threw himself into the novel, and within a week he had the idea for the suicide attack, eight months before Mohamed Atta and his colleagues steered their jets into the World Trade Center and the Pentagon. When he'd finished the opening section, Joel showed it to his wife. "She was a little skeptical of this whole venture, but she read the first three chapters and said, 'Oh my gosh, you can really do this. You should send this to somebody, try to get an agent.' So we began to pray with the kids. 'Kids, we need an agent.' They said, 'Great, what's an agent?' So I sent those three chapters to a friend, Peggy Noonan, who worked for President Reagan and President Bush."

Peggy Noonan wrote some of the best-known speeches of Ronald Reagan and George H.W. Bush. After a stint as a consultant on *The West Wing*, she worked on George W. Bush's reelection campaign in 2004. When she got Joel's manuscript, she sent him to an agent at William Morris who had worked with Mario Puzo on *The Godfather*, and Joel finally found his way to Tom Clancy's agent. "So I said, 'Kids, you're doing good! Keep up the prayers!'"

Then September 11 happened. Although Joel had shopped around his chapters before the attacks, he now thought the book was doomed. "No one's going to want to read a book or sell a book that opens with a kamikaze attack on the United States, least of all a publisher in New York City; these people have just lived and died through this. So it wasn't entertainment anymore, it was too raw, it was too real, it was too painful."

Joel put the book aside until he and his wife watched President Bush's State of the Union address in January 2002. This was the famous speech in which Bush named his Axis of Evil—Iran, Iraq, and North Korea. Joel nearly fell out of his chair. After all, *The Last Jihad* connected the suicide attack with an invasion of Iraq, and now it seemed that President Bush was on the same wavelength. "My wife and I looked at each other as if we were in an episode of *The Twilight Zone*, because up to that point only my novel and I think Paul Wolfowitz were talking about any connection between 9/11 and a possible war with Iraq. And so my agent called back the next day and said, 'Do you work for the CIA?'"

Joel's career as a prophecy novelist was back on track.

The Last Jihad was quickly sold to a big publisher. Soon after its release in the fall of 2002, it hit number one on Amazon.com and spent eleven weeks on the *New York Times* bestseller list. Joel published the sequel, *The Last Days*, a year later, and that novel's description of an American diplomatic convoy coming under fire in the Gaza Strip was also uncannily accurate. Two weeks before the book reached the shops, three American security guards were killed in Gaza by a roadside bomb as they escorted diplomats to a meeting. This was the moment at which *U.S. News and World Report* dubbed Joel a "modern Nostradamus," a moniker that Joel keeps denying but also can't help repeating.

I'M NOT SURPRISED to hear that Joel got interested in prophecy by reading Tim LaHaye. Around 1992, he was settling into his first Washington job at the Heritage Foundation, the leading right-wing think tank in America. He came across a copy of Tim's 1984 book, *The Coming Peace in the Middle East*, and he was intrigued by the discussion of Russia, Israel, and the End Times. I wonder how a nerdy Washington conservative got hold of a copy of Tim's apocalyptic manifesto, and Joel tells me that his wife actually worked for the LaHayes back then.

Tim and Beverly LaHaye had a Washington pad, so they could be close to the political action. Tim offered Joel's wife a job, but then Beverly poached her to work for Concerned Women for America. The Rosenbergs had found their entrée into the world of apocalyptic politics. "And so really I got to spend personal time, and social time, and obviously as you can imagine Dr. LaHaye and I hit it off," Joel tells me. "Totally different generations, and different backgrounds in every possible way, but he was one of the world's foremost experts on Bible prophecy." Their friendship has endured ever since; they had dinner just the week before.

Joel chose to write prophetic novels rather than nonfiction books because "I didn't believe that anybody would listen to me, writing these types of things; fiction was a way of capturing people's attention." He realized that Washington insiders loved Tom Clancy books, and set out to write thrillers that would "connect the dots" (one of his favorite phrases) between today's political crises and the turmoil predicted in the prophecies of Ezekiel. When you read his novels, you'll see just how savvy this is. Unlike the *Left Behind* books, which begin with the Rapture and require a degree of Christian credulity from the get-go, there are only a few overt references to prophecy in Joel's first two books. By the time he gets to *The Ezekiel Option*, his third book, the cat is out of the bag—and the Russian bear is on the march toward Israel.

This is a neat trick. Joel reels in a more secular audience with the promise of a high-octane geopolitical novel, but then points readers toward the unavoidable conclusion that Bible prophecy is being fulfilled in current events. Skeptics abound in the books. White House staffers are wide-eyed with amazement as Christian converts insist that God is going to rain down fire from heaven and consume his enemies. "You've got to be kidding me!" they protest (another of Joel's favorite phrases), before eventually compiling position papers that nudge the president toward an apocalyptic foreign policy.

I mention the *Left Behind* spin-off series, and Joel tells me that his books are rather different. His Washington experience has given him credibility and insight into how government really works. "It's true that I've been here for sixteen years," he tells me, "so I do know a lot of people in this city, and there are people who know of me, not directly, but I worked for someone they knew. So there's maybe an accessibility that I have because I'm not a theologian and I'm not a pastor and I don't live in Texas or California, I'm right here."

Joel's achievement has been to give Bible prophecy a kind of yuppie cool. He's become, in effect, an apocalyptic policy wonk. Joined at the hip to his BlackBerry, he talks about his excitement when it starts to buzz with a news update that may relate to the End Times sequence. On his Web site, www.joelrosenberg.com, you can get "real-time intel," which Joel posts from all over the world—he might upload something about Putin from a Moscow hotel room, for example, or speculate upon Syrian troop maneuvers from an Internet café in the Golan Heights. You can also send Joel your own "intelligence," if you're in a position to provide it. (Joel talks about an "F-16 weapons system officer" who flew combat missions in the 2003 Iraq war and provided "intriguing insights" to Web site readers.) Finally, if you're too busy to keep up with the Web site or Joel's blog, you can subscribe to his e-mail alerts, which he's named FLASH TRAFFIC. (Always in capitals, as if he's getting his tips from the National Security Agency rather than the King James Version.) "They are designed for people who want to have the most important stories delivered directly to their desktop, Palm Pilots, or BlackBerrys without having to be reminded," Joel explains matter-of-factly.

Now that Bible prophecy can be delivered to your inbox without embarrassment, Joel is secure enough about his standing in Washington to produce that nonfiction book he'd shied away from in 2001. In October 2006, just a couple of months after the appearance of his fourth prophecy novel, *The Copper Scroll*, Joel published *Epicenter: Why the Current Rumblings in the Middle East Will Change Your Future*. Like many other prophecy books, *Epicenter* offers the usual caveats about the influence of the Bible on current events. "My intent is not to persuade anyone of what is coming," Joel says in the introduction. On the very next page, however, he qualifies this a bit: "It is the premise of this book that the earthshaking events that lie ahead can actually be forecast with a surprising degree of accuracy."

Epicenter begins with a long account of Joel's political career, including his stint with Benjamin Netanyahu (who seems once again to have been delighted to work with apocalyptic Christians) and Israeli hard-liner Natan Sharansky. What Joel picked up from his political work is that Washington has a serious problem in obtaining and processing intelligence about future events. This is hardly an earth-shattering observation: the 9/11 Commission reported much the same thing in 2004, and the complete failure of American troops to find weapons of mass destruction in Iraq hardly suggests that the problems in intelligence gathering and analysis have been rectified. But Joel's take on this is a little different. The Book of Ezekiel, he claims, is "an intercept from the mind of an all-knowing God." What's more, it can be used "just as a CIA analyst might treat an intercept from the cell phone of a world leader—as a piece of creditable, actionable intelligence."

Joel gives me an example of how he's used biblical "intelligence" when writing his novels. When he decided to write a thriller about Ezekiel's war, he realized that two countries in particular—Egypt and Iraq—were missing from Ezekiel's opaque list of nations that join with Iran and Russia to attack Israel. "Well, Egypt—I can explain that away," he tells me, "because of the 1979 peace treaty at Camp David. But Iraq? How do I explain that? Remember, this is the fall of 2000."

"Saddam Time," I concur.

"Yeah, I mean—is Saddam at Club Med that weekend? He missed the chance to gas the Jews? You know, it wasn't realistic. So I thought I could either write the novel and put him in it, or I'll stick with the Bible and I just don't understand it, and I'll have to come up with some plausible way for Saddam not to be involved. And that's when I realized that I couldn't write *The Ezekiel Option*, the book that I wanted to write. I was going to have to back up the story and write about how Saddam is eliminated."

The prophetic intercepts guided Joel's debut novel. The United States government did the rest by going to war with Iraq in 2003, fulfilling Joel's fictional prophecy and bringing the world into closer alignment with the scenario in Ezekiel 38 and 39. Perhaps it's no surprise that this has puffed Joel up. In *Epicenter*, he makes a lot of his own prescience and the limited vision of the so-called experts in Washington.

Everyone else missed the fact that Saddam was preparing to invade Kuwait in 1990, Joel tells us; but as a pipsqueak at the Heritage Foundation in the months before the August invasion, he was alarmed by the warning signs. Eleven years later, Washington was sleepwalking on the eve of September 11, while Joel was already describing kamikaze attacks in the draft chapters of *The Last Jihad*. Do you see a pattern here? "Too many in Washington today have a modern, Western, secular mind-set that either

EPILOGUE **253**

discounts—or outright dismisses—the fact that evil is a real and active force in history." Joel has policymakers clearly in his sights as he sets up the argument of *Epicenter*. "They insist on interpreting events *only* through the lenses of politics and economics. Yet to misunderstand the nature and threat of evil is to risk being blindsided by it, and that is precisely what happened on August 2, 1990, and September 11, 2001."

The American government relies traditionally upon elites and technocrats to devise its foreign policy: people with Ph.D.s in Middle Eastern Studies or extensive connections in the worlds of politics and business. These people invariably see the world as a very complex place. That's why the State Department was so anxious in 2002 and early 2003 about the war with Iraq: George W. Bush's arguments about evildoers and spreading democracy seemed too simplistic to seasoned observers. But Joel thinks that the existence of evil brings a new urgency and clarity to international affairs.

> While it is fashionable in our times to analyze world events merely by looking through the lenses of politics and economics, it is also a serious mistake, for it prevents us from being able to see in three dimensions. To truly understand the significance of global events and trends, one must analyze them not only through the political and economic lenses but through a third lens as well, the lens of scripture. Only then can the full picture become clearer.

So the "central premise" of *Epicenter* is that the Bible provides "advance warning of future events." If policymakers are willing to look, they can find evidence in the ancient prophecies of "key events and trends that will occur in certain countries," and they can make use of the same divine intercepts that have taken Joel to the top of the bestseller list.

SOME MIGHT SAY that Joel's own rationale for going to war with Iraq in his novels—that Saddam would never sit out Ezekiel's war—looks more solid than either of the Bush administration's principal arguments in 2002, which linked Saddam to 9/11 and insisted that he harbored vast reserves of WMDs. It would be absurd, though, to argue that prophetic logic had anything to do with the U.S. invasion of 2003. Perhaps it's also absurd to imagine that books like *Epicenter* have any real influence in Washington. John Hagee can march his troops into the offices of congressional representatives, but does he really have any pull on the inside of the policymaking machine? *Jerusalem Countdown* and *Epicenter* may have sold hundreds of thousands of copies, but have they had any real impact inside the Beltway?

I went into my conversation with Joel intending to focus instead on his growing career as a media pundit. Since he'd worked for Rush Limbaugh and Sean Hannity, he'd been able to secure a lot of airtime on conservative radio and on Fox News. Joel had even rearranged the publication date of *The Last Jihad* so he could work around Hannity's vacation. Two days after our conversation, Joel turned up with Jerry Jenkins in an interview with CNN; the headline at the foot of the screen read "APOCALYPSE NOW?" Here's how Kyra Phillips introduced the pair: "So, gentlemen, from books to blogs, to the back pews, the buzz is all about the End Times."

But Joel won't let me paint him as a mere pundit. "It's not just talk radio. What's interesting is the growing number of people in government that are asking me to comment, to sit down with them and explain, 'What in the world are you doing? Why do you keep seeing the future?' It's not really Christians that are getting so interested in what I'm finding here. It's government officials who are hearing about the novels, their staffers are reading them, or there's just a buzz about them, and they're saying, well, this is uncanny. In a world where most of our government leaders are so criticized for not connecting the dots, for not seeing the future, for some reason these novels have been capturing people's attention here in Washington."

I suppose Joel's right that there's a crisis of confidence among Washington's political class about America's ability to determine what's going to happen in world affairs. But surely they haven't reached the point at which they're resorting to Bible prophecy to do the work that the CIA, the NSA, or the FBI have been struggling with?

"I want to be clear. Most of the people I meet with don't believe what I believe, or they . . . they're just curious about how a person can seem to foresee coming events with a clarity that to a certain degree would be described to me as enviable. Let me give you some examples. I was invited to the White House in the spring of 2005."

Uh, the *White House?*

"Now, I wasn't invited to meet with President Bush—this was a group of staffers, and for this particular meeting it happened to be a White House Bible study. There are a number of evangelicals that meet, and they invited me to come, because they'd heard about the book, a lot of staffers had read the book. *A lot.*"

Joel pauses here to let this sink in. I haven't said anything, so he qualifies his point.

"I have absolutely no evidence that the president has, I want to be clear about that. A lot of people will say things like, Bush is being driven by these ideas. I have a letter from the president thanking me for a copy of my book, because one of the staffers asked me to sign a copy and give it to him, and I gave it to him through the staffer, but it *doesn't* say, 'I read it and I loved it!' You know."

I find myself feeling stupidly relieved that President Bush's thank-you note wasn't more effusive. But Joel has plenty of other stories about his influence in the corridors of power. Former

Homeland Security secretary Tom Ridge wrote to thank him for *The Last Days*. One of Ridge's staffers had asked Joel for a dozen copies of the book to be distributed among the principals at Homeland Security. Joel knows "senior staff" in the White House who've read his books. And at the State Department. "Interestingly enough, about three weeks ago, I was invited to go meet with a senior official at the CIA. I'd never been invited to the CIA in sixteen years, but this gentleman's wife had read the series, and said, 'Honey, this is just uncanny. You really ought to read these books, and meet with this guy, because he keeps writing books that come true.'"

As we're talking, Joel remembers other people who have recently invited him for a chat. An "Arab Muslim leader" who actually came to Joel's house to talk about prophecy. A former assistant secretary of state who asked Joel to lunch. Two dozen congressional chiefs of staff, each one the principal assistant to a congressional representative or senator, who summoned Joel to a breakfast on Capitol Hill. If people seek him out, he tells me, he's happy to "walk through" the prophecies with them. In *Epicenter*, he mentions a "high-ranking Arab government official," a Sunni Muslim, who invited him to dinner. When he'd heard Joel out, the official sighed and said: "Perhaps God has given you the key to understanding what the future holds."

These encounters have become regular events in his calendar. "This keeps happening. I was invited to meet with members of Congress, a bipartisan group. Off the record, behind closed doors. I can't tell you who was in the room."

I wonder if Joel is overselling this. "Are we talking one or two congressmen here?"

"No, this was eight. They'd heard about the novel. They were curious. I hope you won't characterize it that I'm some sort of guru who people . . . It's just that once you've written books that sell so many, and have media interest, it's 'Wow, this guy's uncanny!' And given the strange and tragic events in the Middle

East, you know perhaps it's not surprising that someone who can speak the political language and understand their world, perhaps differently than a pastor or a theologian, people would want to sit down and say, 'Just give us a sense of it. I'm not saying I agree with it, I don't want it to be in the papers, that I'm being fed all this information about prophecy, but I can't help it.'"

Although I sense that I'm onto some kind of a scoop here, Joel actually includes this story in the final version of *Epicenter*. To my surprise, and perhaps his, the papers don't follow it up.

"Literally," he tells me on the phone, "one of these congressmen, as I was explaining this, said, 'I've never heard this before. Can we just read the prophecy itself?' And so we happened to be in the Members Only lounge, there were some Bibles there, we got them out, everyone took a copy, we opened to Ezekiel 38. I said, 'Why don't I read the first five verses of the chapter; and then, Mr. Congressman, you can read the next five, and we'll just go around and cover the whole chapter, and we can discuss it.'"

HAS JOEL ROSENBERG completed the circuit between apocalyptic Christianity and American foreign policy? When Joel did that interview with CNN two days after our conversation, he'd supplied the producers with a prophecy from Zechariah that they flashed onto the screen: "When all the nations of the earth are gathered against her, I will make Jerusalem an immovable rock for all the nations. All who try to move it will injure themselves." Kyra Phillips, the smiling but increasingly unsettled anchorwoman, asked Joel to make the connection with modern events.

"What are we watching?" Joel asked. "Saddam Hussein or Iranian President Mahmoud Ahmadinejad or Hezbollah leader Nasrallah, they're all drunk with the dream of capturing Jerusalem. That's what *The Copper Scroll* is about, this intense battle to liquidate the Jewish people and liberate Jerusalem. I mean, are we seeing that happen? It's hard not to say that we are."

Joel was wearing a blue shirt, red tie, and dark jacket. President Bush often dresses like this. Joel seemed like every other conservative commentator on television—neat, articulate, ostensibly not insane.

"I mean, that's why I've gotten invited over to the CIA and the White House and Capitol Hill, because people—it's not that they necessarily believe the prophecies, but they want to understand the prophecies in the Bible in light of what's going on right now."

Kyra Phillips, who now had a look of complete bewilderment on her face, began to stab her pen in Joel's direction. "Do you think they're taking what you're saying and incorporating it into *foreign policy?*"

"I wouldn't go that far," he admitted. Kyra let out a relieved laugh at this point, as if they'd all been joking about the relationship between prophecy and politics. Joel didn't seem to think her question was amusing. "But I would say that Bible prophecy is an intercept from the mind of God. It's actually fairly remarkable intelligence, and that's why my novels keep coming true."

WHEN I PRESS JOEL directly on the political usefulness of prophecy, he's much more cautious. "I don't believe that the president or any policymaker should base their decisions on Bible prophecy," he says. "I think they have to base their decisions on American interests." This isn't just pro forma. *Epicenter* makes a long list of political predictions and tells Americans what to expect in the Middle East, but the book narrows toward a pious point. Instead of repeating his suggestion that the U.S. attack Iran's nuclear facilities, Joel concludes with three pieces of advice for the coming cataclysm. "First, have an exit strategy." That would be the Rapture: the easiest way to escape the bad times ahead is to accept Christ. "Second, have a neighborhood strategy." Ensure that your family and friends follow you and join Christ in the air before the Tribulation. "Third, have a global strategy." Support evangelism overseas, especially in those areas—like the Middle East—in which Christian missionaries face the greatest challenges.

Like every other prophecy writer, Joel is interested in winning souls. If the End Times are coming, then the need to embrace evangelical Christianity is especially urgent. But he's become part of a hawkish circle of foreign policy experts who are pressing the Bush administration to view the world through the frame of good and evil. The prophet Zechariah reassures Joel that the leaders of Iran or Hezbollah are hell-bent on capturing Jerusalem, and Ezekiel leads him to conclude that they will inevitably launch an invasion. Apocalyptic Christians like Joel and John Hagee have become mascots for conservatives who want a foreign policy that recognizes evil in the world and confronts the evildoers. No matter, it seems, that both Rosenberg and Hagee believe that the triumph of evil over America—in the shape of the Antichrist's rise to global power—is also inevitable.

Take Joel's views about Russia. He's convinced that the prophecy of "Gog and Magog" refers to the rise of a new tsar, who may or may not be Vladimir Putin. In May 2006, Dick Cheney delivered a speech in Lithuania that stunned many Western observers (and the Kremlin) by attacking Putin and his antidemocratic tendencies. The tone of the speech was extremely aggressive, and attracted a good deal of criticism in America; not least because Cheney then journeyed onward for a friendly meeting with Nursultan Nazarbayev, the dictator of Kazakhstan who'd become a useful U.S. ally in the war on terror.

In *Epicenter*, Joel also took issue with Cheney, but he focused on one of the few conciliatory things in his speech. "None of us believes that Russia is fated to become an enemy," said the vice president. Joel begged to differ: "When one looks at Russia through not only the political and economic lenses but also through the third lens of scripture, one sees that Russia is, in fact, destined to become an enemy of the West, and particularly of Israel, in part because of its alliance with Iran." Hence Joel's persistent references to Russia in his TV appearances, and his determination to paint Putin and Mahmoud Ahmadinejad as partners in crime.

Or consider the contribution of Joel and John Hagee to the conversation in the United States about the Iranian threat. Both men have appeared on Fox News as "Middle East experts" who advocate a preemptive assault on Tehran's supposed nuclear program. Astonishingly, they've been encouraged to offer this advice without being identified to viewers as apocalyptic Christians. Here's Pastor John Hagee on Fox in August 2006:

> I think the United States and Israel should keep their ear to the ground, and the moment they feel that Iran has a nuclear device they need to take out the nuclear capabilities of that country. Make no mistake, Iran will use nuclear weapons against Israel and against the United States of America.

The same month, veteran *60 Minutes* correspondent Mike Wallace secured an interview with President Ahmadinejad and assured Americans that the Iranian president was "reasonable" if combative in his views. Although Wallace pushed Ahmadinejad in the interview until the president threatened to walk out, right-wing commentators back home vilified Wallace for even talking to the Iranians. Joel Rosenberg popped up on Fox once more, billed only as "a Middle East analyst and author of numerous books." Joel had just posted an article on his blog entitled "THE LEFT IS FALLING FOR THE NEW HITLER," and he was angry at *60 Minutes* for conducting the interview in the first place. Reminding Fox viewers that Ahmadinejad had funded Hezbollah and bought missiles from Russia, he added yet another reason to be wary of Iran's president:

> People don't appreciate yet, particularly in the media—Mike Wallace for sure—or understand the evil that is rising in Iran.

And that's what I'm trying to write about in novels. That's what I'm trying to talk about: the religious, end of the world, apocalyptic mind-set that Ahmadinejad has. You can't negotiate with someone, ultimately, who believes it's his mission to end the world.

You have to admire Joel's nerve in decrying Ahmadinejad as an apocalyptic lunatic. But what interested me about this Fox appearance (and another interview with Joel on MSNBC a week earlier) is that the host made no reference whatever to Joel's own apocalyptic views.

It may be true that Mahmoud Ahmadinejad believes in the imminent emergence of the twelfth imam, an Islamic messiah who will redeem the world. The Iranian government has officially denied that this factors into Ahmadinejad's thinking about Iran's foreign or domestic affairs, but he made oblique references in a speech at the United Nations in 2005 that unsettled some observers inside and beyond Iran. At the same time, Ahmadinejad is locked in a struggle at home with the clerical establishment. The mullahs who launched the Islamic Revolution in 1979 were stunned in 2004 when Ahmadinejad—a political and religious outsider—swept to victory in the presidential election. This rivalry has given the new president an incentive to outmullah the mullahs in the battle to appear pious before the Iranian people.

A sober assessment of Iran would focus on this internal struggle for power and legitimacy, and would interpret Ahmadinejad's interest in the twelfth imam and even his saber-rattling toward Israel in this context. This isn't to say that Iran poses no threat under his leadership, or that the country should be permitted to acquire nuclear weapons, but it's clear that the political situation is complex and that the rhetorical lunges of the Iranian government aren't always about their apparent targets: Israel and the United States.

But this kind of analysis is much too nuanced for the "third lens" of Bible prophecy. Joel Rosenberg, John Hagee, and many other apocalyptic Christians see Ahmadinejad as necessarily evil, and very possibly a player in the imminent Middle East war predicted by Ezekiel. Speaking on Fox in the summer of 2006 after Israel concluded its war in Lebanon, John Hagee predicted that the region would soon resume its downward course toward Armageddon: "The moment that Israel determines that Iran has nuclear capability or buys a nuclear weapon from North Korea, they will bomb the nuclear facilities in Iran or go after Iran. And then it is really going to become intense in the Middle East." Once again, the host of the show—in this case, Neil Cavuto—neglected to identify Hagee as an apocalyptic preacher.

So Joel Rosenberg and John Hagee, whatever their caveats about the usefulness of prophecy to policymaking, have been given a prominent place in debates over how America should conduct itself in the Middle East. On numerous occasions, they've been happy to accept the role of "Middle East expert" without coming clean about their apocalyptic convictions. And they've been encouraged and feted by some of the leading lights of the American conservative movement: Sean Hannity, Rush Limbaugh, Neil Cavuto, Joe Scarborough, Peggy Noonan, and others.

I find it hard to believe that this lineup of right-wing stars has actually embraced the apocalyptic perspective. They're attracted to Hagee and Rosenberg not because they share this conviction that the world is about to end but because apocalyptic Christians bring extraordinary moral clarity to messy debates. Why worry about Iran's internal political struggles when Joel Rosenberg is on hand to confirm Ahmadinejad's evil nature, and urge the United States to bomb Iran's nuclear sites? Why linger on the tangled history of the Israeli-Palestinian conflict when Pastor Hagee is on the line from San Antonio to confirm Israel's right to the entire West Bank?

IN OUR CONVERSATION, Joel dismisses the accusation of many American liberals that the U.S. government is being overrun by apocalyptic Christians. Even though his own prophetic confidence has been bolstered by the fact that "there's some early evidence that my novels—and potentially the prophecies—are coming true," I believe him when he tells me that he isn't trying to hasten the End Times or to hijack government policy. What unnerves me, instead, is the effect of Bible prophecy on the thinking of commentators and policymakers at this especially difficult moment.

Since September 11, America has waged difficult and controversial wars against Afghanistan and Iraq and the world has seemed especially unstable. America's standing in the world has been challenged by friends and enemies alike. Critics abroad and at home have vilified the Bush administration for its actions after 9/11, and especially for the invasion of Iraq in 2003. In such a hostile climate, the apocalyptic perspective provides conservatives with a powerful and endless reminder of the existence of evil in the world. Saddam may not have had nukes, but he was *evil* and the United States should be in the business of opposing evil. While the political situation in Iraq or Israel seems to cry out for nuance and expertise— the kind of thing that the old hands at the State Department used to provide, with the benefit of their many years of training and local knowledge—none of that seems necessary when you train the "third lens" of Bible prophecy onto the world's hotspots.

Better still, apocalyptic thinking is brilliantly suited to a world in which things keep getting worse. Of course, the president of Iran is a terrible man who is determined to destroy Israel and the United States—didn't you *read* Ezekiel 38 and 39? Joel tells me in our phone conversation that "there's going to come a moment where more and more people are going to be interested in these prophecies, and these prophecies will start to unfold in a way that becomes unmistakable."

Joel insists that "we're not there yet," but "we're getting closer." He offers an analogy: "Someone takes you to Yankee Stadium and you don't know exactly when the game begins, but there's people starting to fill the stands, there's teams warming up on the

field, and you think, well, there's going to be a game here sometime today!" If one of the signs of the apocalypse is more war and
chaos, and the kind of catastrophe that America witnessed on
September 11, then a bellicose and rigid foreign policy may well
produce yet more "evidence" that the End Times are at hand.
There's a danger here that apocalyptic anxieties and convictions
will fuel an extremely destructive chain reaction: as events get
worse, so it becomes clearer that the End Times are at hand,
and Americans feel ever more justified in seeing the world as the
battleground between God and Satan, good and evil.

THE IRONY IN ALL THIS, as Hagee and Rosenberg tour the news
studios and tutor politicians on Capitol Hill, is that these apocalyptic foreign policy experts have a defiantly negative view of
America's role in the End Times. Joel's not sure exactly how many
Americans will vanish in the Rapture, perhaps just a million, perhaps a hundred times that number. Even if it's on the low end of
the scale, it'll be a much bigger number than the three thousand
who were obliterated on September 11, a day that "changed the
face of America forever." He plays this out for me as if he were
sketching the scene in a novel. (Maybe he will.) "Imagine for a
second, that you're watching the State of the Union address, and
the Rapture happens before President Bush leaves office."

By now I'm an old hand at this kind of thing. "Okay."

"Now you can agree with President Bush, disagree with him,
but he's an avowed follower of Jesus Christ. As is House Speaker
Denny Hastert."

(I interviewed Joel in July 2006. He hadn't foreseen that the
Republicans would lose control of the House of Representatives
in the November elections.)

"Vice President Cheney has never really talked much about
his faith so I don't know where he is. But imagine if the Rapture
were to happen during the State of the Union address next year.

President Bush *disappears*! Denny Hastert *disappears*! Possibly the vice president as well. The whole world's watching. Secretary Rice *disappears*! Most of the White House staff *disappears*! Numerous members of Congress, top generals, key members of our military around the world . . ."

A dark thought occurs to me. "We'll have to bring back Bill Clinton!"

Joel laughs, then thinks better of it. "I don't want to characterize anybody's faith. But as a visual for a moment, you can imagine the level of chaos that would happen, just from a few people disappearing." He tells me that there'll be no time to rebuild America before the Antichrist takes over and neutralizes his opponents. "So that's why I think that America essentially implodes; unfortunately, I too see it as a sad development, except that it would be an indication of the enormous level of faith in this country."

This reminded me of something Joel had told me earlier about the conversation he'd had over dinner with Tim LaHaye the previous week. They were discussing Joel's reasons for writing books about the period before the Rapture rather than afterward, as in the *Left Behind* series. "I agree with you about the Rapture and the events that are going to happen after," Joel told Tim. "But what really interests me is not that. I don't think I'm going to be here for that. What interests me is what might lead up to it."

Perhaps the problem isn't just with prophecy enthusiasts like Joel Rosenberg and John Hagee, but with those conservatives in the media and in Congress who've been willing to entertain the apocalyptic perspective as a way of bolstering their own political agenda. Unless these conservatives are confident that they'll be Raptured, they might consider whether they want to be on the Bible prophecy team as they engage the Middle East and Russia in coming years. Joel Rosenberg and John Hagee may be useful right now in stiffening American moral resolve, in insisting that the war on terror is an elemental struggle between good and evil, but you shouldn't expect apocalyptic Christians to advocate policies that will lead to a Pax Americana or another American century. Committed prophecy believers expect things in the Middle East to get "intense," as John Hagee put it on Fox. They also expect to be out of here before things get really nasty, which should give the rest of us second thoughts about the policies they're advocating.

I CAN THINK of a couple of ways out of all this. The world situation might improve drastically in the coming years, which would certainly blunt the predictions of those prophecy experts who have brought Ezekiel and Zechariah to bear on the Middle East. The *Left Behind* series began in 1995, so there's no reason to think that apocalyptic fervor is entirely dependent on the global crisis that followed 9/11. But it's undeniable that Bible prophecy writers both feed upon and encourage anxieties about where we're heading. If the conflicts in Iraq, Afghanistan, and Israel-Palestine are brought to an end, prophecy writers may switch their attention to the peacemaking agenda of the Antichrist, but they'll have a harder time getting on news networks and bestseller lists when they argue that Ban Ki-moon is the Beast of Revelation.

If, as seems more likely, these conflicts continue and even intensify; if the United States is again attacked by terrorists, or launches another war overseas, the resurgence of apocalyptic interest in America will only continue. The stock of commentators like John Hagee and Joel Rosenberg will continue to rise as things get gloomier on the international stage, and nonevangelicals will have to engage with prophecy enthusiasts and talk them out of their biblical standoffs with the enemies of America and Israel.

I sometimes think that liberals aren't as different from apocalyptic Christians as they might like to believe. When I was finishing this book, a poll was published in my hometown newspaper in Vancouver claiming that two-thirds of the locals—in one of the most liberal cities in North America—believed that the world was going to end in two or three generations. These people aren't on the lookout for Gog and Magog, and they're not writing checks to Israeli settlers; their paranoia feeds on global warming, or the threat of more 9/11-style attacks. Liberals seem just as willing as evangelical Christians to doubt our collective ability to ride out the coming decades, and the outlandish beliefs of many apocalyptic Christians surely feed from these same anxieties. Liberals and conservatives can find plenty of reasons to be scared about what lies ahead, and perhaps it's not surprising that so many Americans see Bible prophecy—especially the idea of the Rapture—as a much more promising escape route than the Kyoto Protocol or a phased withdrawal from Iraq.

Of course, one difference between liberal pessimism and apocalyptic Christianity is that liberals aren't looking forward to the end of the world, and many of them are struggling gamely to prevent it. But it would be a mistake to imagine that those 50 million prophecy enthusiasts are united in trying to move the doomsday clock closer to midnight. I couldn't find anyone who would admit openly to doing this. Many prophecy believers would deny that it's possible to accelerate God's timetable. They're also trying to reconcile what it means to be a citizen of this world—and an American in particular—with the responsibilities of a Christian who may be living in the last days.

The danger comes instead from those ambitious writers and pastors who apply apocalyptic ideas to politics as a way to sell books or to raise their standing in conservative circles. Tim La-Haye, John Hagee, and Hal Lindsey have moved beyond evangelism to political activism. Joel Rosenberg, on the other hand, has transformed a modest career as a political consultant into a much more successful turn as an apocalyptic writer, becoming a crossover phenomenon who addresses church groups and congressional representatives with the same End Times message. ·

These prophecy celebrities have acquired a disquieting influence in Washington. They push the United States government, and especially the Congress, toward positions on Israel and the Middle East that are wildly out of synch with the rest of the world. The idea that Israel has a biblical right to the land, or that Iran and Russia are developing a secret alliance to destroy the Jewish State, would seem fantastical to most nonevangelical observers. John Hagee and Joel Rosenberg are taking these ideas—based on a selective reading of the Bible's prophetic books—and presenting them to members of Congress and the administration as actionable intelligence. What's more, congressional representatives and government staffers are reaching out to prophecy experts, declaring their willingness to speak at meetings of Christians United for Israel or inviting Joel to stop by for a personal chat about Ezekiel.

One obvious strategy for combating this influence is to take Joel at his word, and to insist that evangelical lobbyists come clean about the ways in which their policy prescriptions are shaped by End Times presumptions. In fairness to Joel Rosenberg and John Hagee, the media could simply do a better job of reading their books and correctly identifying them as apocalyptic Christians when they're invited to discuss world affairs on TV.

There may also be reason to hope that some high-profile leaders of the Religious Right will have second thoughts about the fate of the planet. In the summer of 2006, Pat Robertson—a staunch supporter of Israel and a committed believer in the End Times—reversed his position on climate change, and admitted that environmentalists "are making a convert out of me." If apocalyptic Christians can take an interest in global warming, then perhaps some of them may shelve their doomsday thinking and commit to a more hopeful vision of the future.

FAILING THIS, the Bible has some advice about how to reason with prophecy enthusiasts. There are plenty of verses in the scriptures that warn against an obsessive focus on Christ's return.

When I ask Joel Rosenberg about this, he agrees that Christians should not "try to get ahead of ourselves" as they map current affairs onto the Bible. And yet he's convinced that there's a "list of events, and when you see that list beginning to get checked off, Jesus said, 'Then know my return is near.'" Joel is talking about chapter 24 of Matthew's Gospel—the Olivet Discourse—when Jesus talked to his disciples on the Mount of Olives about his return to Earth and their responsibilities in the meantime.

"It's a very specific list," Joel tells me. "I mean, Jesus could have given a Don Rumsfeld answer. When asked, 'What should we be watching for?' he could have said, 'I'm not going to answer that. Next question.'"

This reminds me of that famous Donald Rumsfeld quote about Iraq. "There are known unknowns," I tell Joel. "And unknown unknowns."

Joel ignores me. "But Jesus doesn't! He says watch for wars and rumors of wars, revolutions, famine, earthquakes, pestilence, false messiahs, persecutions, spread of the Gospel, rebirth of the State of Israel, Jerusalem under Jewish control—and that's just a partial list. Well, those events are all happening."

When I push him on this, Joel admits that Israel's rebirth is the "super sign," the most tangible piece of evidence that persuades prophecy enthusiasts that the end is nigh. "Jesus is clear—once you see the birth of Israel and all of these other things happening, he said this generation will not pass away until you see my coming. So I think the clock probably started in 1948, although it may have started in 1967, but essentially within, roughly, sixty to a hundred years of that point, this is the window. And Jesus could have said I'm not going to give you that level of detail, but he did."

Jesus Christ may not be Donald Rumsfeld, but there are plenty of known unknowns in the Olivet Discourse. "Be ye also ready," he says, "for in such an hour as ye think not, the Son of man cometh." Or, a little earlier, "Of that day and hour knoweth no man, no, not the angels of heaven, but my Father only." Jesus then tells some stories that emphasize the need not only to be ready for his return but to do constructive things in the meantime.

One of these, the Parable of the Talents, is a Sunday School classic. A man leaves some money (a "talent" was a unit of currency in the Roman world) with three servants, and two of them use it wisely to make more money for the master. One of them buries the money in the ground. When the master returns, the wise stewards are showered with praise—"Well done, thou good and faithful servant!"—but the cautious fellow gets into a lot of trouble.

I've always found that parable a little tricky. At other moments in the Gospels, Jesus attacks the money changers in the temple and warns against laying up riches on earth. Here he seems to favor an aggressive investment strategy. Meanwhile, the servant who does nothing with the master's money meets a very nasty end: "And cast ye the unprofitable servant into outer darkness: there shall be weeping and gnashing of teeth." But perhaps the message here is more subtle. Even if you believe that Jesus is coming back one day, your mission is to make the most of what he has left you rather than to sit on your talents and wait for his return.

Further Reading

There is a vast literature on the history of apocalyptic thinking. I found the following books especially helpful.

For general accounts of the influence of Bible prophecy on ideas and politics, see Norman Cohn, *The Pursuit of the Millennium*, revised edition (London: Paladin, 1970); Bernard McGinn, *Antichrist: Two Thousand Years of the Human Fascination with Evil* (San Francisco: HarperSanFrancisco, 1994); Eugen Weber, *Apocalypses: Prophecies, Cults, and Millennial Beliefs Through the Ages* (Cambridge: Harvard University Press, 1999); Stephen D. O'Leary, *Arguing the Apocalypse: A Theory of Millennial Rhetoric* (New York: Oxford University Press, 1994); Kenneth G. C. Newport, *Apocalypse and Millennium: Studies in Biblical Exegesis* (Cambridge: Cambridge University Press, 2000); and John J. Collins, Bernard McGinn, and Stephen J. Stein, eds., *The Encyclopedia of Apocalypticism*, three volumes. (New York: Continuum, 1998–2001).

On the origins of the prophecies and the impact of apocalyptic ideas in the early Christian era, see John J. Collins, *The Apocalyp-

tic Imagination, second edition (Grand Rapids: William B. Eerdmans, 1998); John J. Collins, *Apocalyptic Vision of the Book of Daniel* (Missoula: Scholars Press, 1977); Adela Yarbro Collins, *Crisis and Catharsis: The Power of the Apocalypse* (Philadelphia: Westminster Press, 1984); Leonard Thompson, *The Book of Revelation: Apocalypse and Empire* (New York: Oxford University Press, 1990); and Steven J. Fressien, *Imperial Cults and the Apocalypse of John* (New York: Oxford University Press, 2000).

Medieval apocalypticism is discussed in Richard K. Emerson and Bernard McGinn, eds., *The Apocalypse in the Middle Ages* (Ithaca: Cornell University Press, 1992); McGinn, *Visions of the End: Apocalyptic Traditions in the Middle Ages* (New York: Columbia University Press, 1979); and McGinn, *The Calabrian Abbot: Joachim of Fiore in the History of Western Thought* (New York: Macmillan, 1985). For a bleak view of medieval anti-Semitism and its root in apocalyptic thinking, see Andrew Gow, *The Red Jews: Antisemitism in an Apocalyptic Age, 1200–1600* (Leiden: Brill, 1995); a mere nuanced picture of the Jewish role in medieval society is offered by Robert Chazan, *European Jewry and the First Crusade* (Berkeley: University of California Press, 1987).

European views of the apocalypse after the Protestant Reformation are explored in Andrew Cunningham and Ole Peter Grell, *The Four Horsemen of the Apocalypse: Religion, War, Famine, and Death in Reformation Europe* (Cambridge: Cambridge University Press, 2000); Ernest Lee Tuveson, *Millennium and Utopia* (New York: Harper & Row, 1964); Katharine R. Firth, *The Apocalyptic Tradition in Reformation Britain, 1530–1645* (Oxford: Oxford University Press, 1979); C. A. Patrides and Joseph Wittreich, eds., *The Apocalypse in English Renaissance Thought and Literature* (Manchester: Manchester University Press, 1984); and Jeffrey K. Jue, *Heaven Upon Earth: Joseph Mede and the Legacy of Millenarianism* (Dordrecht: Springer, 2006).

The influence of Bible prophecy on American history is discussed in Paul Boyer, *When Time Shall Be No More* (Cambridge:

Harvard University Press, 1992); Nicholas Guyatt, *Providence and the Invention of the United States, 1607–1876* (Cambridge: Cambridge University Press, 2007); Ruth Bloch, *Visionary Republic: Millennial Themes in American Thought, 1756–1800* (Cambridge: Cambridge University Press, 1985); James West Davidson, *The Logic of Millennial Thought: The Eighteenth Century* (New Haven: Yale University Press, 1977); David L. Row, *Thunder and Trumpets: Millerites and Dissenting Religion in Upstate New York, 1800–1850* (Chico: Scholars Press, 1985); Ruth Alden Doan, *The Miller Heresy, Millennialism, and American Culture* (Philadelphia: Temple University Press, 1987); Timothy P. Weber, *Living in the Shadow of the Second Coming: American Premillennialism, 1875–1982* (Chicago: University of Chicago Press, 1987); George Marsden, *Fundamentalism and American Culture* (New York: Oxford University Press, 2006); Kenneth G. C. Newport, *The Branch Davidians of Waco: The History and Beliefs of an Apocalyptic Sect* (Oxford: Oxford University Press, 2006); and Michael Barkun, *A Culture of Conspiracy: Apocalyptic Visions in Contemporary America* (Berkeley: University of California Press, 2003).

On the affiliation of American Christians with Israel, see Yaakov Ariel, *On Behalf of Israel: Fundamentalist Attitudes Toward Jews, Judaism, and Zionism, 1865–1945* (New York: Carlson, 1991); Stephen R. Sizer, *Christian Zionism: Road-Map to Armageddon* (Nottingham: Inter-Varsity, 2004); and Timothy P. Weber, *On the Road to Armageddon: How Evangelicals Became Israel's Best Friend* (Grand Rapids: Baker Academic, 2004).

There are many theological critiques of the End Times thinking; one of the most accessible is Barbara Rossing, *The Rapture Exposed: The Message of Hope in the Book of Revelation* (Boulder: Westview, 2005). For a recent academic study of Bible prophecy enthusiasts, see Amy Johnson Frykholm, *Rapture Culture: Left Behind in Evangelical America* (New York: Oxford University Press, 2004).

A number of liberal authors have recently attacked evangelical

Christianity and berated its influence on American society and politics. These authors have done a lot of very useful reporting, though they often present the Religious Right as coherent, well organized, and menacing; this doesn't entirely square with the Bible prophecy world that I've explored in this book. See, for example, Esther Kaplan, *With God on Their Side: George W. Bush and the Religious Right* (New York: New Press, 2004); Michelle Goldberg, *Kingdom Coming: The Rise of Christian Nationalism* (New York: W. W. Norton 2006); Kevin Phillips, *American Theocracy: The Peril and Politics of Radical Religion, Oil, and Borrowed Money in the 21st Century* (New York: Viking, 2006); and Chris Hedges, *American Fascists: The Christian Right and the War on America* (New York: Free Press, 2007).

I've drawn upon a number of excellent articles and essays in writing this book. There isn't space here to list them all, but I'd like to acknowledge these journalists for their reporting on End Times personalities and issues: Bill Berkowitz, Rob Boston, John Cloud, Robert Dreyfuss, G. Richard Fisher, Michelle Goldberg, Analisa Nazareno, Sarah Posner, Shmuel Rosner, Louis Sahagun, and Craig Unger.

The most important sources for this book were the numerous volumes written by Bible prophecy enthusiasts themselves: from the *Left Behind* novels to *Jerusalem Countdown*. These books may strike many nonevangelical readers as absurd and even offensive, but they offer the clearest window onto the ambitions, the contradictions, and the limitations of apocalyptic Christianity.

Acknowledgments

I'm very grateful to everyone who agreed to be interviewed for this book. I was welcomed by many prophecy enthusiasts who agreed to talk on the record and at length about their views. I didn't manage to include all of my conversations in the final version, and I'd like to thank those people who don't appear in this book but who agreed to be interviewed.

The following readers gave me very helpful comments on the manuscript: Lisa Bailey, Luke Clossey, John Craig, James Cunningham, Michael Fellman, Brandon Marriott, Robert Palmer, and Tony le Vann. I'm especially grateful to Lisa Bailey for her suggestions on medieval apocalyptic thinking; and to John Craig and Luke Clossey for setting me right on the English Civil War, early Chinese ship construction, and a host of other topics.

I received advice, kindness, expert suggestions, or all of the above from Wendy Cadge, Darren Dochuk, Alec Dun, the Graybill family, Stephen Lovell, John Stubbs, Matt Thorne, and Robert Wuthnow. David Rowan asked me to interview John Hagee for the *Jewish Chronicle,* an abortive assignment that nonetheless opened some doors in San Antonio. I'm grateful for the invitation and sorry that I didn't win over the pastor.

I was nudged into writing this book by Lesley Thorne of Gillon Aitken Associates, and Lesley has been extremely helpful throughout the process of researching and writing. I also want to thank Jon Jackson, who was instrumental in shaping the project and pitching it to publishers. Jon knows the name of the wag at Gillon Aitken who came up with the daft title of this book, apparently in the pub. I hope he'll pass along my thanks. In New York, Jeanette Perez, my editor at HarperCollins, has been enormously helpful and encouraging.

My wife has read this book several times, and gamely pretends that she isn't bored by it. My daughter was born two weeks before my final deadline, so I owe her an apology as well as my thanks and love for arriving just in time.

About the author

2 A Conversation with Nicholas Guyatt

3 Meet Nicholas Guyatt

About the book

5 Talking About the End of the World

10 Nicholas Guyatt Interviews Todd
    Strandberg, Founder of RaptureReady.com

Read on

15 Ten Apocalyptic Books, Movies, and
    Games You Shouldn't Be Without

Insights,
Interviews
& More...

A Conversation with Nicholas Guyatt

Let's start with the basics: Where were you born and where did you grow up?

I was born in Bristol in England, and that's where I grew up.

Was your family very religious? What role does religion play in your life now?

My mother was from Dublin, so my brother and I went to a Catholic grade school in Bristol. The school was attached to the local church, St. Patrick's, but they didn't just turn you into a good Catholic—if anything, they placed more emphasis on making you Irish. When I look back on it, it was strange: the principal was Irish, and he encouraged the kids to play the tin whistle and to do Irish dancing. When we had prize days, the guests of honor handing out medals and certificates would be from Aer Lingus. I made it to high school thinking that every kid in England could play "Danny Boy" on the accordion, which turned out not to be the case. Though I can, which is a plus.

I'm not very religious, but I do have a mushy belief in something bigger than us which might care about whether we've done a good job or not in our lives. My wife is nervous that I'll start teaching our daughter about the apocalypse, but that hasn't happened yet.

What is it about this religious American subculture that fascinates you?

I first got interested in apocalyptic Christianity when the *Left Behind* books started to make headlines: the first was published a couple of years before I came to America, but by the time they really took off I was in Princeton and I followed them quite closely. I was fascinated that these books which imagine the imminent end of the world were so popular at the time, especially given the upbeat tone of the late 1990s—the dot-com boom, the idea of the Dow hitting 30,000, Bill Clinton's speeches

> 66 I made it to high school thinking that every kid in England could play 'Danny Boy' on the accordion, which turned out not to be the case. 99

about how globalization would make the world a better place. If America was doing so well, I couldn't work out why so many Americans seemed happy for the world to end.

How do you think your identity as an Englishman helped you investigate apocalyptic Christianity?

I think it helped to some extent, because I didn't seem like an East Coast snot who'd just come to make fun of evangelicals. Many of the people I interviewed see themselves as being in a culture war right now with the secular left, so they feel embattled and a bit wary of journalists. Being from England makes you a total outsider in their eyes, and they don't assume that you come at them with prejudices about how naïve or scary the red states are.

During your travels and interviews around the States, did you ever consider converting?

No. But if millions of evangelical Christians disappear in an instant, and the government issues vague statements about radiation leakages or extraterrestrial signals, then I'll be looking again at the *Left Behind* books.

What type of academic work do you do? Does it tie in with your research for Have a Nice Doomsday?

I've just finished a book called *Providence and the Invention of the United States, 1607–1876*, which tries to explain why many Americans came to believe that God liked the U.S. more than any other country. I pick up this idea with the Puritans, then follow it through the American Revolution to the period of "manifest destiny" and the Civil War in the nineteenth century. That was a big inspiration for *Have a Nice Doomsday*. In my academic book, I'd found a lot of evidence suggesting that Americans had a very optimistic understanding of God and U.S. history in the years before 1876: they believed that the United States had been given a mission by God to help redeem the rest of the world. So I was really puzzled ▶

Meet Nicholas Guyatt

Vic Leung

NICHOLAS GUYATT was educated at Cambridge and Princeton, and he teaches history at Simon Fraser University in British Columbia. Born and raised in England, he now lives in Vancouver. He is a contributor to the *London Review of Books* and *The Nation* magazine. *Have a Nice Doomsday* is his fourth book. ❧

3

A Conversation with
Nicholas Guyatt *(continued)*

by the tens of millions of Christians in twenty-first-century America who seem to have abandoned their faith in the United States as a redeemer nation. That was a starting point for this book.

As a historian, is it a challenge to write a book about the present?

I've never written this kind of book before, and it's a completely different process from researching an academic book. When you're in the archives, you read very slowly and carefully and try to find as much evidence as you can before you write anything. On this project, I knew I wanted to write quickly and to put down my immediate impressions of the places and people I'd visited. It took me nearly six years to write my academic book, and about six months to write this one. But it has made me think differently about how I do historical research. If you write about the period before 1900, you never get to meet your subjects—you just try to figure them out from the writing they've left behind. But when I was researching this book, I had the chance not only to read apocalyptic books and articles but to meet the authors in person and to see how they reconciled their ideas with their everyday lives. You rarely get that as a historian, and after this project I can see how much you miss if you don't have the chance to see your subjects up close.

What are you working on now?

I'm locking myself away to write my next academic book, but I'm also planning a follow-up to *Have a Nice Doomsday*. I'm really interested in the creationist movement, but I'll have to see if I can persuade any evangelicals to talk to me after this book comes out. ❧

Talking About the End of the World

ARE EVANGELICAL CHRISTIANS trying to take over America? That's what a lot of worried journalists and commentators have been saying since 2000, when George W. Bush captured the White House under such controversial circumstances. President Bush quickly embraced many of the cherished dreams of his evangelical base: he was a vocal supporter of restrictions on abortion, gay marriage, and stem-cell research. Meanwhile, in the dark months after September 11, his talk of crusades and evildoers suggested that he might export a Christian agenda around the world.

Something about this never added up for me: if the Religious Right really harbored dreams of a Christian America purged of unbelievers and dissenters, happily submitting to the Book of Leviticus, why did so many evangelicals hope and expect that the world would soon come to a terrible end? Why embrace the apocalypse if you're on the verge of reestablishing the United States as a Christian nation?

It was this paradox that drove me to write the book, and to seek out apocalyptic Christians who might share their perspective. Could you simultaneously embrace a Christian nationalism and an apocalyptic fatalism? How do you live your daily life if you fully expect Christ to Rapture you to heaven any minute? And would you talk about any of this with a complete outsider?

I wasn't sure about the last question in particular, and when I planned my research trips I didn't know how things would work out. I started in San Antonio, and from there I followed my nose and tried to build from one interview to the next. Some people—like Jack Kinsella, the guy who'd moved into an RV to spread his message across America—were very responsive and keen to talk. Others—like ▶

5

Talking About the End of the World
(continued)

Tim LaHaye—were hard to track down. John Hagee and Hal Lindsey wouldn't agree to an interview, though it was easier for me to understand them by actually going to San Antonio and Palm Springs and seeing them in their natural habitat.

I think there's a stereotype among liberal Americans that evangelicals are crazy, scary, or both. This impression is reinforced by distance. When you actually sit down with apocalyptic Christians, what strikes you most is their effort to reconcile these huge and weird ideas about the End Times with a more familiar set of instincts and feelings: rationality, a love of America, and a recognition of the need to live in the moment.

In some ways, apocalyptic Christians have absolutely no need to get involved in politics—remember that things are supposed to get much worse before the End Times arrive, so the moral decay of America or the rise of atheism should actually cheer those believers who can read the signposts toward Armageddon. But, as many people told me, it's hard to give up on a Christian political agenda and to accept that the world is going to hell.

This explains why many conservative Christians argue with one another about theology and politics: which fights to wage, which politicians to trust, which view of the End Times to endorse. The Religious Right is a lot more diverse and unpredictable than many liberal critics have suggested, and the idea that this is a coherent movement that's planning to hijack the government is misleading. Below the big names like Pat Robertson or Tim LaHaye are grassroots believers who are capable of thinking for themselves, including millions of Americans who grapple with difficult questions about faith and society rather than simply singing about a glorious American theocracy or the imminent return of Jesus.

After exploring this world, I'm less

> **❝** When you actually sit down with apocalyptic Christians, what strikes you most is their effort to reconcile these huge and weird ideas about the End Times with a more familiar set of instincts and feelings. **❞**

concerned about the ordinary believers than about the ambitious leaders who attempt to co-opt the grassroots and to bring apocalyptic ideas to Washington. I've introduced some of these leaders in the book. Their influence is growing, though still relatively modest. But in the forging of American policy toward Israel, and now Iran, they have begun to play an inflammatory and unsettling role. These leaders pop up in TV studios or at the Capitol and, very often, are invited to share their views on the latest Middle East crisis without being challenged on their apocalyptic perspective. Politicians and broadcast journalists should be doing a better job of informing the public about this.

One thing I've been asked a lot since I started this book is whether evangelicals and non-evangelical Americans can get along. The presumption, on the part of many liberals, is that we're headed for a showdown: fundamentalist Christians are trying to roll back the Enlightenment, and "reality-based" people of all political persuasions are going to have to confront this religious challenge or surrender America to the theocrats. The clear implication in a lot of liberal reporting on the Religious Right is that Christian conservatives are sworn opponents of reason and tolerance. What's less clear in this reporting is what, exactly, liberals can do about it. Persuade Christian conservatives to move somewhere else? Strip them of the vote unless they can prove that they're sufficiently rational to use it properly?

I have no sympathy with the conservative political agenda of the Religious Right, and I don't think that the apocalypse is going to happen in my lifetime. But, based on my travels and my interviews for this book, I think that non-evangelical Americans have been harboring some unhelpful assumptions of their own about conservative Christians. First, I don't believe ▶

❝ I'm less concerned about the ordinary believers than about the ambitious leaders who attempt to co-opt the grassroots and to bring apocalyptic ideas to Washington. ❞

Talking About the End of the World
(*continued*)

that "faith-based" thinking is necessarily irrational: apocalyptic Christians scan the newspapers closely because they think they'll find evidence there of the fulfilling of the prophecies. The modern prophecy movement would never have existed without the creation of the state of Israel in 1948, the one undeniable "fact" of Bible prophecy which keeps the hopes of apocalyptic Christians alive. One reason I wanted to discuss the roots of Bible prophecy in this book was to give readers a sense of its teasing logic: it *is* rational, if you look at it from the right perspective. The problem, of course, is that this perspective is quite limited and it leaves many things out. But prophecy has been one of the most popular forms of writing for more than two millennia precisely because it can easily seem plausible.

This brings me to the second misconception: the belief of many liberals that it's a total waste of time to talk to evangelicals, or that there's something about the evangelical perspective that's automatically absurd and insane. This kind of thinking easily slides into total dismissal, widening the gap between liberals and religious conservatives. It also persuades conservatives that the country is run by a liberal elite which is condescending and contemptuous toward Americans from the flyover states who don't read sophisticated magazines or have fancy degrees. We've seen this kind of culture clash before. Back in the Scopes trial, the liberal media cheered the attorney Clarence Darrow as he lampooned the southern hayseeds who had challenged Darwin's theories. But the result of this intellectual drubbing wasn't quiet submission on the part of evangelicals. They went away, licked their wounds, and built their own institutions and movements that paid no attention to the *New York Times* or the eggheads at Harvard.

The challenge in responding to apocalyptic Christianity is to reject the political agenda of

66 The modern prophecy movement would never have existed without the creation of the state of Israel in 1948, the one undeniable 'fact' of Bible prophecy which keeps the hopes of apocalyptic Christians alive. 99

John Hagee or Tim LaHaye without dismissing the millions of people who've bought the *Left Behind* books or who listen to Christian radio. This isn't easy, especially if you find yourself on the wrong side of the moral boundaries that evangelical leaders are trying to redraw. But the danger of simply mocking these beliefs, and the faith that underlies them, is that the gap between evangelical and non-evangelical Americans will continue to widen. Right now, many apocalyptic Christians are still torn between a more inclusive vision of America and a future nation that's racked by the Tribulation or ruled by the Bible. I think there's still a chance to talk to these people before their minds are made up. ∽

> 66 The danger of simply mocking these beliefs, and the faith that underlies them, is that the gap between evangelical and non-evangelical Americans will continue to widen. 99

Nicholas Guyatt Interviews Todd Strandberg, Founder of RaptureReady.com

I did a number of interviews for the book that didn't make it into the final version. One was with Todd Strandberg, the founder of RaptureReady.com. For twenty years, Todd has scoured news stories from around the world, looking for indicators across forty-five categories to measure how close we are to the End Times. (These include "False Christs," "liberalism," "Iran," and "plagues.") From these categories, Todd compiles the Rapture Index, a number which is supposed to indicate how close we are to doomsday. (Todd refers to the index as the "Dow Jones Industrial Average of End Times activity.") RaptureReady.com is the most popular prophecy site on the Internet, with around 200,000 unique visitors each month. In December 1993, the index posted its record low score of 57. The record high, 182, was recorded on September 24, 2001. (In the spring of 2007, the index stood at 159.) This is a shortened version of a conversation we had in October 2006.

NICHOLAS GUYATT: *The RaptureReady Web site gets quite a bit of coverage from the liberal media, most of it pretty dismissive. How do you feel about that?*

TODD STRANDBERG: Some people are hostile. Most people who talk to us obviously don't believe a bit of what Rapture is about. I understand that; I've never been offended or disappointed by the coverage we've gotten. I think the nastier they are, the more it entices people to come to the site.

NG: *Does it feel bad when people accuse you of wanting to end the world?*

TS: No, we don't actually want the world to come to an end. The world for most people will come to an end, but there's a lot of complexity. We believe we're going to miss all this nasty stuff that we talk about, and we invite anyone

> 66 Rapture Ready.com is the most popular prophecy site on the Internet, with around 200,000 unique visitors each month. 99

else to join us, and that's what people don't understand. They think, "They're looking to trigger a nuclear war and bring about doomsday!" But prophecy is very complex subject matter. If you don't delve into it, you're going to run into these kinds of misconceptions.

NG: *How did you come up with the Rapture Index?*

TS: Well, I joined the air force in 1987, and in the same year I came up with the index. It was kind of a lark. I thought the best way to compile the End Times indicators would be in an index. There were no fancy graphics; it was just very flat files, and it didn't dawn on me that it was growing into a ministry until the media started contacting me—*Rolling Stone* magazine. We got a big jump when *Time* magazine contacted us, then it just got to a point where we heard from everything: the *Economist*, *Playboy*, *Mother Jones*. The women's magazines, hair magazines. There's a magazine for everything.

NG: *A lark?*

TS: Well, the Rapture Index is not to be taken too seriously, but it is based on a serious approach. People who are out there trying to figure out if the Lord is coming on November 6, 2008, are probably going to be wrong. What I wanted to do was to come up with some sort of working idea of how fast we are approaching the End Times. So we've created a prophetic speedometer. We don't know where the finishing line is exactly; it might be ten miles away or it might be a hundred miles away or it might be a thousand miles away. But if we're going at sixty miles an hour we'll get there twice as fast as if we're going at thirty miles an hour.

NG: *Do you think Bible prophecy has an influence within the Republican Party?*

TS: I think Ronald Reagan's administration was probably the most affected by prophecy. George W. Bush, he's an evangelical Christian, but he's never really to my knowledge said anything that is a direct reference to prophecy. I think he's a friend of Israel, that could be a reflection of ▶

> ❝ I joined the air force in 1987, and in the same year I came up with the index. It was kind of a lark. I thought the best way to compile the End Times indicators would be in an index. ❞

his evangelical Christian beliefs. But you know, it's funny. I've never heard him make a really solid statement on this. On the left, there's been kind of a fear that we got these kooks running the show. But I don't think there is this boogeyman like a lot of the people on the left are claiming.

NG: *Why is Israel so important for Bible prophecy believers?*

TS: For people who are prophetically minded, Israel is probably their number one focus and everything else beyond that is very minor. The funny thing is that End Timers are very much supportive of Israel, but if Israelis knew what kind of stuff we believe they might become somewhat disturbed, because we believe the Antichrist is going to come to power and he's going to befriend Israel and then he's going to betray them in something worse than Hitler's atrocities.

NG: *Why aren't you more interested in Washington politics?*

TS: The only thing that's going to survive this world is people's souls. We have a Christian in the White House right now, we've had control of the Senate, control of the House, the country's still in pretty bad shape, so that hasn't worked, and it won't work. We have kind of a fatalistic mind-set because that's what the Bible says is going to happen, the world's going to continue to get worse and worse.

NG: *Do you think that by warning people about immorality, or the dangers of Iran or Islam, that you can slow down the prophecy clock? You can buy us some more time before the world ends?*

TS: That is an interesting theme, because it creates a conflict of interest for us. What most Christians want is to see the Rapture and to go to heaven, because you're being reunited with your savior. That's an exciting thing; that's

66 The funny thing is that End Timers are very much supportive of Israel, but if Israelis knew what kind of stuff we believe they might become somewhat disturbed. 99

something you look forward to. So the fact that I warn everyone against being so peaceful to Mohammadism, about economic perils, the fact that I talk against those, I'm being counterproductive to our ultimate desires.

NG: *So why not just step to one side and let all the bad stuff go on, while trying to win souls quietly?*

TS: It reminds me of a speech in high school from our history teacher; he had a lot of stock in a tobacco company. He said, "I don't want any of you kids smoking even though it's gonna cost me." So what it is, is a moral conflict. We have to do the right thing now, even though it might cost us a delay in the End Times progression. We want prophecy to move forward, but when we have a conflict, we have to make the right choice here.

NG: *Is it hard to be a Christian expecting the End Times, and also a patriot who loves his country?*

TS: I love the people; I don't love the country—the country is just a landmass. You know, the Statue of Liberty is just a hunk of iron that we got from France. What it represents is one of the first full democracies in the world. It's been a shining example to so many people, it's held back the Soviet aggression, it's done a lot for the world. I respect what a lot of people have died for and what people gave everything for. But to get into the position it's in now, I see a country that is the exporter of a lot of evils to the rest of the world. There's some truth to what these Islamic extremists see in America. A lot of what they say is wrong, but some of the immorality America exports, the materialism, there's a little truth there.

NG: *America seems like such a divided country right now. Is there anything that non-evangelicals can do—apart from* ▶

> " The fact that I warn everyone against being so peaceful to Mohammadism, about economic perils, the fact that I talk against those, I'm being counterproductive to our ultimate desires. "

*converting and accepting Bible prophecy—
to heal some of the wounds in the country?
Is there something they can do to reach out?*

TS: Convert?

NG: *I just told you that you can't have
that one!*

TS: Maybe understand and coexist, but I think
eventually everyone's going to have to face the
fact that what we're talking about is right. I tell
people, pick the point at which you're going to
believe. If we're going to continue toward the
progression of prophecy, either at one point
things will quit happening because this is just
a bunch of nonsense, just a bunch of things that
have coincided with each other. But we believe
things are going to continue, there's going to be
more 9/11s, there are going to be more terrorist
attacks—worse terrorist attacks. So you're just
going to have to put up with us because we're
not going to change, or you're going to have to
say, yeah, these people are right. I really don't
like the coexistence part because coexist means
nothing. If nothing changes on your side, the
liberal side, then we've lost, we've failed, because
it's not us converting to their viewpoint, our
mission is to convert them.

NG: *So there isn't a happy medium where we
can all just get along?*

TS: Common decency is probably the answer.
We should respect each other not because of
our religion but because of our commonality
as human beings. But Bible prophecy affects
everyone whether they believe it or not. If it's
true, then there's no avoiding it. So that's really
our motivation, to get in their face about it,
annoy them. There's a lot of people write me
and say, I'll be glad when you guys are gone.
Well, you probably won't! Maybe for five
minutes, but . . . ∽

> " Bible
> prophecy affects
> everyone whether
> they believe it or
> not. If it's true,
> then there's no
> avoiding it. So
> that's really our
> motivation, to
> get in their face
> about it, annoy
> them. "

Ten Apocalyptic Books, Movies, and Games You Shouldn't Be Without

📖 **THE LAST JIHAD by Joel C. Rosenberg (2002)**

Rosenberg's first prophecy novel, the one that (sort of) predicted 9/11 and the Iraq war. "You have to read this."—Rush Limbaugh. "A tingling triumph."—Steve Forbes. "This stuff could really happen!"—Sean Hannity.

📖 **THE AUTHORIZED LEFT BEHIND HANDBOOK by Tim LaHaye, Jerry B. Jenkins, and Sandi L. Swanson (2005)**

An exhaustive encyclopedia of the *Left Behind* universe, complete with Tribulation timeline and quiz questions. ("You've invited Jesus into your heart . . . but you've also got a head stuffed full of [*Left Behind*] characters and stories. Here's the ultimate insider's trivia challenge.") Contains a separate index of weapons featured in the series, as well as a tantalizing entry for "LSD" (Lake Shore Drive in Chicago).

🎬 **LEFT BEHIND: WORLD AT WAR (2005)**

The third *Left Behind* movie, this one is loosely based on a one-hundred-page section from the second novel in the series. The regular cast is getting quite long in the tooth by this stage, but the main attraction—apart from Nicolae Carpathia's devilish plan of infecting Bibles with an anthrax-like substance to kill off the Christian underground—is the presence of heavyweights Lou Gossett Jr. (*An Officer and a Gentleman*) and Charles Martin Smith (the nerdy accountant from *The Untouchables*). Smith doesn't make it to the second reel, but Gossett gets a wrenching interrogation scene with the unflappable Kirk Cameron.

> 66 'You've invited Jesus into your heart . . . but you've also got a head stuffed full of [*Left Behind*] characters and stories. Here's the ultimate insider's trivia challenge.' 99

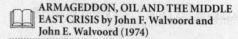

ARMAGEDDON, OIL AND THE MIDDLE EAST CRISIS by John F. Walvoord and John E. Walvoord (1974)

John F. Walvoord was the dean of prophecy study, and from his perch at Dallas Theological Seminary (he was president from 1953 to 1986) he played a greater role than anyone in making End Times speculation seem respectable. *Armageddon* was his one crossover hit, a lurid prediction that the oil crisis of 1973–74 would end with an Israeli peace deal that was advantageous to the Arabs and likely to inaugurate the Tribulation. Notable for Walvoord's magnanimous attempt to deny the obvious implication that Henry Kissinger was the Antichrist. The book was repackaged to tie-in with the first Gulf War in 1991.

RAPTURE UNDER ATTACK: WILL CHRISTIANS ESCAPE THE TRIBULATION? by Tim LaHaye (1998)

Originally published under a different title in 1992, this unusually candid book is very different from LaHaye's more polished output since his *Left Behind* success. Here you can still find him settling old scores with theological rivals, and talking casually about the Illuminati and his early work with the John Birch Society. It doesn't have the novelty value of *Babylon Rising: The Secret on Ararat* or *The Unhappy Gays*, but it tells you more about LaHaye's thinking than either.

LEFT BEHIND: ETERNAL FORCES (2006)

A PC video game based on the LaHaye/Jenkins bestsellers, *Eternal Forces* received some very negative reviews from critics when it was released in late 2006. Left Behind Games, the publisher, subsequently announced that it would try to market the game in Asia; the company declared that Asians were looking

> " A PC video game based on the LaHaye/Jenkins bestsellers, *Eternal Forces* received some very negative reviews from critics when it was released in late 2006. "

for "intellectually stimulating products from the United States" ahead of the 2008 Olympics.

📖 AMERICA THE BEAUTIFUL?: THE UNITED STATES IN BIBLE PROPHECY by David R. Reagan (2003)

Dave Reagan's glum rumination on America's sins and the nation's punishment at the hands of God. (One chapter is called "The Meaning of 9/11: Why Did God Allow It?") A rejoinder to anyone who imagines that evangelicals are rabid nationalists. Features a melancholy cover with the Statue of Liberty looking off toward a setting sun.

📖 SATAN IS ALIVE AND WELL ON PLANET EARTH by Hal Lindsey with C. C. Carlson (1972)

Lindsey's bestselling follow-up to *The Late Great Planet Earth*, SIAAWOPE tapped into the supposed rise of occult religions and devil worshipping in America, especially on college campuses. (Lindsey was especially upset by what he'd seen at the University of California, Berkeley.) A curiosity not only for its focus on Satanism, which now seems quaint, but also for its stirring description of an exorcism (performed by Lindsey himself) involving a comely young woman and a kilt.

🎬 JUDGMENT (2001)

One of many Christian movies from the Lalonde brothers of Canada, *Judgment* is an apocalyptic courtroom drama in which a one-world government puts Christianity itself on trial. Corbin Bernsen of *L.A. Law* has seen better days, but the big surprise in the movie is Mr. T as an impatient Christian freedom fighter. The movie's tagline: "Supreme Court versus Supreme Being."

Ten Apocalyptic Books, Movies, and Games
You Shouldn't Be Without *(continued)*

 **JERUSALEM COUNTDOWN: REVISED
AND UPDATED EDITION by John Hagee
(2007)**

Pastor Hagee returns to his 2006 bestseller,
tweaks some of his original predictions
(including the suggestion that a nuclear
showdown with Iran would take place
before September 2006), and reworks the
subtitle. The original edition of the book
was "a warning to the world"; in spring
2007, it was "a prelude to war." Given
Hagee's multiple appearances on cable
news shows since early 2006, demonizing
Mahmoud Ahmadinejad and talking up
the threat from Iran, the new subtitle
seems well deserved.